WAKING GIANTS

WAKING GIANTS

The Presence of the Past in Modernism

HERBERT N. SCHNEIDAU

New York   Oxford
OXFORD UNIVERSITY PRESS
1991

Oxford University Press

Oxford   New York   Toronto
Delhi   Bombay   Calcutta   Madras   Karachi
Petaling Jaya   Singapore   Hong Kong   Tokyo
Nairobi   Dar es Salaam   Cape Town
Melbourne   Auckland

and associated companies in
Berlin   Ibadan

Library of Congress Cataloging-in-Publication Data
Schneidau, Herbert N.
Waking giants : the presence of the past in modernism
Herbert N. Schneidau.
p. cm.   Includes bibliographical references and index.
ISBN 0-19-506862-9
1. English literature — 20th century — History and criticism.
2. American literature — 20th century — History and criticism.
3. Modernism (Literature) — Great Britain.
4. Modernism (Literature) — United States.
5. History in literature.
6. Memory in literature.   I. Title.
PR478.M6S36   1991
820.9′00912 — dc20
90-19942

9 8 7 6 5 4 3 2 1

Printed in the United States of America
on acid-free paper

For G&G—Giant fans

Preface

This book investigates the ideas of the past that lie behind some of the major works of literary Modernism. As a character in *Ulysses* says, "I would deal in especial with atavism." The play of this figure, the "throwback phenomenon," grew out of plant and animal breeding, in which the recurrence of earlier characteristics in later generations could be easily noticed. In the nineteenth century it gave rise to a host of cultural fantasies about degeneration, reversion to "savagery," and the like. Much ill-informed speculation about races, eugenics, and evolution eventuated in such fearful realities as Naziism. This brings in the connection between Modernism and the political nightmares of our century, which—although sensationalistically exploited by some current critics—is a legitimate and revealing object of study. However, since the Modernists were all atavists in some way, the link here is inverse.

I do not propose to offer a "theory" of Modernism, but I would like to comment on some trends that seem to be relevant to that end. First, we still need some provisional, working theories of literary movements, even when we question the very possibility of such theorization, or of periodization. Not only are they necessary frameworks for discourse, or at least straw men; we as critics are implicated in their cumulative outcomes. None of us is working from a position of pure innocence, and even the most radical calls for revisionary analysis have their backgrounds in previous intellectual histories, including many aspects of the spectacularly germane history of Modernism.

Second, the elitist elements in Modernism have recently called forth a fair amount of self-righteous political criticism. Now Modernism was elitist all right, but its "elect" do not necessarily correspond to the privileged, as some of these critiques imply, nor were these writers cultists in the sense that the gurus of the Sixties were. On the contrary, the works of Pound, Joyce, and Eliot were shockingly transgressive in their time and are far from being totally domesticated even now. Moreover, it is easy to exaggerate the "gentility" with which Eliot, say, was cloaked even in such apparently conservative milieux as Ivy League classrooms in the Fifties (I know, I was there, and those rooms were full of subversive types). "Guilds" and ladies' clubs have used the arts of opera and symphony as occasions for social stratification, but it hardly seems fair to tax music for that; how much less should Modernist literature have to suffer for being made part of the curriculum of various classes and coteries?

Indeed, these writers combined elitism with strong streaks of populism: Pound's economics, Joyce's fascination with clichés of various types (journalistic, musical, obscene, etc.), and Eliot's taste for music halls, Groucho Marx, and low comedy generally all in their different ways bespeak a repudiation of the "refined" and an embrace of the earthy, the vulgar, the unpretentious. It is nonsense to talk of Modernism as being the in-group discourse of the cultivated; its complex allusions were not drawn from nor directed at the store of university knowledge, but from more arcane precincts.

It could even be said—at least in a parabolic sense—that Modernism consisted of a war by Pound and Joyce against the British assumption that the use of the classics was to mark a gentleman's education. Both of them became "Odysseans" partly in order to rescue Homer from the fugitive and cloistered status to which this invidious distinction-making confined him. Such an animus against snobbism gave powerful impetus to the belief that the present had to be atavistically invigorated by a live, earthy past. Even Eliot, although playing the part of an Englishman, worked subtly to undermine the casual misappropriation of the past that occurred in the processes by which the English educational system produced gentility; his fascination with poetry that exposed the tentacular roots of terrors and desires did not pander to the Oxbridge curriculum, even though the Cambridge anthropologists were available there. Nor was the work of Yeats, though bedeviled by dreams of nobility, efficacious at giving aid and comfort to respectable people, especially in its randy last phase; Auden was right to assert that the "parish of rich women" was something he transcended. The "difficult" allusiveness of Modernist texts was not intended to and did not make them into preserves for the privileged, nor were the assumptions of the ruling classes reinforced by the disturbing, haunting indeterminacies that these allusions engendered. The politics of the Modernists have misled many into mistaking their cumulative effect: they sought not to endorse gentility but to affront it, and they succeeded. As for their participation in hegemonic thinking, look at the Pound-Eliot campaign for "tradition," an effort to subvert comfortable insularity and supplant it with awareness of the arts of China, Africa, and the cave painters (with Joyce's "monkish learning" for top dressing). They brought an energetic new cosmopolitanism into Anglo-American literature, and made it ready for the new concept of world traditions.

On the other hand, it is true that there was no romanticizing of proletariat or even "folk" among Modernists, and that their interests in the vulgar and earthy were far more Blakean than Wordsworthian. Indeed, Blake's mystic revelationism is behind all Modernist "difficulty": to find God in a stable or on a cross, infinity in a grain of sand, the sacramental in the trivial or degraded, one had to see through and past the accepted versions of things, and difficulty—as in Pound's remark, examined later, that he wanted to write a kind of "Greek"—served as a necessary defamiliarizing process. This motive is most clearly evident in Joyce's work, in which meaning expands as subjects contract; he found, as did the Bauhaus, that less was more, but in an accretive rather than a minimalist sense. As painters made the still-life into a revelatory motif, so Modernists found the transcendent in the demotic.

The justification for the diversity of topics and approaches in this book is simply that atavism appears in protean forms throughout Modernism; these are sometimes best seen in analysis of particular texts, sometimes in studies of authors' poetics. Indeed, the point is not that this idea "unified" Modernism, nor that it can serve as a litmus test to distinguish true Modernists from false ones. But it does have several other uses. First, it illuminates some vital but obscure relationships: for those fascinated by such puzzles as what Pound admired in Hardy, what connection could exist between Forster and Fitzgerald or Lawrence, why Anderson served as mentor to Hemingway and Faulkner and Wolfe, and how Joyce focused the problem for all of them although he had no interest in "the movement," the theme of the reappearance or resuscitation of the past provides an important answer. Moreover, it suggests readings that haven't been offered before, new ways to look at familiar texts. And finally, this theme opens for probing the major paradox about all the Modernists: their discomfort, in varying degrees, with the very idea of the "modern." The name that we give them (not used by them, of course) ironically conceals a range of attitudes, running from ambivalence to outright hostility, not only toward their own times but also to the sense of belatedness that for them was the consequence of a historical view of the world. Their visions of the atavistic returns of the past turned this paradox into a useful motive for their work. The shared motive not only provides links between individuals but also reveals a constituent element in the "twentieth-century world picture," the premises of the cultural poetics of our time.

In putting together the diverse figures discussed in this book, I have tried to write for a literate but not specialist audience. The chapter on Hardy, for instance, does not discuss his novels, but it would be well to have read one or two, along with the poems in typical anthologies of modern verse. In the case of Pound, I have aimed at a reader who may have tried to read some of the *Cantos* but remains very puzzled by them, and wants to know how they figure in modern literature as a whole. I don't set out to scoff at or offend specialists, but I believe, with Walker Percy, that each thing is too important to be left to the specialist in that thing. And certainly some corners of the study of Modernism lack integration with others.

Finally, the idea — with all its varieties and linkages — raises some compelling questions about the human species. Does our unique dependence on language not entail a constant recovery of the past, which is enshrined in language? What is the role of pastness in the life of the individual? Humankind is the prisoner of its own past in a way that other species are not, yet does not this condition generate its own transcendence? We also are the only animals who can do much about changing our futures, by projecting pasts into them. Modernist visions have some bearing on all such questions, representing as they do acute forms of our self-consciousness.

Tucson   H. N. S.
November 1990

Contents

WAKING GIANTS

Introduction/
The Persistence of Memory:
Joyce's Regress from Mortmain
to Atavism

In 1844 Nathaniel Hawthorne entered in his notebook the following project for the future:

> To represent the influence which Dead Men have among living affairs; — for instance, a Dead Man controls the disposition of wealth; a Dead Man sits on the judgment seat, and the living judges do but repeat his decisions; Dead Men's opinions in all things control the living truth; we believe in Dead Men's religion; we laugh at Dead Men's jokes; we cry at Dead Men's pathos; everywhere and in all matters, Dead Men tyrannize inexorably over us.[1]

Here we can see Hawthorne carried from bemusement to disgust by the inscription of his own thought. His grimace at the appalling spectacle of all those forms of rule from the grave was echoed many times in the nineteenth century; it became characteristic of the age: as Marx said, the past weighed like a nightmare on the brains of the living. Although many intellectuals demurred, progressivism was powerful enough in that century to make many think that the hold of the past was all that kept humankind from true fulfillment. Scientism was in flower; railroads, Crystal Palaces, electoral reform, and the like gave the more hopeful cause to believe in a new meaning for the term *Utopia*.[2]

1. Notebooks of 1842–44, in Malcolm Cowley, ed., *The Portable Hawthorne* (Viking, 1948), p. 568.
2. "Arnold used the word *modern* in a wholly honorific sense," observes Lionel Trilling. "And at what a distance his ideal of the modern puts him from our present

3

We consider ourselves wiser. Although many legacies of progressivism linger on, we have to justify each of them as desirable in its own right, not as parts of any melioristic scenario. Our ambivalence about them is clearly growing: anecdotes about irreparable cars, erroneous but unrelenting computer billings, and the "iatrogenic" (treatment-caused) problems of modern medicine have recently inflamed a long-growing, sullen suspicion that not all innovations have been for the general good. The "inventions" that were going to solve our "problems" — from nuclear energy to automobiles — now seem to trouble and enslave us. We regard bygone hopes of a perfectible future as fatuous, and sneer at their Victorian prophets without considering how mean-spirited such cynicism must have seemed then. At that time, those who proposed reverence for the practices of the past had to bear the burden of proof to show that they were not mere obscurantists. Even the Oxford Movement had a revolutionary quality.

Impatience with the hold of the past on the present was not limited to progressive fantasists. More sober minds also recoiled from blind adherence to precedent; the more tyrannical forms of control by the dead, as in the law, were mercilessly caricatured by Dickens and others. It then became necessary to issue warnings against the anarchy that might ensue if pure social experimentalism took hold; but these warnings were, despite their apocalyptic quality, unable to erase the image of the past as a dead hand, *mortmain*, mindlessly choking the life out of its own sons and daughters. No one ever put this idea into a more repellent and terrifying form than did Henrik Ibsen when he insinuated it into *Ghosts* in the form of heritable syphilis. The old theme of the ancestral curse was incarnated in the unconquerable spirochete, blighting the life of an innocent generation; the sins of the fathers were truly visited on the children, in a morbid adaptation of the Old Testament wording.

To one young man in Ireland, for whom Ibsen was a heroic prophet and the spread of syphilis a powerful threat and symbol, the premise of *Ghosts* seemed to pervade the life of his country. Fear and loathing of mortmain suffuse the early work of James

---

sense of modernity, from our modern literature!" *Beyond Culture* (Viking, 1968), pp. 15–16.

Joyce, who looked on the *passéisme* of his culture as both cause and symptom of "Irish paralysis."[3] Ireland's seedy reverence for the past was for him a form of lotos-eating that narcotized the populace, allowing it to forget the oppressive present but also blotting out the most obvious needs for reform, those that Ibsen blazoned to the world. Appalled by the difference between what his body told him and what Jesuits had taught, the young Joyce concluded that sexual life in Western countries was corrupted by hypocrisy; clearly it needed probing reexamination and discussion, as the syphilis threat testified, yet the hold of the past kept its victims from demanding this. For Joyce, the Irish attitude toward the past created an atmosphere that suffocated souls in their cradles and made escape all but impossible: it was laid on everywhere, like the gas. The twin tyrannies of English rule and priestly domination would have been long ago thrown off, it must have seemed, if only the Irish did not continually opiate themselves against their miseries by rehearsing sentimental eulogies of old times in the barony, or great victories that Ireland would surely have won but for one form or another of betrayal. (Joyce took up the theme of the inevitable traitor and turned it so that the Irish became incurable informers against themselves, in more than one sense. His story "Ivy Day in the Committee Room" is a study in the term *self-betrayal*.)[4] Dwelling in and on the past he saw as all the more enervating for being frequently indulged in barrooms, where the drowning of sorrows could turn into occasions for bittersweet self-indulgence. The memory of defeat and loss was, exasperatingly, just as strong and perhaps even more paralyzing than that of the past's glories. The Irish, forgetting nothing and learning nothing, seemed to luxuriate in it, and thus revealed their inner deadness which the young Joyce grimly but determinedly sought to expose.

Joyce makes it all too easy for us to imagine the chafing impatience of Stephen Dedalus, enduring his father's whisky-logged reunions with cronies, and their endless memorializing of "fine decent fellows" such as "poor little good hearted Johnny Keevers

---

3. See the opening paragraph of the first *Dubliners* story, "The Sisters," and *Letters of James Joyce*, ed. Stuart Gilbert (Viking, 1957), p. 55.

4. For Stephen Dedalus on the "indispensable informer," see Chester G. Anderson, ed., *A Portrait of the Artist as a Young Man: Text, Criticism and Notes* (Viking, 1968; originally published, 1916), p. 202.

of the Tantiles," on the trip to Cork in *A Portrait of the Artist as a Young Man*. How Mick Lacy used to sing a *come-all-you*; how one was a good oarsman, another a good actor and so on and on: no wonder "a faint sickness sighed in [Stephen's] heart," wearied by his father's sentimentality and by his guilty knowledge of adolescent physiology and psychology, stimulated when he sees the word *foetus* carved in a desk. Stephen hears his father patronized as "the boldest flirt in the city of Cork in his day," but he knows what Irish sexuality amounts to: masturbation, whoring for the more adventurous, seduction and betrayal of gullible lower-class girls for the luckiest, entrapment into marriage à la Polly Mooney ("The Boarding House"), and above all endless backbiting gossip. That's what good crowds of lively young fellows were up to.[5]

Stephen is also depressed by the crushing realization that all the chimes-at-midnight rehashing of memories covers over the real purpose of the trip, the degrading liquidation of property, to the end of financing further slides in the family fortunes. His father's progress downhill accords with the ubiquitous sense of decline in the times: naturally everything was better in the old days. Shortly after the journey to Cork, Mr. Dedalus voices the opinion that earlier generations of Irish politicians—Grattan and company—would have had of their successors: "Why, by God, they wouldn't be seen dead in a ten acre field with them." (This sounds like one of John Joyce's sayings that his son found hilarious but epiphanic.) At the end of the book Stephen gives a no doubt well-rehearsed speech in which the father's life encapsulates the theme of decline:

> Stephen began to enumerate glibly his father's attributes.
> —A medical student, an oarsman, a tenor, an amateur actor, a shouting politician, a small landlord, a small investor, a drinker, a good fellow, a storyteller, somebody's secretary, something in a distillery, a taxgatherer, a bankrupt and at present a praiser of his own past.[6]

The last is, of course, a witty variant on the classical *laudator temporis acti*, lauder of the times gone by. Simon Dedalus is Irish, "all too Irish."[7]

5. *Portrait*, pp. 86–96.
6. *Portrait*, pp. 97, 241.
7. *Ulysses* (Vintage Books, 1961; originally published, 1922), p. 623. In Hans Walter Gabler, *Ulysses: A Critical and Synoptic Edition* (Garland, 1984), 16.384.

In Joyce's work the typical Irish gesture is genuflection toward the past even if one's part in it had been shameful In "Ivy Day in the Committee Room," all present agree with old Jack the caretaker when he says of Parnell's era: "Musha, God be with them times! There was some life in it then." But not many of them are forthcoming about what they did in those days. Jack reveres Parnell not for his policies or his skills, but because of the violent controversies that surrounded him; next to the past the Irish love a quarrel best (preferably an old one). Jack's formulation allows even those who opposed Parnell to come in under the umbrella of "them times." "We all respect him now that he's dead and gone," says Mr. O'Connor, revealing more than he intends.

Later Jack regales the group with a scornful anecdote gathered from a porter at the mayoral residence, about the thrifty new Lord Mayor who violates the unwritten laws of Irish hospitality by not entertaining every night: *"Wisha! says I, what kind of people is going at all now?"* The words imply that the group of improvidents listening to him can comfort themselves by reflecting that, if they aren't receiving their due, the fault must be in the times; has not even their employer reneged on his supposed promises to pay them?[8]

Predictably on this anniversary of his death, the group demands to hear an elegy on Parnell, one that consigns him to the grave "with Erin's heroes of the past." As these men, swigging heated stout, revel in the memory of a man whose cause they casually betray, recollected emotions run high, but not in tranquillity. Most gratingly, they allow themselves to excuse the English King Edward as a man of the world for his sexual exploits, forgetting how Parnell was denounced by Church and laity for his one liaison. "In the name of God, said Mr. Henchy, where's the analogy between the two cases?" Indeed there is no analogy, for Parnell was the single-minded lover of an already estranged wife whereas Edward was a notorious womanizer, but Mr. Henchy sees commercial possibilities in welcoming Edward to Ireland. His audience is easily led into shallow rationalization, as easily as they are induced into malicious gossip about anyone who leaves the room. Joyce manages to make

8. Robert Scholes and A. Walton Litz, eds., *Dubliners: Text, Criticism and Notes* (Penguin, 1976; originally published, 1914), pp. 122, 128.

us fear turning our backs to this lively crowd, which prefigures the group in the "Cyclops" chapter of *Ulysses*. No wonder Stephen calls Ireland "the old sow that eats her farrow."[9]

Loathing for mortmain animated Joyce's creation of a gallery of paralytic, melancholic, or vitriolic Dubliners whose spiritual ambitions are limited, like those of "The Sisters," to a last drive through the old neighborhood. It is customary among Joyce critics to suggest that his irritation mellowed somewhat during the writing of *Dubliners*, and that the composition of "The Dead" embodies a new spirit of tolerance and sympathy for his fellow citizens. Yet that story presents a series of images of mortmain that are easily the most powerful in the book: monks sleeping in their coffins, automatic praise for the singers of the past, "young" men of forty dominated and infantilized by mothers and aunts, empty rhetoric eulogizing a moribund generation with hackneyed sentiment, among others. Even the housemaid Lily is eloquent on only one subject: she is sure that "'The men that is now is only all palaver and what they can get out of you.'"[10] She must be a victim of one of the crowd of lively young gallants.

At the climax of the story, Gabriel tries to woo his wife but is shut out of her mind by the memory of a poor pallid young man from many years before, a lover whose supreme amatory gesture was to arise from a consumptive sickbed to stand in the rain under her window—an ultimate gesture of Irish futility, like the monument-circling horse. But, she thinks, "he died for me": that phrase has both obvious Christian overtones, and implications of pointless self-sacrifice. It reminds us of Joyce's letter that says, "How I hate God and death! How I like Nora!"[11] Emotionally Gretta has been possessed by this ghost for all the many years that Gabriel thinks he has been her legitimate lover. Yet he is not angry or appalled, only sympathetic, and as he falls asleep Gabriel's soul surrenders to the ambient forces of the dead, yielding to the tug of the "journey westward." Snow, which falls on the living and the dead alike, is

9. *Portrait*, p. 203.

10. *Dubliners*, p. 178.

11. *Letters of James Joyce*, ed. Richard Ellmann (Viking, 1966), vol. 2, p. 50 [1904]. For a more romantic view of death as "the most beautiful form of life," see the last page of the essay "James Clarence Mangan" [1902]: in *Critical Writings of James Joyce*, ed. Ellsworth Mason and Richard Ellmann (Viking, 1959), p. 83.

"general all over Ireland," settling on "the crooked crosses and headstones, on the spears of the little gate, on the barren thorns" of the churchyard where the dead lover lies buried.[12] For Gabriel the dead become palpable, and as past and present begin to collapse into each other the story insinuates a weird form of re-Incarnation, as the figure of the crucified Christ merges with that of Michael Furey (as later the figures of Odysseus and Leopold Bloom merge). Michael, who was more than half in love with easeful death anyway, extends the hold of the "Dead Men's religion"; it blankets Ireland like the snow. And the Christ invoked is not the one who said "Let the dead bury their dead," but the worshipped corpse, used in Ireland to throttle the spirit of life in favor of sterile sentimentality. Despite the more expansive view taken of Irish hospitality and family life, and of the portrayal of a new fellow-feeling in Gabriel, the story remains a savage indictment of death worship.

Even though the atmosphere of *Ulysses* is far livelier than that in the dusty, ill-lit settings of *Dubliners* and the *Portrait*, reminders of mortmain crop up everywhere. Stephen is assailed by its images, most melodramatically by the ghost of his cancerous mother who turns into a "green crab with malignant red eyes [that] sticks deep its grinning claws in [his] heart."[13] Stephen runs from this bogey into another: facing Armageddon in the form of a drunken belligerent redcoat, he is visited by the apparition of Irish *revanchisme* and abortive heroics.

> (Old Gummy Granny in sugarloaf hat appears seated on a toadstool, the deathflower of potato blight on her breast.)
> STEPHEN
> Aha! I know you, grammer! Hamlet, revenge! The old sow that eats her farrow!
> OLD GUMMY GRANNY
> (*Rocking to and fro.*) Ireland's sweetheart, the king of Spain's daughter, alanna. Strangers in my house, bad manners to them! (*She keens with banshee woe. . . .*)

With more such wails, she urges a phantom dagger on the unwilling Stephen, indicating the soldier and begging "Remove him, acushla. At 8:35 a.m. you will be in heaven and Ireland will be free." Here

12. *Dubliners*, pp. 223–24.
13. *Ulysses*, p. 582; Gabler ed., 15.4220.

mortmain appears in the black-humor form of "death's madness," demanding yet another futile, suicidal assassination, according to the code still heeded by the IRA. Stephen protests that he doesn't want to die for his country, but would rather let it die for him.[14]

But it would not die for Joyce, so he transmuted his contempt into the source of all his work: if he could not get rid of the Ireland in his head, then he would ransack it for the sake of his art. He would recall, examine, and augment each of his memories, finding more and more in less and less, constricting his subject to the most banal and trivial events but finding radiant significance in them, as Blake saw infinity in a grain of sand. Even Irish poverty, which he had revealed so unsparingly, he could now see as a source of the riches of meaning. The principle is linked to that in Flaubert's work: as Ortega observed, to meet a real Madame Bovary would be thoroughly boring, but the revelation of her in the novel is fascinating. Through the art of memory, Joyce could transform Ireland with a sacramental vision, without the self-searching that accompanies a similar strategy in Proust. To the end of his life Joyce would question Irish visitors to Paris on all sorts of mundane information that a lesser artist would have "made up" as he went along; for Joyce Irish trivia, and above all Irish words, were laden with talismanic significance. Frank Budgen observed his friend's conviction that people were "strangely ignorant of the value of the words they used so glibly," and saw that Joyce had embodied it in Stephen: "To most boys words are convenient counters and no more. . . . But to Stephen they were mysteriously alive. In a sense, they were much more potent than the objects, actions and relations they stood for."[15] This is not linguistic mystification, but the premise of Joyce's process of sacramental transformation.

In the *Portrait*, Stephen evades a priest's vocation and chooses instead the secular priesthood of art, in which the "daily bread of

14. *Ulysses*, pp. 595, 600, 591; Gabler ed., 15.4578, 4586, 4737–38, 4473.

15. See Brenda Maddox, *Nora: A Biography of Nora Joyce* (Hamish Hamilton, 1988), p. 421; and also my *Ezra Pound: The Image and the Real* (Louisiana State University Press, 1969), chap. 3. Budgen, *James Joyce and the Making of* Ulysses (Indiana University Press, 1960; originally published, 1934), p. 57; see also Joyce, *Stephen Hero*, ed. Theodore Spencer (New Directions, 1959), p. 26. José Ortega y Gasset, *Meditations on Quixote*, trans. Evelyn Rugg and Diego Marin (Norton, 1961), p. 161.

experience" can be transmuted by fanatical linguistic precision and factual accuracy into "the radiant body of everliving life."[16] Just as Joyce turned the central images of the Church he feared and despised into instruments of his purpose, so he determined to do with Irish life as a whole. He saw that epiphanic revelations could be made of the tawdriest details. By means of Flaubertian discipline and economy of language he could realize his eucharistic project, which was at the same time Daedalian, "the artist forging anew in his workshop out of the sluggish matter of the earth a new soaring impalpable imperishable being."[17] No one has ever mined his memories so closely and profitably, wresting from the daily bread of Irish experience and the sluggish matter of its earth the raw material of an art that set many readers and writers in quest of their own personal pasts. So well did Joyce fulfill his goals that he made recovery of the past seem the gateway to a lost country, a realm of infinite meaning where those questions and longings of childhood, that stay with us forever, are satisfied.

When we read the Hell sermon in the *Portrait*, we realize that Joyce has turned the Jesuits' weapons against themselves; by closely mimicking the preacher's use of "composition of place" he lets the Irish Church reveal itself as a purveyor of lurid religious pornography, a motif compounded throughout the work with sentimental Mariolatry. Joyce then shows how to put Loyola's "spiritual exercise" to work for aesthetic ends in recreating his Dublin, a place more vivid than the one that can be visited. The sacramentalist use of Irish *passéisme* grew out of this cunning strategy, and then took over the oeuvre. The change in tone in *Ulysses* chimes with the fact that here sacramental transformation is not only strategy, but also theme and image. From Buck's mock-eucharistic shaving bowl to Molly's chamberpot the theme runs, borne by what Bloom calls a "language of flow" that traces all the images of flux, from human excretions to (and into) the Protean, transforming sea. Through gleefully exploited *passéisme*, 1904 Dublin suffers a "seachange into something rich and strange."

Joyce's fanatical use of autobiographical and Irish material is obvious; what is less so is that in putting it to use he was turning

16. *Portrait*, p. 221.
17. *Portrait*, p. 169.

the backward tropism of Irish memory into an animating force. In this sense the critics are right, there is a new spirit in "The Dead": not that Joyce grew any more tolerant of Irish failings, but that in the writing of that story he began to see clearly the potentialities of *passéisme* consciously and ironically adopted as artistic strategy. For the force of "The Dead" comes not only from the strength of Joyce's fear and contempt for mortmain, but even more from the painstaking reconstruction of the Misses Morkans' annual dance and the world it implicates. The loving cares that Joyce lavished on this effort are evident in every sentence. Each word carries forward some aspect of that sprightly yet death-centered ambience, fitting as if into a mosaic of detail and nuance that is utterly convincing. It makes us feel as if we are in that ballroom. There is no labored symbolism; even the snow, and the gas, are as natural and unforced as anyone could wish, and as potent: no one can assign reductive meanings to them. Joyce made the story from luxuriant revels in the riches of his own and Nora's memory banks; he transformed himself, as it were, into his past-praising father indulging in memorial reconstruction—which is one reason, besides the wit and the prodigalism that his brother Stanislaus hated but that he himself loved—why Joyce revered the old man and even felt that his own verbal genius was somehow tied up with the extravagantly spendthrift habits he "inherited." "Old father, old artificer, stand me now and ever in good stead."[18] Read as literally as Joyce was wont to do, this means that his father took his place as creator.

From then on, in his work Joyce looked for new possibilities of using the past: the *Portrait* cunningly exploited his own autobiography, but also, with the Daedalus symbolism, opened up the strategy of overlaying the past, like a template, on the present. *Ulysses* was the triumphant result: beginning life as a *Dubliners* story, it languished until the parallel between the ancient hero and the twentieth-century advertising canvasser was seen in the light of yet another twist. Once more Joyce was mimicking a form of Dublin *passéisme*, but this time a more pretentious kind; as Hugh Kenner remarks, "*Ulysses* takes as if literally the talk of Yeats and his friends about metempsychosis."[19] The Dublin Theosophists and

18. See Richard Ellmann, *James Joyce* (Oxford University Press, 1959), pp. 656–57; and the last sentence of the *Portrait*.
19. *The Pound Era* (University of California Press, 1971), p. 271.

spiritualists endlessly discussed reincarnation (a craze that has itself been reincarnated in California: no wonder Yeats received the first spoken communications from his *daimon* [through his wife] in Southern California).[20] Joyce wanted not only to mock them openly—as he does in the book—and to show that he could bring the theme into artistic fruition better than anybody else: the best joke was to imply that fashionable mysticism, like the Gaelic Revival and all the other forms of highminded nationalism, was really only a variant of the commonplace, lower-middle-class Irish theme of past-worship. The identification of Michael Furey with Christ had been rather tentative, but Bloom could be made to reenact Odysseus in a far more hilariously full-blooded way because of this joke.

And then the joke went a quantum leap further. Joyce began to see that he had found a way to turn Irish backwardness into a tribute to the universal human interconnectedness of past and present, the very bond that makes the past spring up again like mummy wheat (to use one of Yeats's favorite metaphors) simply because it is deposited in language.[21] Contemplating what he was able to do with Homeric parallels in *Ulysses*, Joyce saw that patterns from earlier eras affect the lives of humans in all sorts of unacknowledged as well as obvious ways: language enshrines these for us, whether we like it or not. Even in the most futuristic or past-ignoring cultures, as in America in the Sixties, there are strong implications of repeating history (as farce, usually), because of the grip of verbal paradigms or what were called then "mental sets." Neither cultures nor individuals can reinvent themselves by an act of will—though some remarkable self-delusions of such grandeur have been produced—given the ineluctable modality of the way language circulates. To achieve total emancipation from the past would require babies to be born and then abandoned on remote islands, or some such Platonic scenario. Humans are the only animals who, by using language, can pass on images from the past to newer generations, which happens with the spontaneity with which

20. See Yeats, *A Vision* (Macmillan, [New York], 1961; originally published, 1938), p. 9.

21. See Yeats's poems "On a Picture of a Black Centaur by Edmond Dulac" (1922) and "Conjunctions" (1934); see also "All Souls' Night" (1920), l. 86: "I have mummy truths to tell."

language acquisition takes place anyway; it is impossible to keep children from learning language, and the past likewise cannot be kept from us. Moreover, quite aside from the collective heritage, by means of language we store images from our own personal histories in a unique way, whereas animals live essentially in a continuous present as if doing everything always for the first time; they have no real sense of what we would call repetition, that unique and problematic gift (and constitutive element) of language.

For human life, language, and thus retrospectivity, is sine qua non; and experience represented or mediated, in the form of imagination, is uniquely important to humans. With a past we can imagine futures, other people's lives, all kinds of things. In fact — a fact that Proust exploited wonderfully — represented experience in many ways governs our lives, overshadowing direct experience, if indeed there is any such thing: we have reason to believe that what we call consciousness is a way of instantaneously *representing* external events to ourselves, giving them a quasi-linguistic processing that turns mere sensation into "experience," something we can deal with in our minds. Things never just happen to us; they always have potential "meanings" that are ultimately linguistic. Consciousness seems to turn stimuli and perceptions into a running, subverbal but latently articulate narrative, a "story" of our lives that gives us a chance to think things over, change them (within limits), and so on. We know that this is true of memory, and when we try to remember simple sensations — for example, how we sat down in our present seats — we are recalling "created imagery," what it *must* have been like. If consciousness is simply instant memory — the ongoing transformation of "events" into a video with latent voice-over — then we are producing "created imagery" all along; that is, for language-using beings, all experience is mediated. This would help explain many things, from dreams and hallucinations to why consciousness interferes with motor skills (in sports, musical performances, and the like.)[22]

It would also explain the importance of art to humans. Art is the

22. Several of these points have been adapted from Julian Jaynes, *The Origins of Consciousness in the Breakdown of the Bicameral Mind* (Houghton Mifflin, 1976), bk. 1, chap. 1.

(more or less) masterful, emotional organization of images and representations whose power to evoke vicarious experience in auditors is related to the dominant roles that represented experience and retrospectivity play in our consciousness and our lives generally. Art can augment the context of and the sense of insight into our lives and actions, which sounds like an aesthete's credo but equally well describes what happens at a rock concert. (The premise that this, among other evidence, suggests is that all music, including the most abstract, owes more for its power to wordless emotional tones of the human voice, and to repetition and recall, than is generally acknowledged: "All a kind of attempt to talk," as Bloom thinks in "Sirens.")[23] These augmentations do not always have to be pleasurable in the obvious sense: the tragedians have always known the desirability of fear and pity, while comedy can exploit anxiety and discomfort in hilarious ways. Such Joyceans as Samuel Beckett illustrate and draw on anxieties of meaninglessness such as those that arise in writing itself — as in the anxiety over the blank page. This anxiety involves facing not only the infinity of possible ways to say things, but also all the ways in which language has been used before. The reverberations of the past, as always, have the power to stultify the present. This brings us back to Ireland, and Joyce's solution to his own blank-page problem by electing to enshrine its nostalgic language with passionate care.

Joyce ascribed sacramental power to names, phrases, and verbal motifs, so that his work becomes an epiphanic manifestation of a *logos*, albeit a parodic one, with his recollection of the past. He pored over the most minute turns of Dublin phrase, reproducing them in his works with exact fidelity and amazing sensitivity — surely the greatest in world literature — to idiom; the spontaneity and freshness of his characters' speech disguise the fact that their energy is that of a reawakened corpse.[24] He saw that present words and acts reverberate endlessly against bygone models, and that there was high comedy to be enacted in the setting of these in relation to one another. His intense, even manic, verbal precision and his zany inquiries to travelers and to his native informants,

23. *Ulysses*, p. 288; Gabler ed., 11.1196.
24. Cf. Hugh Kenner, *Dublin's Joyce* (Indiana University Press, 1956), p. 1.

such as his aunt (he asked her to go to 7 Eccles Street and measure the railings) aimed to perform the feat of reincarnation itself, the flesh made word.[25]

Proceeding thus singlemindedly with hardly a thought of what other writers might be doing (though Yeats was often in the back of his mind), Joyce anticipated a basic strategy of the Modernist movement, the recovery of the presence of the past: as T. S. Eliot was to say in his famous essay on tradition, not the pastness of the past but its presentness, its presence *in* the present.[26] This attitude is reminiscent of many Western revitalization movements, from the Renaissance and even before (e.g., in the concept of the *translatio* from Troy to Rome),[27] but it acquired a new depth in the light of evolution, archaeology, and related developments. In the nineteenth century, fear of the past's hold caused a proliferation of theories of degeneration and atavism, the recurrence of ancestral characteristics in later generations, the "throwback" phenomenon. Harmless enough in the genetics of flowers or dogs, it became a threat like that of syphilis in the writings of Lombroso, Nordau, and others, as if civilization were endangered by misbreeding and the human race precariously perched on a precipice of brutality. But in the imaginations of the Modernists, unafflicted by melioristic fantasies of progress, atavism was rehabilitated, and became the matrix of a new energy in art. Joyce's evolution, from fear of mortmain to cunning and resourceful use of metempsychosis, stands for the shaping of the movement generally, with his discovery transmitted by Ezra Pound and transmuted by Eliot (who called it "the mythical method").[28] But the return or revival of the past in the present had already found many forms in proto-Modernist works; the foundations were laid by many figures, including Hardy, Forster, and Conrad.

25. Gilbert, ed., *Letters*, p. 175; cf. pp. 135, 136, 174; *Ulysses*, p. 391 (Gabler ed., 14.293).

26. "Tradition and the Individual Talent," in *Selected Essays of T. S. Eliot* (Harcourt Brace, 1932), p. 4.

27. See Ernst Robert Curtius, *European Literature and the Latin Middle Ages*, trans. Willard Trask (Harper & Row, 1963), pp. 29 et seq.; also see Walter Burkert, *Structure and History in Greek Mythology and Ritual* (University of California Press, 1979), p. 25.

28. "Ulysses, Order, and Myth," *Dial* 75 (1923): 483.

Ulysses is, as Kenner says, the decisive or "pivotal" work of the era, and the most florid manifestation of the new view, because for one thing Homer himself appeared to have a strong streak of *passéisme*.[29] Homer's mighty warriors and grave counselors might at first have seemed very different from the enervated Irish, but as Joyce explored the comic possibilities he saw more and more parallels, including the supreme one: that as he was immuring a Dublin day of 1904 in amber, Homer too had preserved a past. The Achaeans were as remote in time from Homer as were the Geats from the author of *Beowulf*, and Homer's characters in turn talked endlessly themselves about the past, particularly but not only Nestor. Moreover, the Greeks seemed to be as loquacious as the Irish, as prone to speechify on any subject. These similarities suggested delicious satiric angles to be developed.

Homer, we now know, retailed with amazing precision features of the dead Mycenaean culture, obsolete armor and funeral rites and the names of towns long since razed, that were meaningless to listeners of his own day.[30] These were buried apparently in the fragments of formulaic language out of which the epics were made, handed down by generations of bards. The more they mystified his audience, the better for Homer's purposes of evoking a lost world, and for getting them to believe him when he said that two men of his own day could hardly lift the rocks these ancient heroes threw at each other.[31] Joyce had little trouble finding Irish verbal equivalents for those forgotten artifacts, or for those missiles.

Verbosity proved to be the richest parallelism. The modern reader might well conclude that Homer's characters, like Bloom, could talk about a straw for an hour and talk about it steady (yet Bloom is not a tenth as garrulous as the Thersitean "Nameless One" who says that about him).[32] The warriors are fantastically articulate; indeed, in Homer a combatant with laryngitis would be under a severe handicap, for the fighting cannot proceed without taunts, boasts, pious reflections, anecdotes, and other verbal forms. As among apes and baboons, intimidation substitutes for

29. *Joyce's Voices* (University of California Press, 1978), p. xii.
30. Denys Page, *History and the Homeric Iliad* (University of California Press, 1959), pp. 218–19.
31. Iliad, 5.302–4.
32. *Ulysses*, p. 316; Gabler ed., 12.894–96.

much real fighting, and war cries often dominate the battle. Achilles, unarmed, routs the spoilers of Patroclus' body with his great cry, and when Athena "bellows" in support of him, such consternation is produced that twelve Trojans are killed falling back on their own ranks.[33] At the end of the Odyssey, Athena's mighty cry is the only thing that can stop the outbreak of civil war in Ithaca. The war cries then merged with or were expanded into battle songs, death songs, and other constituents of tribal warfare, and eventually became the nuclei of the epics that immortalize these battles. This point allows Homer many self-reflexive touches: for example, the bard Demodocus' songs about Odysseus, which he sings to the hero himself in disguise. *Ulysses*, naturally, is full of self-reflexive ironies.[34]

Most important for Joyce's purposes, Homer intertwined the human voice with the past. Mr. Dedalus and his cronies ape, without knowing it, Homer's choric figures who murmur sagely about the high deeds of the old days. Thus Joyce's project, of delineating Dublin in a way so vivid that it could be re-created from his work, mimics Homer's preservation of the Mycenaean world and uses the elegiac mode so congenial to the Irish and the Greeks alike. Indeed, all audiences of epic must love it, for weeping is as characteristic of epic as insult, quest, or slaughter; perhaps even more so, since it typically accompanies the other frequent action of storytelling. Heroes weep like women when they hear mighty deeds including their own recited, as all do when the past is recalled. Weeping frames the Odyssey: at the beginning Odysseus's tears come from thoughts of home while he languishes in Calypso's benevolent captivity, while his return home at the end cues enough scenes of pathos to float a ship. (Thinking of the linkage of tears to oceans, we note that it was a Greek philosopher who said that all things flow.) Homer does not omit the pitiful death of the faithful old dog, who wags his tail for his disguised master as he lies dying on the dunghill, forcing Odysseus to hide more tears. The Odyssey is a poem strangely compounded of exotic terrors and domestic nostalgia, but the comparatively bloodthirsty Iliad contains equally

---

33. Iliad, 18.215–31.
34. Odyssey, 8.71 ff. On self-reflexiveness, see Brook Thomas, *Joyce's* Ulysses: *A Book of Many Happy Returns* (Louisiana State University Press, 1982).

heartrending scenes, from the metaphor of the terrified baby birds about to be swallowed by the snake to the final scenes of Priam begging the body of Hector—at which Achilles weeps with him, thinking of his own father, of Patroclus, and of himself.[35] Nor is this river of tears stanched when we leave Homer; from *Gilgamesh* to the *Song of Roland*, epics are pervaded by themes of loss, grief, and mortality, and by the lamentations of men and women.

Homer's audiences must have wept as freely as his characters did. The audience's tears implicitly recognize that culture itself passes away like human life, that indeed it is but an image—not only in the epic, but even when it flourished. A culture is a group of people trying to conform to an image of how life should be lived, yet another manifestation of the power of represented experience in human life. And as the shade is latent in the hero, so also the culture is mortal, and must be memorialized. The recognition in epic of a culture's transitory nature is an acknowledgment that it is always already insubstantial, a set of relations and representations. The recurrent Ozymandian drive in cultures, to try to immortalize themselves in deathless marble or bronze, betrays the anxiety caused by this recognition.

Cultures after all are creatures of language, like everything human. As Claude Lévi-Strauss put it, who says man says language and who says language says culture.[36] This interidentity is implicitly the theme of the epic, explaining the prevalence of themes of loss, which can be overcome (and then only partially, like mortality) by memorial reconstruction, by representation in language. Epics are not philosophical statements about loss, but performative utterances: "They shall not be forgotten." The grief is bound up with the very images that allow it to be transcended. Images of the past cause weeping because they remind us of what is already lost, but assuage grief because we can remember it. The days that are no more can live again, in the very refrain that they can never live again.

This formulation fits very well the Irish mood depicted throughout Joyce's work. *Ulysses* carries his appropriation of *passéisme* as strategy to its extreme, for to write of 1904 Dublin in World War I

35. Iliad, 2.308–20, 24.507–12.

36. See G. Charbonnier, ed., *Conversations with Claude Lévi-Strauss*, trans. John Weightman and Doreen Weightman (Jonathan Cape, 1969), pp. 149–50.

Trieste or Zurich was already an elegiac act. Joyce had sensed the
yawning rift in cultural continuity that opened as the war shattered
the old epoch: after 1916 he had to reckon with the possibility, as
British gunboats bombarded the Post Office, that his work might
indeed have to serve as a blueprint for rebuilding. He knew he was
memorializing a way of life that had already passed. The Great
War created our world by freeing us from that old one, which is
why the Twenties still seem modern though everything before it
is impossibly remote. Joyce anticipated the "change" in human
character that Virginia Woolf postdated at about 1910.[37] In that
year, it must be remembered, the large majority of the earth's
inhabitants still lived under the rule of emperors: how far away
that seems! What has such an outdated political contrivance to do
with the twentieth century? In one of the great all-time gestures of
mortmain, the British held on to India until after another world
war, but the culture to which that empire belonged had been crum-
bling since 1914. Hence Joyce's sense of what he was writing about:
the seventh city of Christendom, and second of the British Empire,
as representative of a gone world—with the reverberation that
worlds are always in a sense gone.

D. H. Lawrence was much more right than he knew, but for the
wrong reasons—he was a great misreader—to object to *Ulysses*
because "it's all so *dead*":

> My God, what a clumsy olla putrida James Joyce is! Nothing but old
> fags and cabbage-stumps of quotations from the Bible and the rest,
> stewed in the juice of deliberate, journalistic dirty-mindedness—what
> old and hard-worked staleness, masquerading as the all-new![38]

Lawrence never understood the nature of Modernism, though he
dabbled in some of its procedures. He meant all this as crushing
dispraise, but like Jung's complaint that the book could be read as
well backwards as forwards, it turns into ironic tribute. All that is
new comes from "old stumps," as Joyce and the Modernists realized; hence Joyce was totally unembarrassed in his procedures.
"Ultra-modernist Joyce always turned back to the classics. . . .

---

37. Woolf, "Mr. Bennett and Mrs. Brown" (1924), reprinted in Michael Hoffman
and Patrick Murphy, eds., *Essentials of the Theory of Fiction* (Duke University
Press, 1988), p. 26.
38. Aldous Huxley, ed., *Letters of D. H. Lawrence* (Viking, 1932), p. 750.

History, Vico, and *Finnegans Wake* all say that each impulse of new life is a *re*vival."[39]

While most Westerners were still living as if they had to accept Tennyson's admonition to "move upwards, working out the beast,/ And let the ape and tiger die," the Modernists were ready to look on the primordial past as the source of long-stored energy.[40] Joyce encapsulated it all by making the dominating image of his last work the waking corpse of a giant who falls like Humpty-Dumpty and lies buried in the Dublin landscape:

> The great fall of the offwall entailed at such short notice the pftjschute of Finnegan, erse solid man, that the humptyhillhead of humself prumptly sends an unquiring one well to the west in quest of his tumptytumtoes: and their upturnpikepointandplace is at the knock out in the park where oranges have been laid to rust upon the green since devlinsfirst loved livvy.[41]

The giant Finnegan's toes stick up at the knock or hill in Phoenix (how appropriate!) Park, while his head is Howth ("head") on the sea.

So Joyce's work in progress forms the constitutive parable of Modernism, even though he would have been wryly disdainful of such a notion. Thus came about the further irony that a movement named (by us, not them) for its aggressively avant-garde experimentalism was founded on the premise that the dead can be revived, and are themselves the source of the reviving energy. Literary movements are in a way overrated, the creations of critics rather than writers, but Plato rightly noted that the walls of the city are undermined when the modes of music change. No one can fully understand the works and days of Joyce, Pound, Eliot, or any who followed them without some concept of Modernism. It was a movement that coalesced out of several energies, not only in literature but also in the plastic arts and music, and even—though there's less here than meets the eye—in philosophy. Because of the interaction of all the arts, and their cultural implications, we can use Meyer Schapiro's summation of the total picture:

39. Fritz Senn, "Remodeling Homer," in Heyward Ehrlich, ed., *Light Rays: James Joyce and Modernism* (New Horizon [New York], 1984), p. 71.

40. "In Memoriam," sec. 118, ll.27–28.

41. *Finnegans Wake* (Viking, 1939), p. 3.

The years 1910 to 1913 were the heroic period in which the most astonishing innovations had occurred; it was then that the basic types of
the art of the next forty years were created. . . . About 1913 painters,
writers, musicians, and architects felt themselves to be at an epochal
turning-point corresponding to an equally decisive transition in philosophical thought and social life. This sentiment of imminent change
inspired a general insurgence, a readiness for great events. The years
just before the first World War were rich in new associations of artists,
vast projects, and daring manifestos. The world of art had never known
so keen an appetite for action, a kind of militancy that gave to cultural
life the quality of a revolutionary movement or the beginnings of a new
religion.[42]

This revolutionary quality remains the most visible mark of the
writing that this period set in motion, as it is of the painting;
although it is true in both fields that the efforts of the next forty
years consisted of attempts to work out the "basic types" created
then, in many ways the works were so startling that they have never
been outmoded, or even copied. In spite of Cubism's formidable
influence, it produced no direct successors, and the same is true of
works like *Finnegans Wake* or Pound's *Cantos*. Such work at-
tempted to be not merely new but unrepeatable, as if perpetually
revolutionary. Given this, we might fall into the mistake of thinking of the deep impulse of such movements as purely innovative;
nowadays we connect the revolutionary impulse with the idea of
blotting out the past. But Schapiro discerns that, across the spectrum, awareness of the past did not decline, but rather grew:

> The fact is that the young moderns had an insatiable hunger for past
> art; the new movements were accompanied by a revaluation of forgot-
> ten epochs and an extraordinary expansion and deepening of historical
> research, often by scholars who drew from their experience of modern
> art a quicker sympathy for the old.[43]

This observation would have especially gratified someone like
Pound. His point, and Eliot's in the essay on tradition, was that
we cannot accept either the conventional view of past art or some
totalized "lump or bolus" of it without selectivity: on the contrary,

---

42. *Modern Art: 19th and 20th Centuries: Selected Papers* (Braziller, 1978), pp.
137–38.
43. Schapiro, pp. 152–53.

forgotten epochs and works must be revitalized, and a view of the past created that would see the alignments connecting old and new.

The shape of our era is still largely determined by the component conceptions of that "heroic period" in which consciousness of the past and its meanings were the catalyzing force for the most revolutionary activities, and the awakening of the past in the present was a model of true vitality. We have not yet exhausted the potentialities of the paradox in this sense of things, partly because the Modernists made us ready for a vastly expanded sense of the past that has come to us through archaeology, anthropology, and their attendant sciences. All social scientisms run the danger of declining into studies of their own methodology, but they have helped give us new understandings of humankind and its role in the order of things.

The enabling act of Modernism may well have been the treatment of the "chthonic" religion of Greece by the Cambridge anthropologists, especially Jane Harrison. Seeing that the Olympian religion that appears in Homer was itself merely a flower in sand, she searched out the obscure local, earth-centered cults that preceded it. In line with the generalized social Darwinism of the time, she might have been expected to treat these cults as a "stage" of Greek religion later transcended and outgrown. But instead she treated them more as life-giving soil, without which the Olympian religion appears merely etiolated.[44] This embrace of the archaic started many trains of thought, eventuating in a new fascination with such phenomena first as "roots," and then as objects of interest in their own right. Now we have come full circle. Words like *primitive* have become in many contexts (the most important ones) more honorific than pejorative; this is an index of a great paradigm shift, and no more far-reaching intellectual revolution has occurred in the Western world. Unlike the Victorians, who treated "primitive survivals" (peasant superstitions and the like) as products of perversely backward habits, we do not recoil from them: instead, we tend to see the continuity between ancient humans and the newest achievements. Even in its most popularized form (as in *2001*) this insight is a giant step, although it may be itself too easily thema-

---

44. *Prolegomena to the Study of Greek Religion* (New American Library, 1955; originally published, 1903); see p. viii.

tized as a form of progress. The differences in the two centuries'
views of the past should not be made a matter for facile self-
congratulation, but these differences cannot be ignored either. Guy
Davenport's formulation is that "what is most modern in our time
frequently turns out to be the most archaic."[45] Not even the most
cynical degenerationist would have said that in the last century.
We can now see that the Modernists made a discovery rivalling
that of Columbus: like him, they found the New by seeking the
Old.

45. *The Geography of the Imagination* (North Point, 1981), p. 21.

1

The Century's Corpse Outleant: Hardy and Modernism

> On ne peut pas porter *partout* avec soi le cadavre de son père.
> EZRA POUND, quoting Apollinaire[1]

Thomas Hardy wrote "The Darkling Thrush" in December 1900, the last month of the old century. Here is the second stanza:

> The land's sharp features seemed to be
>   The Century's corpse outleant,
> His crypt the cloudy canopy,
>   The wind his death-lament.
> The ancient pulse of germ and birth
>   Was shrunken hard and dry,
> And every spirit upon earth
>   Seemed fervourless as I.

Hardy himself was sixty years old, and in a position to consider the changing of the calendar as something more than a mere convention — here, it seems to be a mournful anxious rite for something passing irrevocably. Though most of the critical attention devoted to this poem has centered on the thrush, who sings with implausible hope in the next stanza, the original title was "By the Century's Deathbed," which points us toward gloomier conclusions.[2] But those who, like Hardy here, felt anxiety deepening to trepidation about the new century did not necessarily want the old

---

1. From "Vorticism" (1914); see Pound's *Gaudier-Brzeska: A Memoir* (New Directions, 1960), p. 82.
2. See *The Complete Poetical Works of Thomas Hardy*, ed. Samuel Hynes (Oxford: Clarendon Press, 1982), vol. 1, pp. 187–88.

one back. Not nostalgia but a sense of omnipresent failure pervades this stanza, and the figures of stiffening impotence add to
the funereal tone. Something is dying, not in the way of all flesh,
leaving a patrimony to a new generation; rather, here the image is
of extinction, entropy, stillbirth, abrupt discontinuity. The word
ancient recalls the features of the wizened death mask in the landscape, even before it reminds us that the "pulse of germ and birth"
has a time-honored status, so that *ancient* here in effect means
"worn-out." Bacon had written in *The Advancement of Learning*:
"These times are the ancient times, when the world is ancient,"
making paradoxical play with the quarrel of ancients and moderns,
but Hardy's appropriation of the trope adds to the sense of enerva-
tion in the poem.[3] The process of death making way for new birth
is itself here in danger of senile decay, and of the abhorréd shears.
The corpse is "outleant," a Hardyism suggesting that it is not only
prostrate but also somehow unstable, leaning or hanging uselessly
out into the landscape. Indeed, some reverberations of this word —
though strictly speaking irrelevant — further deepen the tone of sterility: the homophonic echo of "lent out" dimly recalls a dubious
financial adventure, and yet another entangled association gives
thoughts of pointless competition, in that the corpse outleans others, notably the speaker himself in the first stanza, who "leant
upon a coppice gate." (Hardy was attentive to postures; see, e.g.,
his wife's assumption of a crucified posture in "Near Lanivet,
1872.") As to verbal associations, in later decades the reproductive
sense of "germ" that Hardy intended was muddied by overtones of
microbes and disease — but this meaning was already common in
his time, and if read there it complicates interestingly the connotations of morbidity.

   The sexual connotations in the latter part of the stanza would
surely have appeared morbid to a good Victorian reader, and
Hardy must have anticipated that his readers would be too of-
fended even to acknowledge the disturbance to themselves. On the
one hand the lines have a confessional spirit — Hardy's marriage
had just about dried up, emotionally and sexually, and the stiffening of the corpse suggests sexual frustration as well as rigor mortis.
Hardy knew, better than anyone else, that an audience whose pruri-

   3. Quoted in Matei Calinescu, *Faces of Modernity* (Indiana University Press,
1977), p. 24.

ent squeamishness had helped drive him out of novel-writing by objecting to *Tess* and *Jude* could not miss the implications of "shrunken hard and dry," but would be unable to say so. In this light the word *pulse* bespeaks not only the rhythms of birth but even those of the sexual act itself, all of them now slowing and shrinking into sclerotic paralysis.[4] Against the throbbing pulses of reproduction, the poem opposes a force that retards and rigidifies them, leaving an image of shrunken tumescence, shriveled gonads, dried seed. This sense is shared by the corpse and the speaker, who feels impotent and spiritless.

The degeneration of Hardy's marriage into something that would produce such images of frustration is a well-known story. His first wife grew jealous of his success—like Zelda Fitzgerald or Vivien Eliot—yet felt she had married beneath her. The combination proved lethal to domestic life, and she grew very distant and uncommunicative, as many of Hardy's most plaintive poems tell. An allegory of the situation may be found in the poem "The Ivy-Wife," in which he portrays parasitic ivy as clinging to, and thus killing, the tree she finally "marries." The ivy "longed to love a full-boughed beech/ And be as high as he," and though he evades her, as does a plane, she finally strangles an ash, and both perish in his fall. Not unnaturally, Hardy's wife objected to the poem. Even more revealing, and a clear link to the images of "The Darkling Thrush," is the poem entitled "The Dead Man Walking." The speaker, obviously Hardy himself, has been "inched" to death-in-life by successive disappointments, of which the failure of love is the culmination:

> And when my Love's heart kindled
>   In hate of me,
> Wherefore I knew not, died I
>   One more degree.

He is changed into a "corpse-thing," a zombie who walks and talks but "live[s] not now." This complex of feelings seems to make explicit the morbid overtones of "shrunken hard and dry." Indeed,

---

4. Surely Hardy did not intend the archaic sense of "pulse" as a kind of soup. On his marital situation, see Carl Weber, *Hardy of Wessex: His Life and Literary Career* (Columbia University Press, 1965), pp. 216–18; and J. O. Bailey, *The Poetry of Thomas Hardy: A Handbook and Commentary* (University of North Carolina Press, 1970), pp. 21–26.

in view of the implications of priapism, one has to wonder if there isn't a sly though anguished duplicity to the title of that apparently parliamentary poem, "The Rejected Member's Wife."

So Hardy saw himself in the image of the stiffened, phallic corpse of the century, both of them drained of life by desiccated desires. Of course Hardy was a man ready to be disappointed by any course of life, and acknowledges in the poems that "he never expected much." "For life I had never cared greatly" is, if anything, an understatement. Still, the period of his wife's estrangement seems to have been especially traumatic: why should Time have brought this to him? Earlier he had complained that events were governed by "purblind Doomsters"; now the arbitrariness of what had befallen his marriage was a final sting. Yet had he not foretold it unawares? Throughout his work the sexual process is likely to lead to disaster of one kind or another. In the poems even more than the novels, poignant feelings of love and desire are almost always recalled in moods of loss, remorse, and sorrow, with Hardy's famous retrospectivity: the poems have an interestingly monotonous elegiac quality, relieved occasionally by tart, sardonic cynicism ("The Ruined Maid" and "Ah, Are You Digging on My Grave?") but dominated either by loss or by touches of pathos: "No Buyers" simply gives an image of poor hapless peddlers; "Snow in the Suburbs" means a picture-book scene for the human observers but a brush with death for a starving cat. Hardy was a connoisseur of the transiently painful miseries we appropriate from the lives of others, in whom we see ourselves but for whimsical turns of fate. But he had plenty to wince at in his own life, and poems like "Neutral Tones" are as harrowing in their portrayals of crossed or baffled love as anything in our confessional century:

> The smile on your mouth was the deadest thing
> Alive enough to have strength to die;
> And a grin of bitterness swept thereby
>   Like an ominous bird a-wing. . . .

This Frostian monodrama is conducted at a "pond edged with grayish leaves" fallen on "starving sod," under a wintry sun "white, as though chidden of God." These form the landscape for love in Hardy. This poem was written even before he met his future wife, but whatever stillborn affair it chronicles — probably that with his cousin Phena—taught unforgettable "keen lessons that love deceives,/ And wrings with wrong."

In the famous "Convergence of the Twain," the collision of the *Titanic* with the iceberg is figured as a marriage arranged by the fates; the great ship built by humans has a "sinister mate" prepared by nature in "shadowy distant silence." And the "consummation" shakes the world—another of Hardy's barely submerged sexual images, with the iceberg standing for the imaging process as well as for the fatal misalliances that chance provides to dog humanity's most elaborate plans and hopes. So the poem is as much about Hardy's idea of marriage as about public events. This makes it all the more remarkable that one of the features of the poem is the absence of human figures. Somehow Hardy has anticipated the television pictures we were recently able to see, showing the eerie emptiness of the great artifact on the ocean bottom without any of the usual signs of human habitation. But in fact this characterlessness is typical of Hardy poems; they form a veritable roster of missing persons. As David Perkins puts it,

> One need not demonstrate Hardy's urgent preoccupation in his poetry with the hurt of aloneness. Its importance is marked not only by open statement in his poems, but also by the fact that the protagonist almost always appears as a solitary, an outsider, or an individual alienated from the life of his fellows.[5]

But there is more here than hurt, or Hardy's feelings of being the skeleton at the feast in his society, especially in the love poems. Most often the speaker is Hardy with his memories, but even when other characters appear, it is as if they were alone on earth. In these landscapes one feels, as it were, deserted by humankind: sometimes "Wessex" seems an uninhabited country, which as Hardy's creation it was. There is a tremendous loneliness in these poems, an isolation almost autistic. If crowds or multiple characters are mentioned, they are insubstantial—more often than not, they are ghosts. This characteristic must be composed of complex feelings, but surely one component is the idea that marriage is fruitless (as his were), an isolation of two who may become antagonists when they had hoped to be helpmates. He saw it as a process

5. "Hardy and the Poetry of Isolation," in Albert Guerard, ed., *Hardy: A Collection of Critical Essays* (Prentice-Hall, 1963), p. 143.

not of participation in the ongoing of generations, but of a detachment, a stepping out the swirl of life, perhaps into a long struggle
so intense that it would blot out all other individuals and absorb
all awareness.

The striking absence of the sense of a peopled world is especially
marked in the series of poems addressed to his wife's ghost that
Hardy wrote after her death in 1912. Because most critics judge
these to be among his best, their features are particularly revealing.
First, the wife's almost willful disappearance is what enkindles his
old love for her again; since no poems so tender survive from the
years of their marriage, clearly her absence was more stimulating
than her presence. Second, the isolation of the two in remembered
scenes is remarkable. As they appear in the landscapes of "Ly-
onesse," they might as well have been on the moon. Indeed, it
becomes clear that places — not only in this series but in all the
poems — are more important than other people. No doubt many
lovers have had this feeling, but the presentation of it in these
poems is so stark as to be a little chilling, even frightening. What
Hardy remembers and desires to re-create is not merely seclusion
with his beloved, but a metaphysical alienation from all others.
That Hardy was in several ways glad to turn from novel-writing to
poetry is widely acknowledged: a major advantage of poems may
have been that they enabled him to dispense with the characters
obligatory for novels. Yet even the novels are chronicles of isolated
individuals, and have nothing of the swarming sense of life in
Dickens, or even in Eliot or Thackeray. And what marks the poems
about Emma Lavinia Gifford is only slightly less intense in those
about other women, other affairs unpursued or unconsummated;
the relationships are compressed down to essences that are, in effect, out of life. Phena is named in the poems only after her death.

Such presentation of scenes of life as enervated, insubstantial,
and devoid of filiations to others contributes much, obviously, to
the sense of Hardy as a relentless pessimist. His "obsessive ideas,"
in Samuel Hynes's words, are "infidelities of all possible kinds, the
inevitable loss of love, the destructiveness of time, the implacable
indifference of nature, the cruelty of men, the irreversible pastness
of the past."[6] Yet there is a sense in which all this is balanced by

6. *The Pattern of Hardy's Poetry* (University of North Carolina Press, 1961),
p. 4. Hynes is wrong about the irreversible pastness of the past, as shall be seen.

another theme, that of a chthonic vigor of life beyond the grave. If the living in Hardy's poems tend to be etiolated shadows, whether as speaker-observers or as memories, the dead have a peculiar power and significance in their being. They are indeed adept at seeing and saying what the living cannot see and say. "There are so many poems in which dead men speak that it must be defined as a normal occurrence in this poetic universe," observes J. Hillis Miller. "The dead are not only still conscious, but they have a more unclouded and far-seeing vision than they ever had when alive."[7] Miller's delineation of the dialectic of distance and desire in Hardy's work, typically yielding a view from a perspective both near and far simultaneously, accounts for much of the strangeness of Hardy's poems, and opens speculation about the singular feature of the articulate dead. Other critics have elaborated rationales for this feature: James Richardson compares Hardy's dead to gods who possess an Olympian *apathein*.

> The dead cannot lose. They cannot be disappointed or disillusioned. They are not subject to self-division, to the round of loss and return. The Hardy who was fond of dying before he was out of the flesh, and who found the passing of life unbearable, embraces the dead, who, like the ghost he sought to make of himself, have presence but no present. Just as he viewed himself as not solid enough to influence his environment, so the dead in their indifference, in their renunciation of power, become invincible.[8]

But this does not explain the more red-blooded ghosts who appear in the poems. The paradox is wholly Hardyesque: the dead are often more vigorous than the living. The ultimate form of the distance-and-desire phenomenon entails living beings, haunted by ghosts and loss, becoming zombies living in the past (as Hardy in

7. *Thomas Hardy: Distance and Desire* (Harvard University Press, 1970), p. 226. In Hardy's poems, even the dog Wessex spoke after his death. See also Miller, "Topography and Tropography in Thomas Hardy's *In Front of the Landscape*," in Mario J. Valdés and Owen Miller, eds., *Identity of the Literary Text* (University of Toronto Press, 1985), pp. 73–91. Miller shows how the poem's rhetorical structures recapitulate the theme of the insubstantiality of the present and the presence of the past.

8. *Thomas Hardy: The Poetry of Necessity* (University of Chicago Press, 1977), p. 123. Richardson's paragraph paraphrases a famous passage in Hardy's autobiography, which appeared under his second wife's name: see Florence Emily Hardy, *The Life of Thomas Hardy 1840–1928* (Archon, 1970; originally published, 1928–30), pp. 209–10. This work is hereafter referred to as *Life*.

old age was said to do by visitors such as T. E. Lawrence, Virginia
Woolf, and E. M. Forster), while the dead enjoy an expanded
existence, often in haunting the living.

Miller traces the set of ideas involved here into a conclusion
about Hardy's belief in the persistence of the past, to which we
shall return. Meanwhile, one important motif connected with the
vigor of the dead is often overlooked: the power of the chthonic
itself. In one of the most intriguing of the poems to or about the
dead Emma, "I Found Her Out There," Hardy recalls her life in
Cornwall, where he met her on church-architecture business in
which he was engaged before his writing career. Then he turns her
"roots" from spiritual metaphors into literal growths into the earth
by speculating that "her shade, maybe/ Will creep underground/
Till it catch the sound/ Of that western sea." If we ignore the image
of Emma as an old mole — can'st work in the earth so fast? — we
find the focus on the power of spirits to return to their former
places, an ancient folk belief that we have reduced to a joke, but
that Hardy like Forster treats as expressive of important truths.
Vivified by the call of her western home-shore, the ghost finds
itself with a power the living lack, and will work its way back from
a Dorset grave to the landscape of originary significance.

This poem is emblematic of many in which interment in the earth
energizes humans who were failed or pallid or insignificant in life.
In the prophetic "Channel Firing" the dead rise at the false alarm
of naval gunnery practice, which can be heard as far inland — and
as far back in time, it is implied — as Stonehenge and Camelot, and
which they take for the Last Judgment. (The poem was written in
April 1914, and Hardy could not have known how the ancient
heritage of Britain was to be shaken by the guns of August.) But
the dead wish only that they had not wasted so much effort on
earth; the parson would have stuck to pipes and beer instead of
preaching if he'd had the knowledge of the gravedweller, that no
amount of human effort makes the world saner or war less horri-
ble. And there are several other poems in which the souls of the
slain or other spirits rise in transcendence of their earthly futilities.
Since Hardy consistently resists any Christian imagery of resurrection — the joke about The Last Judgment in "Channel Firing" is as
close as he comes to that vocabulary — the source of his ghosts'
power, the earth itself, is all the more noteworthy.

Sometimes the dead are said to survive only in loved ones' memories, as in "Her Immortality," but it takes a rather lively and forthright shade of a lover to make this known to the speaker. Otherwise, as in "Wessex Heights," the only escape from the importunate messages of such ghosts is to avoid the places they haunt. For the power of the dead is in their all-too-literal connection with place. Just as the places are more important than transient others in the memories of courtship, so also the dead draw strength from their rootedness in particular places; or, as in "I Found Her Out There," from their desire to return to the places. In one memorable poem, "Transformations," Hardy literalizes the root figure as far as it can go:

> Portion of this yew
> Is a man my grandsire knew,
> Bosomed here at its foot:
> This branch may be his wife,
> A ruddy human life
> Now turned to a green shoot.

The grass is a lady who longed for repose, and the rose is a sought-after maid. They are no longer underground, but open to sun and air, and they take in the energy of the cosmos in a new form. In life we may flit about ineffectually, but in death we merge with more permanent things. So the immense significance of place in Hardy's work is not merely a matter of his regionalism, or of his nostalgia for a preindustrial landscape. Place absorbs and encodes in memorable form the human efforts that are frustrated in mere life. Even Drummer Hodge, killed in the Boer War, has his "homely Northern breast and brain/ Grow to some Southern tree," although he never really knew where he was or why he was there.[9]

The intertransformation of the earth and the dead is of course a Romantic *topos*, and the Lucy motif must have been on Hardy's mind often (see, e.g., "Rain on a Grave"). But whereas Lucy is ambiguously silent for Wordsworth, in Hardy burial is regenerative: being rolled round in earth's diurnal course with rocks and

---

9. Ironically, and against his express instructions, Hardy was not buried in his native place; his ashes were interred in Westminster Abbey. However, his heart was removed, placed in a biscuit tin, and buried with his first wife in Dorset. And a spadeful of Dorset earth was sprinkled on the casket in the Abbey.

stones and trees gives articulatory powers. In this sense, Hardy is a graveyard poet. "Voices from Things Growing in a Churchyard" is a revealing title, anticipating *Spoon River Anthology* and *Our Town*, with the dead singing their stories in turn, "All day cheerily,/ All night eerily!" In fact he was capable of sport with graveyard clichés: in "1967," the speaker looks a century ahead and dismisses all thoughts about progress in favor of a wish that "thy worm should be my worm, Love!" This puts to lively use Marvell's worm (that tried long-preserved virginity), Donne's buried lovers, and Hamlet's graveyard musings.

Hence it may be said that the average denizen of a Hardy poem illustrates the transvaluation of life and death: the speakers are typically — especially in the dialectic of distance and desire, voyeurism and enactment — dying, dead-in-life, wanting to die ("A Sunday Morning Tragedy"), wraiths, or shadows. But if they die then they live, usually by being joined to the ever-living earth and becoming "significant soil," as T. S. Eliot was to call it in "The Dry Salvages." Given his obsession with these inversions of value and force, we may wonder why Hardy did not more often think of suicide. But this appears only as a passing motif: he, like most of his living characters, was too languidly taciturn for such a decisive act. He couldn't work up the energy.

All of this complicates mightily the figure of the century's corpse in "The Darkling Thrush." Hardy, who was fond of imagining such things as "God's Funeral" and "Earth's Corpse," possessed deeply equivocal attitudes toward such images. Despite the unsettling implications of discontinuity in the first two stanzas, that the "fervourless" speaker whose ill spirit blights his surroundings should then encounter a quixotically irrepressible singing bird seems now a characteristic gesture. The poem is itself a suspended question, the obverse of a question like "Did she put on his knowledge with his power/ Before the indifferent beak could let her drop?"[10] In the Hardy poem, the speaker is tempted, but only tempted, to believe that some force of regeneration can be sensed through the thrush. He cannot be sure. He is related to the speaker in "The Shadow on the Stone" or "The Oxen," who fears to resolve his doubts and would rather leave them suspended. Yeats, on the other

10. "Leda and the Swan," in *The Collected Poems of W. B. Yeats* (Macmillan [New York] 1957), p. 212.

hand, is quite sure that the brute blood of the air infused the whole ancient era through the impregnated Leda, so though we may wonder in passing if Leda got a glimpse from a godlike perspective, the real point of the lines is precisely the incarnation asserted: the question disguises a statement. (This is fitting for the modern poet who hated rhetoric above all, associating it with the endless debates of Irish politics, but was himself the most rhetorical of his age and made great use of triumphant nonquestions: how *can* we tell the dancer from the dance?) Hardy, in contrast, "could think" that the thrush proclaims "some blessèd Hope," but this statement ends, in effect, with a question mark.

The thrush's ambiguity extends that of the century's corpse. Is Hardy saying that the song of the "aged . . . frail, gaunt, and small" bird reproaches the speaker's self-pity, or that his paradoxical cheerfulness is simply an automatism of Nature? In "The Blinded Bird," Hardy eulogizes a bird whose eyes have been put out with a red-hot needle to make it sing, "resenting not such wrong":

> Who hath charity? This bird.
> Who suffereth long and is kind,
> Is not provoked, though blind
> And alive ensepulchred?
> Who hopeth, endureth all things?
> Who thinketh no evil, but sings?
> Who is divine? This bird.

We are meant to think, with a squirm, of our own habit of complaining. Not even 1 Corinthians 13 escapes a touch of the satiric lash here. No doubt Hardy, who was an antivivisectionist and RSPCA member and wrote often of the inhumanity of man to animals, was condemning those who make manifest the bird's divinity by such repulsive means, but the further implication is that self-styled Christians ought to realize that the image of divine, all-forgiving love is all around them in their pets. His many texts on the subject (see "The Mongrel," "The Puzzled Game Birds," and young Jude with the birds) make it clear that he saw in people's treatment of animals the image of what the fates do to humans: as flies to wanton boys, so are we to the gods. It's not so much cruelty as institutionalized insensitivity, malign neglect, the Crassness of Casualty, so that we fail in our trust in both senses: we can't trust gods, and animals can't trust us, we who are as gods to them. "The

Blinded Bird" may also imply that we crucify our gods whether in Nature or not. But in all this, ambiguity still exists: what are we to think of the birds' resolute and uncomplaining songs? They sing, literally, because they don't know any better. We have not that excuse, we do know that better is possible. Their ignorance may be a blessed condition, but we cannot aspire to it; instead, we must sing more querulous songs, which is what Hardy's poems are.

To speak of the thrush's song and its relation to Hardy's song is one of many ways in which to bring the discussion round to a comparison with Keats's nightingale. Several critics have asserted that Hardy was answering, or even undercutting, Keats's "at-oneness" with the bird. They point out the similarities in diction: compare Keats's "Darkling I listen," "spectre-thin" youth, and "pouring thy soul abroad" with Hardy's title (which of course also echoes Arnold's "darkling plain"), "spectre-gray" Frost, and "fling-[ing] his soul/ Upon the growing gloom." David Perkins says that the nightingale "becomes a symbol of the visionary imagination, or of the soul in secure possession of vision and so lifted into ecstasy, and the speaker then aspires to an identification with the bird. . . . in Keats, the identification seems for a moment to take place."[11] Hardy does not even contemplate such an identification. The bird may know of some providential blessing hidden within the cheerless barren scene—just as some animals are said to be able to sense impending earthquakes—but even if it does, this cannot do humans any good at all; in fact, it emphasizes their alienation.

Hardy seems sometimes to have felt that he was a Romantic (or at least an epigone) condemned to live out the maturities that Keats and Shelley did not attain and, as such, obliged to qualify their visions of transcendence, to bring them down to earth. In "Shelley's Skylark," Hardy hunts for the dust of the skylark that inspired visionary flight, so as to give it an adequate grave, but the true emphasis seems to be on our need to acknowledge that the bird did indeed become dust; the Biblical overtones are clear. Like the articulate dead, it lives only by becoming chthonic. So also in "Proud Songsters," they will return to the earth from whence they

---

11. "Hardy and the Poetry of Isolation," pp. 151–52. See also Charles E. May, "Hardy's Darkling Thrush: The Nightingale Grown Old," *Victorian Poetry* II (Spring 1973): 62–65.

came: a year or two ago they were "only particles of grain,/ And earth, and air, and rain." Hardy wants to stress a biological basis for these birds' immortality, as if to say to Keats and Shelley that they had neglected this. This motive probably reflects the influence of geology and Darwin. Indeed, it may be said that Hardy participates in a great shift of what we may call the concept of mythology, from the aerial and visionary overtones it had among the Romantics to the chthonic and artifactual ones of Modernism. This may be seen even more clearly in the century's corpse, for it is related to archaeology as, say, Blake's Albion is not. There are earth-bound figures in Romanticism, but they are drawn from mythographic, allegorical tradition, from the moralization of such figures as the Titans: as much as the birds, they are visionary. From Augustine and Boethius onward, Christian fathers had appropriated pagan mythology and decoded it into Stoic precepts, thus "despoiling the Egyptians" (Exod. 14), using techniques from Plato and Philo to show that all wisdom was ultimately Christian. That these practices still colored Romanticism is evident in the latter's internalizing tendency, in which myth portrays moral forces in conflict within the individual: out of the medieval psychomachia, the battle of vices and virtues, came the Romantic psychodrama. In contrast, Hardy's figures are seen from "the Victorian perspective of a newly acquired sense of geological time," and Hardy was an eminent Victorian in that sense. He was an antiquarian and a folklorist, avid for archaeology, very conscious of the fact that a spadeful of Dorset earth was likely to turn up Roman coins or prehistoric skeletons. He was "fond of placing human destiny against a background of millennia."[12] "Wessex" is as much an extension back in time as a

12. Both quotations from Norman Page, *Thomas Hardy* (Routledge, 1977), pp. 2, 57. If Hardy's century-corpse is not much like Blake's Albion or Shelley's Prometheus, it is equally unlike figures from a familiar Western tradition in which the landscape-body is feminine. These stem not from Christian allegorizing of classical myth but from much older sources: see, for example, Vincent Scully, *The Earth, the Temple, and the Gods* (Yale University Press, 1962) and G. Rachel Levy, *The Gate of Horn* (Harper & Row, 1963). Shakespeare's *Venus and Adonis*, lines 229ff., is a memorable example of this tradition, but the best-known adaptation appears in the American frontier mythos: see Henry Nash Smith, *Virgin Land* (Harvard University Press, 1971), and Annette Kolodny, *The Lay of the Land* (University of North Carolina Press, 1975). Insofar as this tradition colored Wordsworth's view of mind interpenetrating or "marrying" Nature, Hardy avoids that too.

fictionalization of space. Of all this, the brooding presence of the corpse—contrasted to the uncertainty of the bird's message—is an emblem.

Hardy was particularly attracted to giants and their works in the earth, as interpreted by legend: for example, the Cerne Abbas giant (a hill figure), Maiden Castle (a Celtic earthwork), horse figures, and other uncanny shapes that abound in his part of England. Avrom Fleishman points out his fascination with motifs that included "an animate (or once-animate) being dormant in the earth, whether in the form of a buried skeleton incarnating the ghosts of the past, or of a quasi-human figure underlying or constituting certain topographical features (usually hills), or of a *genius loci* residing not in an aerial or other evanescent medium but in the soil of the place itself."[13] One can see how Hardy's vigorous dead tie in with these interests. The giants are the most compelling form of the belief in the persistence of superhuman energies embodied in the landscape. Ironically, they even fulfill the phraseology of the King James Bible—"there were giants in the earth in those days"— which Hardy knew minutely, although he had lost the faith. Of course the century's corpse is an equivocal image of these forces, as it is funereally developed and symbolic of impotence. Nonetheless, both it and the thrush are parts of what looks very much like deliberate anti-Romanticism on Hardy's part.

It is worth noticing that hardly ever—and certainly not in this poem—is Hardy's Nature full of the ministering presences that it might have in Wordsworth. On the contrary, he is as likely to emphasize starving or freezing animals, and fungoid or parasitic growths, as more reassuring kinds. The storm-battered thrush is an obvious example. Nature is as cruel as humanity, and the fates are as indifferent to its creatures as they are to humans. Surely this effect was calculated by Hardy as a reply, if not a reproof, to the Romantics. Even if Harold Bloom is right that what looks like Nature poetry is really "antinature," or if we have missed the ironies in Keats's treatment of the nightingale, Hardy probably saw them in the more obvious way. Certainly he is careful to exclude

13. *Fiction and the Ways of Knowing: Essays on British Novels* (University of Texas Press, 1978), p. 111.

all thoughts of the transcendence that we associate with Romantic concepts of imagination.

It may be that "The Darkling Thrush" is even more anti-Romantic than most critics think. One common reaction to the poem is that it must record an actual experience. As Ralph Rader puts it, if we feel that

> Hardy had invented the thrush's song for the sake of the effect, rather than creating anew for us what it was like in the midst of that wintry bleakness to hear that unexpected burst of song, we would feel that the effect was spurious, like the streaks of sunlight which break through the dark clouds of a Hollywood ending.[14]

Does it follow that he encountered the thrush on the last day of the century and hurried home to write about it? Doubtless Hardy's presentation makes us think that the experience was real—he himself had no doubt that Shelley's skylark was real—and Hardy critics so regularly resort to terms like *honesty* and *sincerity* that it seems malicious to question the point. But there are some difficulties, for it has long been known that the characterization of the bird bears an unsettling resemblance to a passage in W. H. Hudson's *Nature in Downland*, published in 1900:

> Mid-winter is the season of the missel-thrush. . . . when there is no gleam of light anywhere and no change in that darkness of immense ever-moving cloud above. . . . If you should observe him in rough or gloomy weather, perched on an elmtop, swayed about this way and that by the gusts, singing his best, you must believe that this dark aspect of things delights him; that his pleasure in life, expressed with such sounds and in such circumstances, must greatly exceed in degree the contentment and bliss that is ours. . . . The sound is beautiful in quality, but the singer has no art, and flings out his notes anyhow; the song is an outburst, a cry of happiness.

The last phrases especially could have inspired Hardy to play a subtle variation on the theme that art lies in concealing art. Once we start seeing that many of the poems are disguised, evasive autobiography, we think less about honesty and more about creative deviousness. Incidentally, in editions of his poems Hardy dated it

14. "The Dramatic Monologue and Related Lyric Forms," *Critical Inquiry* 3 (Autumn 1976): 144.

"31 December 1900," but its first publication in a magazine came two days before that date (under the early title).[15] So much for actual experience. Taking the poem prima facie resembles closing the book and going off to seek impulses from a vernal wood, as per Wordsworth's instructions. Wordsworth obviously knew that we see Nature, like everything else, through language, or not at all in a human sense.

If Hardy was aware of the "Aeolian Harp" motif in Romanticism and its attendant figure of the "correspondent breeze," the *ruach* that blows through mind and Nature and unites them, then the poem contains a vivid anti-Romantic gesture in the notation that "The tangled bine-stems scored the sky/ Like strings of broken lyres." Not only is the harmonic correspondence destroyed, but the remains of wiry strings lacerate the firmament as if to make the theme painfully obvious. This figure seems as calculated as anything in the poem; it is difficult to believe it unintentional, although Hardy could have perhaps drawn it from more general sources, with music as a figure for universal coherence. But because Hardy's attitude toward Romanticism is implicated in so many other ways in this poem, there seems little reason to make an exception here. His sense of the poem's position in literary history is obvious, and ties in with the self-conscious emphasis on the date. Clearly he saw it as a boundary-marker poem, although he could not have foreseen the go-between character it would be assigned in histories of modern poetry.

No one seems to have felt comfortable in classifying this simply as a Victorian poem. Yet it hardly seems to belong among the difficult and demanding idioms of Pound, Eliot, and Stevens; why then does it so often have pride of place in anthologies of modern poetry, which proliferated in and since the 1950s as ancillae to the classroom effort to domesticate these disturbing if oracular figures? Of course in the anthologies Hardy simply represents the "early twentieth century." But some serious case can be made for his status as a modern poet, one that emerged from the chrysalis of the Victorian novelist.

"The Darkling Thrush" has several features that make it argua-

15. See Bailey, *The Poetry of Thomas Hardy*, pp. 166–67. Hudson, *Nature in Downland* (Longmans, 1900), pp. 249, 252.

bly at least Janus-faced in relation to its time. For instance, its anti-Romanticism falls in with the general Modernist debunking. Eliot called Keats, Shelley, and Wordsworth "poets of assured though modest merit," although this was in fact a slap at the hero worship of the Georgian poets — Rupert Brooke and others — rather than a necessary program for Modernism.[16] That the poem does not celebrate Nature, nor even some evolutionary fantasia, makes it seem not only post-Romantic but post-Victorian: Hardy does not say to the thrush, as Tennyson did to the flower in the crannied wall, that from it man and God could be deduced. The chthonic element in the poem, and in Hardy's work generally, also emerges from anti-Romanticism and takes on a proto-Modernist significance. Even if not noticed as such, it must have contributed a sense of uncanniness to which modern readers were learning to respond. Similarly, the poem's ambiguities would have seemed congenial to New Critical sensibilities when those came along. On the other hand, the confessional touches in the poem are not so salient as to make any new departure apparent, although the unpleasing sexual innuendo would have been counted as "modern" in a pejorative sense by any who discerned it.

The ghostly, graveyard quality in Hardy's work was undoubtedly seen as quaintly Victorian by most of his readers, and would still seem so if it were not tempting to explore his transvaluation of life and death by post-Nietzschean modes of critical approach, those that emphasize a text's phenomenology of attitudes and figurations and how they are sedimented out of still older figurations. We need to know not so much Hardy's psychobiography but a series of entangled affiliations that the ideas of "life and death" could have had for him. Particular embodiments of the theme may make the point best: lines like those in "Neutral Tones" — "The smile on your mouth was the deadest thing/ Alive enough to have strength to die" — not only need close reading, and an alertness to confessional possibilities, but also are too transgressive to be handled by older modes that are determined to make the text yield univocal, ultimately moralistic meanings. Here, where life consists of having strength to die, a smile sits on a mouth as if pasted onto a mannequin, and takes its place among a gallery of moribund objects of

16. "Observations," *Egoist*, May 1918, p. 69. Signed "T. S. Apteryx."

comparison. *Beyond the Pleasure Principle* would be a good place to start with this text. And the thrush singing over the century's corpse would be illumined thereby.

The simple fact is that we enjoy many benefits from our distant perspective: remoteness emphasizes the shadows and fault lines in the text that will reward investigation but that were not so noticeable to contemporaries, too close to the subject. Oddly enough, an emblem of the process can be found in the sumptuous photographs now appearing in books turned out by the Hardy industry to illustrate his "country." These views of gently rolling heaths and woods, dramatic cliffs, and so on, de-emphasize the human figure — they avoid showing today's inhabitants, obviously — and thus enable us to see the landscape as Hardy saw it in his inner eye, as a gigantic graveyard. They reveal to us the isolation and chthonic power of Hardy's unhumanized landscape.[17]

Hardy, especially as poet, seems more modern by thus being brought into the scope of our preferred kinds of criticism. But this does not exhaust the arguments by any means. A more empirical inquiry could stress the debt of twentieth-century poets to him. Along these lines a case is sometimes made for the novels too, but it seems to be a back-formation from criticism of the poetry, which has often proceeded in this way to enroll Hardy as at least a precursor of the moderns. Usually specific lines are drawn only to British poets, however. Donald Davie was able to say in 1972: "In British poetry of the last fifty years (as not in American) the most far-reaching influence, for good and ill, has not been Yeats, still less Eliot or Pound, not Lawrence, but *Hardy*."[18] Samuel Hynes gives a list of influencees that includes both Frost (but counts him as "the best of the Georgians") and early Lawrence, and ends with Philip Larkin.[19] To show Hardy's role in this inheritance is fairly easy, and these critics do the job well. More difficult to discern is Hardy's influence on early, international Modernism, but that deserves some discussion.

As we can now see, a premise of Modernism was the foreground-

17. For example, Denys Kay-Robinson, *The Landscape of Thomas Hardy* (Webb & Bower, 1984).

18. *Thomas Hardy and British Poetry* (Oxford University Press, 1972), p. 3.

19. "The Hardy Tradition in Modern English Poetry," in Norman Page, ed., *Thomas Hardy: The Writer and His Background* (Bell & Hyman, 1980), p. 189.

ing of language: Hardy gets both merits and demerits here. On the one hand, his diction is idiosyncratic (*outleant* is typical of many coinages of which the most striking are, predictably, negative: *unbloom, unbe, unhope*) and, together with his cramped and strange syntax, succeeds in drawing attention to itself. William Archer made the perceptive remark that he saw "all the words in the dictionary on one plane," thus mixing archaisms with neologisms, which often creates a peculiar appearance.[20] James Richardson aligns him here with Browning, in that for both "language is a highly volatile substance which vaporizes without constant stretching, cramping, and roughing up. . . . Their poems are artifacts—they assert their madeness, their physicality."[21] So Hardy does certainly foreground his language, but on the other hand rarely achieves the colloquial, spoken idiom that Modernists praised in opposition to artificial poeticisms; he gets a part score. It would have pleased the moderns that Hardy was uninterested in the kinds of euphonic fulsomeness associated with Swinburne and Tennyson, while also steering clear of the indifference to actual words of Arnold (such unfortunate titles as "The Sick King in Bokhara" or "Sohrab and Rustum" tell of a poet whose discursive earnestness has eroded the sensitivity with which he analyzed the phrase "Wragg is in custody"). Moreover, Hardy avoided the vigorous grotesqueries into which Browning sometimes fell through excess of colloquialism—his hearty or "red-blooded" streak, as Pound called it—in the excitement of painting a character. The very attenuated nature of Hardy's personae precluded this, as did his instinctive reserve and reticence in wielding any of the techniques of poetry. Though he spent long years mastering the craft, he never let any of it run away with him.

Hardy never competes excitedly for the reader's attention; he seems diffident about offering himself as a poet at all. Though he wrote on topical occasions, such as the sinking of the *Titanic*, he really preferred slighter and more private subjects, and sometimes said that in poetry he was writing for himself. This allowed him another way to foreshadow Modernism at least dimly, by participating in the dethronement of subject in favor of style. The ad-

20. Quoted in Hynes, *Pattern*, p. 93.
21. *Poetry of Necessity*, pp. 78–79.

vancing of critiques of representationalism in art made it important
to notice that pictures are made of paint, and a corollary was that
no longer need an important picture require an important subject —
indeed the choice of topical subjects came to be seen as spurious
appeal. So also, as Mallarmé told Degas, poems are made not
with ideas but with words. Hardy might not have understood the
anecdote, for he certainly had no thought of writing exercises in
style. Nonetheless, his diffidence about his art and his willingness
to write from inward, apparently trivial experience set him apart
from the great Victorians with their public-mindedness, their sense
of being responsible for man's fate. Compare Hardy's private rumi-
nations to Browning's self-dramatizations, his sense that great issues are being played out through him: two poets' uses of themselves in their works could hardly be more different.

Against these somewhat distant connections with Modernism,
we must remember that to a poet like Eliot, working out the heritage of Symbolism, Hardy was in effect invisible. Only a few years
after "The Darkling Thrush" was written, Eliot was writing lines
that are far less dated, that indeed today's undergraduates can and
do read as if they were written yesterday: "Preludes" and "Prufrock" do not date, in spite of their cab-horses and skirts that trail
along the floor. The effect is due not only to Eliot's sense of modern idiom, but even more to his adaptation of Symbolist practices,
so that whatever is mentioned seems to be a dream object rather
than an actual referent. A frequent question is whether Prufrock
encounters anything, or imagines it all. Eliot's echo chamber makes
the outside world, and hence the date, moot. His settings are as
haunting and as timeless as those in a de Chirico painting, a fact
that allows "I have measured out my life with coffee spoons" to
bring a response from those who've never seen a coffee spoon. To
a poet like this, Hardy would have seemed stilted and depthless,
and thus the dismissal in *After Strange Gods*: "At times [Hardy's]
style touches sublimity without ever having passed through the
stage of being good."[22] Indeed, Eliot testified that no one writing
in English in the first decade of the century was then worthy of
study. He went to other languages.

22. *After Strange Gods: A Primer of Modern Heresy* (Harcourt Brace, 1934), p.
59.

When Eliot's cosmopolitanism set the tone and Pound was also known primarily for exoticism, Hardy was eclipsed and counted among the insular. In British poetry, he came into favor again only because a generation arose that began to suspect that Modernism was an American—or worse, an Irish—trick. But before that there occurred the most puzzling phenomenon of all: the extravagant admiration of Hardy by Pound the revolutionary, the friend of Brancusi, Picabia, Gaudier-Brzeska, Joyce, Eliot, and Yeats— what linkages could Hardy have to that group?

Pound's flowering in the milieu of Edwardian–Georgian England surprises those who know of him only as the arch-Modernist. His reverence for Henry James, Swinburne, and a host of lesser ghosts and near-ghosts, however, appears in his work, and through them he wanted to have a laying on of hands that would put him in touch with the great Victorians and Romantics in what he called an "Apostolic Succession" of poetry. In his youth Pound had worshipped Browning as his chosen father figure, as many of the early poems testify, but later he came to let Hardy eclipse the older poet and judged that Hardy had "pruned away" or "shed" Browning's excesses and "improved on" his best qualities. These phrases are from his most sustained tribute to Hardy, printed as an appendix to the anthology *Confucius to Cummings* (1964). Pound begins with observations very characteristic of his own predilections, and works up to his absolute vote of confidence:

> Clear page or palimpsest, Hardy registered an age. Of conventional mind, apparently, but of a very particular sensibility; whether he saw ghosts or thought them useful to his record, he liked the feel of the past and dissented with remarkable ubiquity and vigor from the era he lived in. . . .
>
> . . . No one trying to learn writing in regular, formed verse can learn better than in observing what Thomas Hardy accepted from Browning and what he pruned away from his more busteous or rambunctious predecessor.[23]

This note also contains the clues to why Pound was drawn to Hardy in the first place. It is actually a double tribute, to Hardy and to Ford Madox Ford, the latter supremely meaningful to

---

23. Ezra Pound and Marcella Spann, eds., *Confucius to Cummings: An Anthology of Poetry* (New Directions, 1964), pp. 325–26.

Pound as conservator of "the prose tradition." On going to London
in 1908 primarily to learn from Yeats, Pound found to his surprise
that he could learn more from Ford the prose writer. After a short
period of resistance, Pound was won over completely to Ford's
doctrines, "living language and *le mot juste*," that is, unbookish,
unpretentious, nonantiquated diction and clear Flaubertian *constatation* or "presentation." To Pound, Ford also stood for the cult of
craft and hard work, and exemplified, against genteel amateurism,
a devotion to writing that amounted to obsession. Before 1912
Pound's work had been entangled in problems of archaism and
poeticism, which for him were survivals of adolescent enthusiasm,
and gave his juvenilia an old-fashioned "cloak-and-dagger" tone,
as Eliot put it. After Ford ridiculed the archaisms, however, Pound
decided to "modernize" himself, and from that time on, the very
word *modern* in Pound's writing usually meant the influence of
Ford, who became "the critical LIGHT." In Pound's version of
literary history—for instance, in "How to Read"—the art of writing
"went over to prose" with Stendhal and Flaubert, with Ford as the
transmitter of the tradition from which, Pound insisted, poetry had
henceforth to learn: Hardy took a place in this "prose tradition," as
did Hudson.[24]

In his tribute to Hardy and Ford, Pound remarks that "it should
be known that Ford Madox Ford started *The English Review* in a
rage that there was no place in England to print a poem by Thomas
Hardy." The poem was "A Sunday Morning Tragedy," in which
desperate resort to an abortifacient kills a pregnant girl. Like most
legends that Ford put out, this account of the founding is far too
simple, but Pound believed it, and for him the connection not only
brought together two great prose artists but also confirmed his

24. See "How to Read," in *Literary Essays of Ezra Pound*, ed. T. S. Eliot (New
Directions, 1954), esp. pp. 31–32; "Hudson: Poet Strayed into Science," in Ezra
Pound, *Selected Prose*, ed. William Cookson (New Directions, 1975), pp. 429–32;
and my *Ezra Pound: The Image and the Real* (Louisiana State University Press,
1969), chap. 1. The championing of Hudson by Pound and Ford shows up in
Hemingway's *The Sun Also Rises*, in which Hudson mesmerizes Robert Cohn; this
is part of the satire on "Braddocks" (Ford). See the much more savage treatment of
Ford in *A Moveable Feast*, caused by guilty feelings of indebtedness. Hemingway
learned about "prose" not only from Ford but also from Pound's adaptations of
Ford. He was always willing to acknowledge Pound but was afraid to reveal his
debt to Ford. See Chapter 4 in this book.

deep suspicions about the persecution and alienation of writers —
which, after all, is what *Hugh Selwyn Mauberley* is all about. Thus,
Ford's brief tenure (1908–1909) at *The English Review* became for
Pound a crux in history. After a glorious couple of years, in which
he printed many of the great writers of Europe, Ford was found
to have run up large debts. His mistress Violet Hunt thereupon
persuaded Sir Alfred Mond, a wealthy Jew, to buy the *Review* —
but he then fired Ford. After retelling by Ford, this story combined
in Pound's mind with growing convictions that "financiers" and
"munitions makers" had caused the Great War, so that after 1918
he gradually became an anti-Semite (the Mond brothers appear
unfavorably in Cantos 78, 80, and 104). Hardy with Ford became
symbolic of the life of the mind and of the art of writing, under
pressure from an uncomprehending Philistine public manipulated
by sinister forces. As Pound's note implies, Hardy's "dissent" from
his age could be seen as a form of heroism, and his anticonven-
tional treatments of sex, the goodness of life, and so on, as manifestations of the artist's power to see through the pretenses of his
time. As it happened, Pound must have been delighted by Hardy's
reading of "that moderate man Voltaire," since he greatly admired
all who tried to puncture an era's clichés.[25]

Pound credited Hardy's achievements in poetry, like those of
Ford, to prose training: "The lifetime spent in novel-writing gave
him a magnificent tool-kit." This echoes what he had said decades
earlier about Hardy's *Collected Poems*: "Now *there* is a clarity.
There *is* the harvest of having written 20 novels first."[26] We may be
amused at the idea that the novels were only preparatory to the
poems, and of course Hardy didn't wait to write poems until his
novel-writing career was over, although very few were published
until the twentieth century. But Pound's point was that poetry in
that day was menaced by the general use of poeticisms, signs of the
tacit contract between writer and reader that it was safe to admire
works if they used *o'er* and the like. Pound recapitulated Words-

25. The line is from "The Respectable Burgher"; see Pound and Spann, *Confucius to Cummings*, p. 328. Voltaire's anti-Semitism should also be noted. On *The
English Review* and Mond, see Arthur Mizener, *The Saddest Story: A Biography of
Ford Madox Ford* (World, 1971), p. 195.
26. *Letters of Ezra Pound 1907–1941*, ed. D. D. Paige (Harcourt Brace, 1950),
p. 294; cf. Pound and Spann, *Confucius to Cummings*, p. 326.

worth's disgust at such mutual indulgence, and prescribed the "prose tradition" as a cure for flowery rhetoric, jingling euphony, thumpingly regular rhythm, and the other ills that attended a poetry of contrived sentiment, as exemplified by Alfred Noyes's "The Highwayman." In 1912 Pound started the Imagist movement, to have H. D.'s poems printed and "to bring poetry up to the level of prose," in other words to disseminate the precepts he had learned from Ford (see Chapter 5). From those days on, he believed in the efficacy of writing prose as preparation for poetry—not as Yeats sometimes did, by first writing out the poem in a prose draft, in the manner of Ben Jonson, but rather as training in the sense of his comment on Hardy. "Flaubert and De Maupassant lifted prose to the rank of a finer art, and one has no patience with contemporary poets who escape from all the difficulties of the infinitely difficult art of good prose by pouring themselves into loose verses."[27]

Hardy's poems are not really prosaic, either in the common pejorative sense or in the way that Pound would have admired, but they are distinctly unpoetic, and their frequent awkward and strange uses of language have led some to call them prosy. What counts is that like Wordsworth, Hardy ran the risks of the prosaic very willingly. (Wordsworth had believed that there could be no "essential" difference between verse and prose.)[28] Hardy's reserve, his spareness and lack of showmanship, his very reticence and evasions contribute to this effect of lack of poeticism. Pound did not find what he called "rhetorical din," which he abominated, in Hardy. Moreover, Hardy was far more of a craftsman than most were aware, though he took pains to conceal it. But Pound saw it, especially his "undergraduate efforts to use ancient metres—no man ever had so much Latin and so eschewed the least appearance of being a classicist on the surface."[29] Pound knew about the ancient meters because he himself tried to adapt them to modern uses, and he no doubt sympathized with Hardy's reason for hiding his classicism—not having been accorded a university education,

27. *Gaudier-Brzeska*, p. 83.

28. See the 1800 Preface to *Lyrical Ballads*: "There neither is, nor can be, any *essential* difference between the language of prose and metrical composition," and so forth.

29. Pound and Spann, *Confucius to Cummings*, p. 325.

Hardy would not have flaunted his Latin and Greek in fear that he would seem to be posing as a gentleman. Pound resented the fact that in England the classics were used as markers of social class.

Hardy even anticipated in a way some of Pound's Imagist principles. In a well-known autobiographical passage, Hardy ascribed his sense of poetic form to his early architectural training:

> Years earlier he had decided that too regular a beat was bad art. . . . He knew that in architecture cunning irregularity is of enormous worth, and it is obvious that he carried on into his verse, perhaps in part unconsciously, the Gothic art-principle in which he had been trained, [seeking for] poetic texture rather than poetic veneer; the latter kind of thing, under the name of "constructed ornament," being what he, in common with every Gothic student, had been taught to avoid as the plague.[30]

Compare the Imagist prescription for "cunning irregularity": "to compose in the sequence of the musical phrase, not in sequence of a metronome." Even more striking, compare the general Modernist abolition of ornament, urged throughout Pound's writings: "The point of Imagisme is that it does not use images *as ornaments*. . . . One is tired of ornamentations, they are all a trick, and any sharp person can learn them."[31]

Experimental translation of Gothic irregularities into a poetics, with its consequent risk of appearing uncouth, is most revealing of Hardy's procedures as a poet. He, like Pound, valued the attempt at new explorations more than success in more established and complacent modes. In another important autobiographical passage, Hardy remarked,

> I prefer late Wagner, as I prefer late Turner, to early (which I suppose is all wrong in taste), the idiosyncrasies of each master being more strongly shown in these strains. When a man not contented with the grounds of his success goes on and on, and tries to achieve the impossible, then he gets profoundly interesting to me.[32]

To some extent, this is a disguised credo and apologue. Davie quotes Edmund Blunden as remarking that Hardy's faults were those of a "zealous experimenter" whose materials were sometimes

30. *Life*, p. 301.
31. *Gaudier-Brzeska*, p. 88; *Literary Essays*, p. 3.
32. *Life*, p. 329.

intractable or unfitting; certainly that could be adapted as a description of the poet of the *Cantos*.[33]

Almost all of the critics have commented on the frequent jarring effects in Hardy's poems, usually counting them as uncouth. Hynes says the poems often seem "awkward, halting, and often ungrammatical," and many vary these words.[34] Yvor Winters, who should have known better, even called Hardy a primitive. Several reasons have been discussed already, as to why the poems do sometimes give these effects, why Hardy seems sometimes to be forcing himself into poetry as a farmer forces himself into a new suit. His instinctive reticence, about revealing his life and about appearing to show off as a poet, makes a major contribution; his lack of inner conviction that he was really a poet, at least of the inspired-bardlike, Romantic or Browningesque, type, is clear; his belief that language must be cramped and stretched, as Richardson puts it, was innate; but undoubtedly the most powerful reason that he wrote as he did was his experimentalism, his need to try out more of the resources of language and form, in which he drew as Pound noted on his early training, in architecture and then in prose. Along this line of thought we may as well admit the deposition of W. H. Auden, who congratulated himself on having run into Hardy as his "first Master": "He was a good poet, perhaps a great one, but not *too* good. Much as I loved him, even I could see that his diction was often clumsy and forced and that a lot of his poems were plain bad. This gave me hope where a flawless poet might have made me despair."[35] So it was not his success rate as an experimenter that made Hardy a father to the moderns; his mere effort was instructive. Auden also learned from "his metrical variety [and] his fondness for complicated stanza forms," but the most important contribution was the mediation of literary, intellectual, and spiritual history through the poems' Janus-faced role.

> Whatever its character, the provincial England of 1907, when I was born, was Tennysonian in outlook; whatever its outlook the England of 1925 when I went up to Oxford was The Waste Land in character. I

33. *Thomas Hardy and British Poetry*, p. 16.
34. *Pattern*, p. 57.
35. *The Dyer's Hand and Other Essays* (Random House, 1962), p. 38.

cannot imagine that any other single writer [but Hardy] could have carried me through from the one to the other.[36]

So Hardy seemed to the young Auden "good . . . but not *too* good," and "modern without being too modern." There is more in this parallel than may at first be seen.

Hardy's experimental thrust, his reticence and avoidance of poet-icisms, his disdain for fluency and for fully worked-out articula-tions, all combined creatively: not only did they produce that un-polished, unfinished, phlegmatic, homemade character that so many deplore, but they also proved inspirational to younger poets even when these were as different as Auden and Pound. By down-playing the accepted tokens of poetic competence in favor of at-tempts to transcribe insight and feeling in inventively analytical ways, Hardy put himself into a role somewhat like that of the Impressionists clearing the way for twentieth-century painters — or one might compare the relationship of Cézanne to Picasso. In both cases we have an older artist who is willing to ignore *idées reçues* about facility, who in his own work may seem to many to retro-gress to an elementary level of workmanship. Picasso was enabled to put aside his own immensely impressive facility — at the age of twelve he could outdraw anyone in his father's art school — by heed-ing the example of Cézanne and those who were willing to incur public contempt and ridicule, accusations of incompetence and even fraud. The phenomenon of Philistine derision at the new and seemingly clumsy has indeed become a cliché of art history. Its significance is that new schemata, in the terms of E. H. Gombrich, will usually look barbarous next to the facile ones that they bypass. To achieve them the uncompromising artist must deform his or her own work, by giving up the quest for facility and fluency, finish and polish. And their successors are then enabled to explore newer forms of representation, even to enlist forms that appear to the public to be wild and distorted, terms that were used of both Pi-casso and Pound. In other words, in reading Hardy's poems Pound did not find specifically modern schemata, but he found incentives to create them himself.

36. "A Literary Transference," in Guerard, ed., *Hardy: A Collection of Critical Essays*, p. 139.

It might be interesting to go further in comparing Hardy with the Impressionists, since some lines of criticism have depicted him as a poet of perception and observation.[37] He himself wanted to be remembered as one who "used to notice such things," meaning apparently trivial but perceptually interesting phenomena (see "Afterwards"). But the main point is that he was willing to jettison what William Carlos Williams called "pleasing wraiths of former masteries," and that was inspirational for Pound, Auden, and those who came after. By 1915 Pound was putting words into arrangements that bewildered and infuriated a public accustomed to Alfred Noyes, John Masefield, A. E. Housman, and the like. Then poets whose natural gift was emphatically not fluency, such as Williams, began to see that they had not to learn it, but even to unlearn such as they had. Pound, who had known Williams since youth, once called him *the* most bloody inarticulate animal that ever gargled," but soon realized that his strength was in that inarticulateness. His lack of glibness forced Williams to atomize American speech to find a poetic idiom, a process that often made him look clumsy or *faux-naïf*, but that produced one of the most important legacies to contemporary American poetry. Pound's 1928 essay on Williams praised his scorn for "the 'accomplished.'" In a letter Pound wrote "The thing that saves your work is *opacity*, and don't you forget it. Opacity is NOT an American quality. Fizz, swish, gabble of verbiage, these are echt Amerikanisch."[38] The current generation of American poets has tried to live down Pound's accusation, largely by finding inspiration in Williams. Though Williams, irritated by Eliot's cosmopolitanism, often posed as an ideological nativist, he thus owes a debt to Hardy for putting fluency into question, and so then does American poetry in general.

But along these lines, it is Pound's debt that remains clearest. Without Hardy's abandonment of the ideals of mellifluous and fluent speech, he might never have been moved to declare his own independence of these criteria so vigorously. Pound drove himself sometimes to the edge of aphasia, as it were, in order to get clear of third-hand masteries and to achieve his own highly individual

37. For example, Tom Paulin, *Thomas Hardy: The Poetry of Perception* (New York: Macmillan, 1975).
38. Pound, *Letters*, pp. 124, 131; *Literary Essays*, p. 396.

registrations. He wanted to place himself in positions where the words would not come too easily, or as derivative reflexes: "It is only in the flurry, the shallow frothy excitement of writing, or the inebriety of a metre, that one falls into the easy—oh, how easy!—speech of books and poems that one has read."[39] Pound's Puritan streak appears here, as it does in the hatred of ornament, to reinforce the drive against fluency, which is of course basically derivative. His ideal for his own work was so thoroughly to eschew fluency that the reader would have to struggle: "The reader must not only read every word, but must read his English as carefully as if it were a Greek that he could not rapidly be sure of comprehending."[40]

Hardy's influence was also fateful in that he led Pound to be as impatient with aestheticism as with poeticism. His referentiality, which contrasts so obviously with Eliot's evasion of it, encouraged Pound to put his own Symbolist heritage to uses more Rimbaldian than Mallarméan, in comparison to Eliot. From Ford, too, Pound learned a preference for *res* over *verba*: this inclination may seem backwards in the context of Modernism, and is certainly ironic given Hardy's participation, however slight, in dethroning the "subject" in art as argued above, but, at that time, appeared necessary in order not to fall back into Ninetyish or decadent aestheticism. Whereas this latter movement had suited Yeats well, Hardy cannot be even remotely related to it, and Pound (like Williams) derived therefrom a revolt against loose symbolism and even against the idea of poetry as fiction. The *Cantos* proclaim that they are "not a work of fiction" (99) and *Paterson* obviously has a similar aim, both poems using *collagiste* techniques to make the point.[41] In Pound's diagnosis, aestheticism had led to a "taste for the unreal," and the cure was Hardy: "He woke one to the extent of his own absorption in *subject* as contrasted with aesthetes' preoccupation with 'treatment'" (this also is a theme of *Mauberley*). The strenuous

---

39. *Letters*, p. 49; for his self-induced aphasia, see my "Wisdom Past Metaphor: Another View of Pound, Fenollosa, and Objective Verse," *Paideuma* 5 (Summer 1976): 15–29.

40. Quoted in Ronald Bush, *The Genesis of Ezra Pound's Cantos* (Princeton University Press, 1976), p. 11.

41. *The Cantos of Ezra Pound* (New Directions, 1973), p. 708. Subsequent references combine canto number and page number of this edition, as 99/708.

didacticism of the *Cantos* followed from Pound's conviction that Hardy showed the way to dealings with the realities of the world. His distillation of an *ars poetica* in 1934 asserted that there are only "two roads" to poetic achievement: one was "music," as he concisely put it, meaning to him not only sound but certain mystical, visionary practices; the other was "the old man's road (vide Tom. Hardy)—CONTENT, the INSIDES, the subject matter." Reading Hardy prompted him to reject art for art's sake, and to say "it's all rubbish to pretend that art isn't didactic."[42] What Hardy showed was that slight, private subjects could be revelatory, and could mix with more topical "contents." Could these words not be adapted, *mutatis mutandis*, for a description of the *Cantos*?

Very probably, in Pound's eyes, it was Hardy's restrained handling of personae (as contrasted to Browning's vigor and rambunctiousness) that led to his healthy "absorption in *subject*." Pound moved away from the method of Browning's dramatic monologues, in which the persona turns into a developed character, toward personae that were frankly "masks of the self," transient creations that took fleeting form in the "'search for oneself'. . . . One says 'I am' this, that, or the other, and with the words scarcely uttered one ceases to be that thing."[43] In other words, Pound played down the dramatic element, in line with his derogation of the theater as a place of misleading diffusion of force: "Anything that asks the reader to think of effect or how it wd. be on stage distracts from reality of fact presented. Even if it does appeal to the ballet russe or charlotte russe instincts of the beeholder. Means the author not obsessed with reality of his subject."[44] Here it is again, Pound's Puritanism: identifying the theatrical with the meretricious, he insists on an obsessive "reality of the subject." The influence of Hardy merged with this latent Puritanism to produce the Pound who strove to ground his long poem in reality rather than in his bardic vision. (Of course, it should be remarked that for him reality included much "music"; see his views on the truth of myth.)

Mauberley is a good example with which to sum up. The figure Mauberley is, deliberately, the slightest of personae: a "mere sur-

42. *Letters*, pp. 178, 180, 248. See also Davie, *Ezra Pound* (Viking, 1975), pp. 43–48.
43. *Gaudier-Brzeska*, p. 85.
44. *Letters*, p. 306.

face," Pound called him, certainly not a character in the Browning sense; to make him any more substantial would distract from the "reality of fact presented." Many readings of the poem have come to grief because they lose this point, look for characters, and try to assign all the sections to specifiable speakers. But Pound is merely holding up "masks of the self," and does not want us to get entangled in the seductions of responding to the masks, creating lives and backgrounds for them, indulging in the kind of fantasizing that, carried to its absurd extreme, produces *The Girlhood of Shakespeare's Heroines*. Pound's speakers resemble the attenuated personae of Hardy's poems because Pound wants to make sure we keep our eyes on the subject, which is the degradation of British artists by the Philistine public and their escapist retreat from reality (and "the relation of the state to the individual") into aestheticism. In illustrating that process, Mauberley is the antithesis of Hardy.

These many facets of influence help explain Pound's reverence for Hardy, despite the obvious dissimilarities in their poems and in their poetics; yet to complete the picture, indeed to center on its most important feature, we must return to Pound's words about Hardy and the past: "Whether he saw ghosts or thought them useful to his record, he liked the feel of the past and dissented with remarkable ubiquity and vigor from the era he lived in." Clearly, for Pound, dissent from the age and response to the vigor of the past went together in Hardy: the retrospectivity and temporal voyeurism, the attenuation of the present and the sense of frustration in life, merged with the presentation of the power of the dead and of the chthonic to form the other, intrinsically related, side of the coin of Hardy as critic of the Victorian era. Given the intensity of Pound's convictions about the artist as alienated prophet, it is unsurprising that Hardy's "feel for the past" was not only a corollary of his dissatisfaction with the present, but also the motive power of his work in Pound's reading of it. He makes this clear in several different ways. In his most unreserved tribute to the poems themselves, he stated: "No man can read Hardy's poems collected but that his own life, and forgotten moments of it, will come back to him, a flash here and an hour there. Have you a better test of true poetry?"[45]

45. *Guide to Kulchur* (New Directions [1938]), p. 286.

Those who know the *Cantos* will hear an echo:

Le Paradis n'est pas artificiel
                                         but is jagged,
For a flash,
                      for an hour.
Then agony,
                        then an hour. . . . (92/620)

Pound is saying, then, that the reader of Hardy's oeuvre acquires a
cumulative retrospectivity that opens up to him the closed-off passages of his own life, and that this resembles certain experiences of
spiritual illumination. (Echoes of Pascal and of Revelation are also
present.) In other words, the power of Hardy as poet is in his
ability to unearth the past in the present.

In one of the most self-revealing passages in his *Life* Hardy
wrote: "I believe it would be said by people who knew me well that
I have a faculty (possibly not uncommon) for burying an emotion
in my heart or brain for forty years, and exhuming it at the end of
that time as fresh as when interred."[46] The ostensible subject was
how he came to write "In Time of 'The Breaking of Nations'" in
1914, although the emotional experience belonged to 1870, the year
of the Franco-Prussian War. But the text opens up a far more
illuminating series of insights when we look at the burial metaphor,
the exact fulfillment of the pattern of transvaluing living and dead,
and the atavistic sense of the past's power to revive after interment.
The passage also shows why Pound's comment on Hardy's "true
poetry" was a genuine penetration into the secrets of its power.
For if that is the way Hardy's poems work cumulatively on us as
we read them — that they revive our own buried memories — then we
can see why so many have sought to pay tribute to Hardy as poet
without being able to account for his worth in terms of mastery and
technical skill. The poems provoke our own hidden emotions to return to us from the forgotten or even repressed past, because they are
so often the bearers of exhumed emotions themselves.

It is intriguing that one of the poems Pound chose for *Confucius
to Cummings* was "Under the Waterfall," in which it is Emma who
is said to undergo the Proustian experience of having her courtship
come alive whenever she plunges her arm into cold water, because
she and Hardy once lost a drinking glass in a small waterfall, on a

46. *Life*, p. 378.

picnic, and thrust their arms repeatedly into the water without success. The lost "chalice" moves her because "No lip has touched it since his and mine." The glass is itself an emblem of the past, which is more emotionally laden when recovered in memory than it was when it was present. Though gone forever, it has a dynamic life that cannot be touched by routinization, or even by the decay of love itself.

The Hardy–Pound relation thus comprises a variety of influences, from the opening up of new poetic schemata to the exhuming of buried memories and emotions. Hardy showed the way to a kind of poetry that would be realistic and antiartificial, referential and antiaesthetic, prosaic and antipoetic. It would be experimental rather than polished, "broken speech" rather than fluent, uncouth rather than facile. But above all it would dissent from the present, and accepted ideas and standards, and it would make the past wake. Pound conceived his own lifework in that image.

The *Cantos* even resembles *The Dynasts* in aspiring to be "an Iliad of Europe," a true tale of the tribe. And those will not be wanting who will say that they are equally unreadable. Certainly Hardy would have agreed with Pound that an epic is "a poem including history." Pound's admirers agree that the achievement of the *Cantos* is the presentation of history as live and concrete, not remote and antiquarian, though few would agree that Hardy accomplished that. But consider how Pound was able to do it: according to Hugh Kenner, he first had to abolish the "tone of time," the perspectival and inevitably patronizing view of the past as either quaint or abstract. Kenner shows how Pound strove toward this in his work, and how *Homage to Sextus Propertius* was a decisive step. Quoting a few lines, Kenner comments:

> There is no "point of view" that will relate these idioms: neither a modern voice ("bristle"; "frigidaire patent"; "collective nose") nor an ancient one ("Phaeacia"; "Marcian"). . . . In transparent overlay, two times have become as one, and we are meant to be equally aware of both dictions (and yet they seem the same diction). The words lie flat like the forms on a Cubist surface. The archaizing sensibility of James's time and Beardsley's has simply dissolved.[47]

47. *The Pound Era* (University of California Press, 1971), p. 29. See also pp. 138–42 and other references to Cubism throughout the volume for Kenner's insights into this important comparison.

Here let us remember William Archer's comment that Hardy saw all the words in the dictionary on one plane. His mixing of archaisms and neologisms was very different from Pound's mixing of demotics with documentary quotations; yet the one practice could plausibly, when fitted among the many other influences with a similar tendency, have helped suggest the other.

Their interests in the past turn out to be strangely parallel. Pound, the poet as archaeologist, made his heroes in the *Cantos* those who recover and preserve vital parts of the cultural heritage that are in constant danger of being effaced, thanks to the forces of usury: he must have counted Hardy among these heroes. He implies that "Wessex" was a labor of preservation of a "record," to which the "ghosts" may have been "useful." None of this is surprising if we go back to Pound's "Apostolic Succession," mentioned above, of London days. As in Canto 82, "Swinburne my only miss/ and I didn't know he'd been to see Landor," which means that youthful diffidence kept him from approaching Swinburne before his death in 1909, and that he thus missed a chance to grasp a laying on of hands that linked back to Landor.[48] But Swinburne was his only miss: from Yeats, Ford, Henry James, Blunt, and many others he received the tradition of the ghosts. Hardy often thought along the same lines. James Richardson pulls together some instances:

> Because the past is always present, Hardy is intensely, even superstitiously, excited by coincidences in space. He is drawn to the graves of poets and other ancestors; he speculates that he and his mother have stayed in a room once occupied by Shelley; he writes a poem about Keats's brief sojourn in Dorset on the way to Rome and then finds himself on a committee whose purpose is to acquire one of Keats's homes. Space, too, can be collapsed, and when it is, he is concerned with coincidence in time: "It bridges over the years a little to think that Gray might have seen Wordsworth in his cradle, and Wordsworth might have seen me in mine."[49]

Norman Page observes that Hardy "was present at Palmerston's funeral in Westminster Abbey, characteristically noting in a letter

48. 82/523. For the "Apostolic Succession," see "How I Began" (1913), reprinted in Noel Stock, ed., *Ezra Pound/Perspectives: Essays in Honor of His Eightieth Birthday* (Chicago: Regnery, 1965), p. 1.

49. *The Poetry of Necessity*, pp. 116–17.

to his sister that the former Prime Minister was a link between their own age and that of Pitt and Burke."[50] Both Hardy and Pound at times apprehended an almost palpable past, in places and survivors and relics.

Indeed Hardy's concern with atavism, with the continual return of the past in the present, was perhaps his strongest conviction. J. Hillis Miller demonstrates this at length, notably in a reading of *Tess*.

> The idea of a present which is a repetition or reincarnation of the past recurs through the novel like a refrain with many variations. The narrator at his first introduction of Tess tells the reader that, "for all her bouncing handsome womanliness, you could sometimes see her twelfth year in her cheeks, or her ninth sparkling from her eyes; and even her fifth would flit over the curves of her mouth now and then." . . . The nature she inherits forces her to enact involuntarily a new version of a life which has been lived over and over again by her ancestors, as if she were no more than a puppet of history, or an actor in a play already performed a thousand times before, just as Henchard repeats the life of Saul or Cain.

Thus, the "murder is not her act, but is performed by her ancestors acting through her." And her capture at Stonehenge "is a fitting climax for a novel which has been dominated by a brooding sense of man's atavistic kinship with what is oldest, darkest, and most irrational in nature."[51] Miller concludes: "In all Hardy's work, then, history is present not just objectively in old roads, houses, utensils, the debris of past generations, but is also able to enter into the lives of people living in the present, to force them to act and feel in ways that it imposes." But this sense of the past is not always doom-laden. Hardy does not merely have the conventional Victorian fear of atavism, for the past is also the source of spiritual significance. As Richardson puts it: "All memory is sacred, and Hardy cares for it as for a nearly extinct species." In fact, the last chapter of Miller's book is entitled "Literature as Safeguarding of the Dead," and it elaborates the characteristic Hardy trope: "In the act of describing all he has lost the speaker brings it back again in the words of the poem, enshrining it there in the remembering immortality of

50. Page, *Thomas Hardy*, p. 8.
51. *Distance and Desire*, pp. 102–4.

words."[52] Hardy's speakers ironically parallel Joyce's maudlin Irish rememberers.

So Hardy's complex sense of the past anticipates in important ways that of Modernism. It is fitting, then, that the century's corpse in "The Darkling Thrush" in its very ambiguity comprises a feeling of failure in himself and in his time, an anxiety about the future, and yet some hope that the very deadness of the past will revitalize that future. In this variant of the Antaeus myth, the past draws strength from being buried, and thus has the power to reappear in the present.

Hardy has somehow anticipated his own status as a father figure for Modernism but, even more surprising, also has anticipated the parricidal nature of that movement: he knew that he had to be a *dead* father. One of the most marked characteristics of the twentieth century has been its need to disown and discredit the nineteenth. Ironically, it now mocks the very myth of progress which was a powerful force giving rise to this need for dissociation. Modernism, far more openly than comparable movements of other ages, demanded that predecessors be consumed rather than accepted on their own terms. Even Pound's unabashed reverence for Hardy contains the premise that the best ways of paying homage will not enshrine but rather outmode him. For a father figure, after all, is not someone to copy, but someone to go on from. Hence Auden's comments on the dynamic impetus he received from Hardy because he was "not *too* good." The time-consciousness of Modernism demands the notion of a literary history in the full disintegrative sense of that term: to say "here is where we started from" is to say "we are not there any more." Modernism obliges us to write a periodized history, and at the same time it spawns a ubiquitous revisionist impulse that recurrently erodes all positivist generalizations about periods. The clash typifies its ambivalence toward the past, and a major reason it wants to have done with the Victorian age is that it finds that age wanting in a true sense of the past—except for a few figures like Hardy.

Our revisionism is part of our Western heritage; the Bible is the most revisionist of all works, and in this sense Modernism is simply hyperbolical Westernism. It gives us a powerful sense of the tran-

---

52. Miller, pp. 105, 252; Richardson, *The Poetry of Necessity*, p. 117.

sience of such things as the meanings of texts: Borges' Pierre Menard is as typical as Eliot's remark that we cannot read the Shakespeare that Dr. Johnson read. We know that texts do not stay identical to themselves. We are more concerned than ever with what the past has given us, but we no longer see it as something fixed; we know that it must constantly be recovered and revivified. In short, we find ourselves living out Eliot's admonitions about tradition: we cannot take it for granted, but must work for it with great effort.

Hardy's sense of himself as a dead father coincides with the crisis in the concept of patriarchy that was evident, but only to a few, in 1900. We can see clearly now just how anxiety-ridden were the treatments of fatherhood as the central problem of the age. Think of Freud and his Laius complex, as it should be called; of Dostoevsky, constantly reliving his father's death at the hands of his serfs; of Turgenev (perhaps the Russians were acutely conscious: they foresaw that their "little father" had not long to reign, that his fall would be far and the crash resounding); of Ibsen's *Ghosts*; of Kafka, who stuttered only in his father's presence. It can now be seen that the European ethnocentrism that was exploded in 1914 was based on metaphors of patriarchy — compare the paternalism of the British Empire — and that we are still sweeping away the debris of both. When Stephen Dedalus says in *Ulysses*, nervously and protestingly, that "paternity may be a legal fiction," he sounds the death knell of all the sureties that patriarchalism had promised. But he also suggests that acknowledging our fathers forces us to give up our stubborn fantasies of self-creation and come to terms with our own contingency and mortality. This double sense survives in Modernism. For the legacy of atavism, which motivates so many Modernist works, is partly a confession that we are not self-begotten or self-created, sufficient in our beings, no matter how much our Stephen-selves want to be. We must admit the power of the past within us, and turn it into a source of life rather than try continually to exorcise it. In this, preeminently, Hardy shows the way.[53]

---

53. *Ulysses* (Vintage Books, 1961), p. 207; Gabler ed., 9.844. For more on the metaphors of patriarchy, see my *Sacred Discontent: The Bible and Western Tradition* (Louisiana State University Press, 1976), chap. 4.

Hardy qualifies as a father for all the reasons just recounted, and he qualifies as a dead father because although he lived well into the modern era he knew he could really never participate in it. Alienated from his own time by his refusal to knuckle under to conventions or to play the Victorian sage, he yet could not comfort himself with futuristic fantasies. Though he insisted on being called an "evolutionary meliorist" rather than a "pessimist," he had very few illusions about human betterment in the future, and the Great War destroyed even these. His sense of the nineteenth century as a corpse having become all too real in the debacle, he lived on until 1928 as if in a time capsule, watching himself revisit the past. Yet he was not wandering between two worlds, but rather uneasily bridging them. Recall Auden's comment on how he facilitated the journey from Tennysonian England to the Waste Land, and that phrase "modern without being too modern" becomes deeply suggestive.

On this bridging activity, Norman Page comments:

> Hardy was born when Victoria had been on the throne for only three years, and survived to welcome her great-grandson (as the Prince of Wales) into his home. He began his schooling in the year in which the *Communist Manifesto* was published, and he lived to see the Russian Revolution; he was already a young man when Darwin's *Origin of Species* appeared, and in his old age he took an interest in the theories of Einstein; he belonged to the generation which was overwhelmed by the poetry of Swinburne, he heard Dickens read, and met Tennyson and Browning; but he lived to ponder the poetic techniques of T. S. Eliot and D. H. Lawrence, and to discuss his work with Virginia Woolf.[54]

But the life was remarkable not so much for its length. Rather, its interest is in the dissent from the age to which his multiplex sense of the past impelled him. Whether or not he was totally "unaffected by the progress myth," as A. O. J. Cockshut says, he was out of step with his times in many ways, and in his ambivalence toward the nineteenth century he merited the interest of the twentieth.[55]

Pound began Canto I, in the final version, with the blood rite

---

54. Page, *Thomas Hardy*, p. 3.

55. "Hardy's Philosophy," in Margaret Drabble, ed., *The Genius of Thomas Hardy* (Weidenfeld & Nicholson, 1976), p. 147.

that gives voice to the ghosts: his acknowledgment of the power of the chthonic includes the belief that a sacrifice must be performed to make the dead live again. By implying his own identity with the century's corpse, Hardy makes himself both priest and victim. He offers himself, in his art, as a father who makes way for the new by imaginatively counting himself among the dead. Pound was not the only legatee, nor even the British line that runs to Larkin. Hardy also made way for the compelling interest in the chthonic that arose in Forster and even Lawrence, and his Wessex, together with his insight into the force of long-buried memories, forecasts a series of successors from Joyce's Dublin and Lawrence's Midlands to Sherwood Anderson's Winesburg and Faulkner's Yoknapatawpha. He knew that in creating imaginary regions out of personal history, the artist could infuse them with the Proustian power of memory. Above all, his sense of atavism in memory and history carried him, straddling two worlds, into an artistic life beyond his own, for which he had never cared greatly.

2

Safe as Houses: Forster
as Cambridge Anthropologist

> Can what they call civilization be right, if people mayn't die
> in the room where they were born?
>
> RUTH WILCOX

Many agree with Lionel Trilling that *Howards End* is "undoubtedly
Forster's masterpiece."[1] *A Passage to India*, written much later,
may have reached a wider audience, partly because of the topicality
of its antiracist and anticolonialist sentiments, and of course Forster enthusiasts can make cases even for the earlier works. But for
those interested in the twentieth-century novel, this creation of
"1908–1910" counts as a high-water mark for Forster and the
genre. The British novel just before the Great War attained a level
it has not, in general, reached again, and the best novels of the
1920s were written by those who had attained maturity and mastery
before 1914. The War harrowed English sensibilities and sent several of its writers into spiritual exile, ironically imitating James
Joyce's prewar remove. Their later works belong to International
Modernism, not British literature. There was no surge in the number of new British writers after 1918, as in American, because those
writers who stayed at home had trouble assimilating Modernism
and especially could not embrace *Ulysses*, its pivotal work. Even
Virginia Woolf called it the book of a "queasy undergraduate
scratching his pimples," a remark that says nothing about Joyce
but tells all about the mental paradigms of Bloomsbury.[2]

1. *E. M. Forster* (New Directions, 1943), p. 114.
2. Woolf, quoted in Richard Ellmann, *James Joyce* (Oxford University Press,
1959), p. 542.

By 1918 the urge toward uncompromising "truth telling," the frankest possible presentations of social and sexual issues, was overpowering. The War in its official version (no photos or veridical reports had been allowed from the front), and the society out of which it had grown, were nothing but "old lies and new infamy."[3] This too figures in the ascendancy of the American novel and the stasis of the British: for the former, the uncensored aspect of Modernist writing was congenial to its prophetic–puritanic impulses, while the circumlocutory preferences of the latter, typified by Forster's genteel evasions in matters of sexuality, seemed dated or even duplicitous. Here again *A Passage to India* seems belated, and perhaps the years of novelistic silence before and after it appeared were Forster's tribute money to the presiding spirits of a world that had passed him by. Moreover, Forster's methods did not conform to Flaubertian and Jamesian proscriptions of authorial "comment." Indeed Forster revelled in addresses to "dear readers."

Forster and Modernism were thus sundered by powerful forces and beliefs. But in a cautious way he prefigured the world of Joyce and the others, in his deployment of what T. S. Eliot would later call, in regard to *Ulysses*, the "mythical method."[4] The parallels with mythological episodes in *Howards End* do not call attention to themselves, and there are few obviously classical motifs in the novel, in contrast to Forster's earlier works. But Forster does dramatize, through the motifs of the house and the land around it, an ideology that we, can call that of sacred space, or autochthony, that is, the belief that spiritual powers, which Forster reticently calls "the unseen," inhere not in heavens or in ethereal forms but in the earth; that they are beings, incarnate in landforms or dwellings or tombs; and that they forcefully affect even godless lives. In many tribal societies, powers such as conception are credited not solely to sexual intercourse but to ancestral spirits who reside in groves, rocks, trees, and the like. Such was the legacy of autochthony, and it persisted into Hellenistic culture in the cult of the *genius loci*, the spirit of place.[5] After this, it became merely "po-

3. Ezra Pound, "Hugh Selwyn Mauberley," IV.

4. "Ulysses, Order, and Myth," *Dial* 75 (1923): 483.

5. See my *Sacred Discontent: The Bible and Western Tradition* (Louisiana State University Press, 1976), pp. 69–77. See also Geoffrey Hartman, "Romantic Poetry and the Genius Loci," in his *Beyond Formalism: Literary Essays 1958–1970* (Yale

etic." Forster wants us to suspend disbelief; without going over
into fantasy, he wants it to occur to us that these archaic beliefs are
true in ways that we, under the dominance of materialist heritages,
cannot acknowledge. He means to persuade us to lower our skepti-
cal guards and to take literally such offhand metaphors as Margaret Schlegel's "'Houses are alive. No?'" For in the story the house
is alive — it has a heart, and in a revelatory moment the heart is
heard beating — and the land too lives: "England was alive, throbbing through all her estuaries, crying for joy through the mouths
of all her gulls, and the north wind, with contrary motion, blew
stronger against her rising seas."[6] In context, Forster always gives
us the chance to write off such remarks as characters' or author's
"fancies," but the totality of the design makes it clear that he intends a "logic of the imagination" to work on us, so that the figures
have a cumulative or accretive effect. His personal beliefs are of
course not necessarily determinative of the novel's imaginative
structure, but he did want to be known as one who had tried
various spiritual adventures, and his Clapham Sect ancestors revisited him in the form of an ambition to be a spiritual mentor to his
age.

Most of the criticism on *Howards End* has centered on "personal
relations," on the epigraph "only connect" and the other mottoes
that cue a reading of the work as a bourgeois-liberal drama. "Panic
and emptiness," "telegrams and anger," and other phrases are used
by the Schlegel sisters to signal their rejection, whether contemptu-
ous or forgiving, of the way of life represented by the Wilcoxes:
domineering, crass, impersonal, and complacent; life by the code
of the successful businessman and the dutiful colonial, highminded
and coarsegrained. Here they are businessmen, in *A Passage to
India* colonials; Forster may have said that he wanted to "connect"
with such people, but he really wanted to stamp them out. In
any case the book is not simply a tragicomedy of manners. "The
personal" in this work is absorbed and eventually eclipsed by the

University Press, 1970), pp. 311–36. Hartman covers the older literary allusions to
the idea but does not bring in autochthony. See also Jane Chance Nitzsche, *The
Genius Figure in Antiquity and the Middle Ages* (Columbia University Press, 1975),
which also knows nothing of autochthony.

6. *Howards End* (Vintage Books, n.d.; originally published, 1910), pp. 155, 175.
Subsequent page references in the text are to this convenient edition.

drama of "the unseen"; the salvageable characters are separated out from the hopelessly obtuse by their intermittent insights into this development, which in turn involves dim awareness — all that any of them are ever vouchsafed — of the theme of autochthony.[7]

Trilling's elegant reading of the book on the social level is now several decades old but remains typical in many ways. He regrets the "mythical fantasy" of Forster's early stories, remarking that "surely the Greek myths made too deep an impression on Forster," and regrets further the persistence of these elements into the earlier novels. The implication is that *Howards End* advances beyond these by subordinating the mythical elements, reducing them to the dominant social criticism. The truth in this is that the autochthonic theme is implicitly critical of the modern consciousness, but it is misleading to imply that myth is subordinated: actually, it is less obvious but more pervasive. Moreover, Trilling supposes that the motifs of house and land are essentially political.

> *Howards End* is a novel about England's fate. . . . England herself appears in the novel in palpable form. The symbol for England is the house whose name gives the title to the book. Like the plots of so many English novels, the plot of *Howards End* is about the rights of property, about a destroyed will-and-testament and rightful and wrongful heirs. It asks the question, "Who shall inherit England?"[8]

Trilling insufficiently signals his irony. Not only might the unwary suppose that Schlegel liberalism is an adequate answer to Wilcox crudeness, but to frame the question legalistically is wholly inconsonant. The novel asks, "Is it credible that the possessions of the spirit can be bequeathed at all?" (pp. 98–99) The concept of "rights of property" is firmly associated with the Wilcox mentality; and when the odious Charles Wilcox goes to prison for killing a man, his sentence grossly misrepresents the situation: but "the law, being made in his image," (p. 334) is incapable of truth.

Forster does labor to make us fear that Wilcox ideals will overwhelm the modern world, but as for inheriting Howards End, the Wilcoxes were never in the running. They are too stupid and insensitive, and are easily outmaneuvered by the powers immanent in

---

7. See p. 338: "Don't drag in the personal when it will not come." Critics should heed Margaret's advice.

8. *E. M. Forster*, pp. 38, 118.

house and land. They are caricatures whose genial or generous moments are somehow the results of misapprehension (except for those female Wilcoxes who "marry in" and are thus not real ones), and projects to "connect" with them are absurdly misplaced charity, at best. Forster's inveterate tendency was to practice novelistic overkill against the type of Englishman he feared and resented: clubbable, self-possessed, aggressively conventional. He will set up such a figure and then kill him off quickly and painfully—the revenge of the timid, sensitive, bullied schoolboy, which Forster remained to the end of his life.[9] The Wilcoxes are so grotesque that we may miss the fact that the Schlegel nostrums for progress and social change are likewise caricatures. The sister are saved only because their openness gives more scope to the force of "the unseen."

In thus dramatizing mythological themes, Forster connects not only with Modernism in general but specifically provides a link between his friend Hardy and his other friend (despite plebeian origins) D. H. Lawrence, in whose works the whole idea flowered rather showily. For Forster it was thus "in the air." His years at Cambridge are best known for his membership in the Apostles and for other friendships that prefigured the Bloomsbury mystique, but his education in classics also enticed him with its promise of recovering a lost world and turning it into a merely misplaced one. He may even have heard something of Jane Harrison and the other Cambridge anthropologists, though he never manifested firsthand knowledge. In a sense his work uncannily recapitulates Harrison's discovery that underneath the Olympian pantheon there was a layer of chthonic, local traditions, cults, and numens of place.[10] The goal of *Howards End* was even more ambitiously revisionist than was Harrison's: he aimed to change not only our understanding of ancient religions but also our thinking about the nature of our lives and their relation to the earth on which they are carried out.

The grandiosity of these ambitions and their thematic conceptualizations surely gave Forster pause, and hesitancies appear even in the famous diffident opening: "One may as well begin with Helen's

9. The obvious example is Gerald Dawes in *The Longest Journey*.
10. *Prolegomena to the Study of Greek Religions* (see note 44 to the Introduction).

letters to her sister." This effete tone—"Oh dear yes, the novel tells a story"—betrays Forster's fear of seeming "hearty," unforgivable in British gentility with its decayed ideal of *sprezzatura*: "A country in love with amateurs . . . where the incompetent have such beautiful manners," as Ezra Pound put it.[11] Forster like other well-bred Englishmen disguises his own seriousness, so that the first episodes are dominated by the sisters' goodhearted playfulness and by the comic distractions of Aunt Juley, the interfering relative whose blunders land both families in an awkward misunderstanding. When Helen Schlegel and Paul Wilcox tryst—Helen being perversely attracted to Wilcox manliness—Aunt Juley and Charles Wilcox, Paul's older brother, turn the affair into a shouting match, a "game of Capping Families, a round of which is always played when love would unite two members of our race. But they played it with unusual vigour, stating in so many words that Schlegels were better than Wilcoxes, Wilcoxes better than Schlegels. They flung decency aside" (p. 21). These early pages of sub-Wildean farce are disguise, distraction, sleight-of-hand; Forster is already insinuating hints that will open out as the story progresses and especially as we reread. The very first pages of the book are disguised as an inconsequential letter from Helen to her sister Margaret, describing the house and its trees and grounds, but every detail comes to be part of the book's spiritual pattern. The letter introduces the person Helen cannot know is the presiding genius of the place, Ruth Wilcox, nee Ruth Howard at Howards End, later prevented from dying there only by her husband's habitual insensitivity and underhandedness (p. 283):

> This long letter is because I'm writing before breakfast. Oh, the beautiful vine leaves! The house is covered with a vine. I looked out earlier, and Mrs. Wilcox was already in the garden. She evidently loves it. No wonder she sometimes looks tired [later we learn that she was dying even at this time]. She was watching the large red poppies come out. Then she walked off the lawn to the meadow, whose corner to the right I can just see. Trail, trail, went her long dress over the sopping grass, and she came back with her hands full of the hay that was cut yesterday—I suppose for rabbits or something, as she kept on smelling it. (p. 4)

11. "The Prose Tradition in Verse" in T. S. Eliot, ed., *Literary Essays of Ezra Pound* (New Directions, 1954), p. 371.

The smelling of the hay, like her lack of concern for her dress, is symbolic of Mrs. Wilcox's affinity for the earth, and in the final chapter the Schlegel sisters enact half-consciously her bequeathed awareness: the chapter is framed by an opening in which the "sacred centre" (p. 335) of the hay field is about to be harvested, and an ending in which Helen says more than she knows: "'The field's cut!' Helen cried excitedly—'the big meadow! We've seen to the very end, and it'll be such a crop of hay as never!'" (p. 343) The "very end" is not only the end of the book but also a long perspective that looks back through and past time, all the way back to the eternal present of ancient man and *la pensée sauvage*, which Forster calls "the Now" (p. 249, cf. pp. 315, 323). Thus the hay participates in a double framing, of the last chapter and of the book, and it identifies the first appearance of Ruth Wilcox in Helen's letter as the theophany of Demeter: the hay is her cereal icon. Demeter was Forster's favorite mythological figure, who "alone among gods has true immortality."[12] The hay reappears so often that critics who do not grasp autochthony find it obtrusive—Mrs. Wilcox is said to be "a wisp of hay, a flower" (p. 74)—and at the climax the same phrase refers to "death" (p. 330). She therefore represents fructifying, sacrificial death, and in that sense plays the role of Persephone as well as that of Demeter: she disappears to emerge in renewed forms of life, organic and inorganic. She is incarnate in the house and field as well as some of the characters, notably Margaret Schlegel, who becomes "Mrs. Wilcox" and is pointedly so addressed at the end, even by the defeated, hostile Wilcoxes themselves.

Not surprisingly, the real Wilcoxes all have hay fever. Helen's letter continues:

> Later on I heard the noise of croquet balls, and looked out again, and it was Charles Wilcox practising; they are keen on all games. Presently he started sneezing and had to stop. Then I hear more clicketing, and it is Mr. Wilcox practising, and then, "a-tissue, a-tissue": he has to stop too. Then Evie comes out, and does some calisthenic exercises on a machine that is tacked on to a greengage-tree—they put everything to use—and then she says "a-tissue," and in she goes. And finally Mrs. Wilcox reappears, trail, trail, still smelling hay and looking at the flowers. (p. 4)

---

12. Forster, "Cnidus," in *Abinger Harvest* (Harcourt Brace, 1936), p. 176.

Much later the book's sibyl, old Miss Avery, cackles maliciously at the thought of the Wilcox hay fever. "There's not one Wilcox that can stand up against a field in June—I laughed fit to burst while he [Henry] was courting Ruth. . . . This house lies too much on the land for them" (p. 273).

To the Wilcoxes, Howards End is merely an ungainly and useless property—"'one of those converted farms. They don't really do, spend what you will on them,'" says Henry Wilcox (p. 135)—and they hold on to it only from a grasping instinct. That the house has been in the Howard family for generations means nothing to Henry; for him it is hay fever and problems. To Ruth, on the other hand, it is "a spirit, for which she sought a spiritual heir" (p. 98), and her "one passion . . . the Holy of Holies" (p. 85), though she herself understands this only vaguely and nonintellectually. Throughout she is characterized as dim, evasive, and remote, out of focus with the everyday and the material, although loving and generous and above all majestic. She is in short a figure from another world. Her wisdom comes from atavism, from the voices of her ancestors sounding in her brain (as in Julian Jaynes's theories of "schizophrenic" ancient man).[13] When Aunt Juley and her son Charles have quarreled bitterly at "Capping Families," she settles all, first defusing Charles's efforts to play inquisitor:

"Paul, is there any truth in this?"
"I didn't—I don't—"
"Yes or no, man; plain question, plain answer. Did or didn't Miss Schlegel—"
"Charles dear," said a voice from the garden. "Charles, dear Charles, one doesn't ask plain questions. There aren't such things."
They were all silent. It was Mrs. Wilcox.
She approached just as Helen's letter had described her, trailing noiselessly over the lawn, and there was actually a wisp of hay in her hands. She seemed to belong not to the young people and their motor, but to the house, and to the tree that overshadowed it. One knew that she worshipped the past, and that the instinctive wisdom the past can alone bestow had descended upon her—that wisdom to which we give the clumsy name of aristocracy. High-born she might not be. But assuredly she cared about her ancestors, and let them help her. When she

13. *The Origin of Consciousness in the Breakdown of the Bicameral Mind* (Houghton Mifflin, 1976).

saw Charles angry, Paul frightened, and Mrs. Munt ["Aunt Juley"] in tears, she heard her ancestors say: "Separate those human beings who will hurt each other most. The rest can wait." (p. 22)

Her instincts contrast vividly not only with her family's obtuseness but also with Aunt Juley's self-satisfaction and itch to interfere. After the contretemps,

Mrs. Munt soon recovered. She possessed to a remarkable degree the power of distorting the past, and before many days were over she had forgotten the part played by her own imprudence in the catastrophe. Even at the crisis she had cried: "Thank goodness, poor Margaret is saved this!" which during the journey to London evolved into: "It had to be gone through by someone," which in its turn ripened into the permanent form of: "The one time I really did help Emily's girls was over the Wilcox business." (p. 23)

So it is delicious irony that we are introduced to still more symbols of "the unseen" through this unseeing person. On her train trip to the village where Howards End stands, "a series of tiled and slated houses passed before Mrs. Munt's inattentive eyes, a series broken at one point by six Danish tumuli that stood shoulder to shoulder along the highroad, tombs of soldiers" (p. 15). These mounds, called the Six Hills, grow in significance as the novel progresses, and link the landscape's eternal "Now" with the historic past. Margaret Schlegel responds to the Six Hills with instinctive admiration: "Beneath them she settled that soldiers of the best kind lay buried. She hated war and liked soldiers—it was one of her amiable inconsistencies" (p. 198).[14] She looks often at them, "tombs of warriors, breasts of the spring" (p. 309). At the crisis of the book, she is sitting on the "glebe," all that is left of the old farmland: "Henry's kind had filched most of it. She moved to the scrap opposite, wherein were the Six Hills." When Henry confesses to her that the Wilcoxes have been utterly defeated, "Margaret drove her fingers through the grass. The hill beneath her moved as if it was alive" (pp. 333–34).[15] They symbolize the renewing vitality of the earth,

14. Miss Avery says that Ruth should have married a "real soldier" (p. 275) instead of Henry, the degenerate imperialist descendant of "warriors of the past."

15. Even critics trying to illuminate Forster's mysticism frequently ignore such passages: for example, Denis Godfrey, in *E. M. Forster's Other Kingdom* (Oliver & Boyd, 1968), though alert to the "instinctive mysticism of the English soil," does not quote it (pp. 137ff.).

again uniting life and a fructifying death. In another connection, Forster notes another local "myth": "Six forest trees — that is a fact — grow out of one of the graves in Tewin churchyard. The grave's occupant — that is the legend — is an atheist, who declared that if God existed six forest trees would grow out of her grave" (p. 323). If we share the Wilcox mentality, we stick to facts. Henry writes off the Six Hills with a passing remark: "'Curious mounds,' said Henry, 'but in with you now; another time'" (p. 204). He is handing Margaret into his "motor" and has no leisure for tourist speculations, but his "another time" is of course a major dramatic irony: he does not know that he is evoking what he himself so grievously lacks, the sense of the Past, the sense that the modern "restless civilization" that seems to him the *telos* of all the ages is simply a phase in the real life of the earth. For Wilcoxes the time is always out of joint, but they like Mrs. Munt are fatuously unaware of it, "incapable of grouping the past" (p. 259). Henry's "mental states became obscure as soon as he had passed through them" (p. 178).

Forster works many more landscape details, such as trees with "healing powers" and other legendary attributes, into his mosaic of the living land and house, but these examples should suffice; the others can easily be tallied if we reread the book with open minds to what the text pointedly says. The cumulative effect of the motifs is an interesting adaptation of the literary impressionism that is more familiarly associated with Ford and Conrad: it requires us to pay attention to minute details, to remember motifs, to put them together by looking again and again, varying our perspectives.[16] As in *pointillisme* the details can hardly be seen for what they really are until they cohere into Gestalten. Forster's techniques culminate in scenes that suddenly irradiate many details with revelatory significance. Possibly the best managed is the entry of Margaret, after years of strange delays and frustrations, into Howards End. She is not consciously aware that she is entering a sacred space, but is

16. A textbook example of impressionism is this passage from Joseph Conrad's *Heart of Darkness*, in which Marlow's steamboat is ambushed by natives: "Sticks, little sticks, were flying about. . . . Arrows, by Jove! We were being shot at!" Bruce Harkness, ed., *Conrad's* Heart of Darkness *and the Critics* (Wadsworth, 1960), p. 39. Compare the passage in which Leonard, about to be struck by a sword, sees only a "stick, very bright," descend (p. 324).

unaccountably moved by the landscape as she stands on the porch. A Hardyesque "fancy" pops into her mind: "How Helen would revel in such a notion! Charles dead, all people dead, nothing alive but houses and gardens. The obvious dead, the intangible alive, and—no connection at all between them! Margaret smiled" (p. 200). Then the house opens itself up to her, though it had seemed locked to Henry (he's gone to get the key), and she enters full of "fancies" she doesn't grasp, like Adela Quested going into the Marabar caves.

> She paced back into the hall, and as she did so the house reverberated.
> "Is that you, Henry?" she called.
> There was no answer, but the house reverberated again.
> "Henry, have you got in?"
> But it was the heart of the house beating, faintly at first, then loudly, martially. It dominated the rain.
> It is the starved imagination, not the well-nourished, that is afraid. Margaret flung open the door to the stairs. A noise as of drums seemed to deafen her. A woman, an old woman, was descending, with figure erect, with face impassive, with lips that parted and said dryly:
> "Oh! Well, I took you for Ruth Wilcox."
> Margaret stammered: "I—Mrs. Wilcox—I?"
> "In fancy, of course—in fancy. You had her way of walking. Good day." And the old woman passed out into the rain. (pp. 201-2)

Forster has designed the scene so that with the words *old woman* we are ready for a ghost: "'Did you take her for a spook?'" asks the crude but insightful Dolly Wilcox in the next chapter (p. 202). In consequence, the line, "'I took you for Ruth Wilcox'" might have confused Margaret even more than first appears, because it voices her own reaction to the descending figure. This is no spook but the "eccentric" Miss Avery. The momentary confusion is expertly planned: the three women instinctively share much, and at this point their identities actually interpenetrate. Margaret, we learn, was "clutching a bunch of weeds" (p. 202) when she saw the apparition. Near the end of the book, Margaret—by then being called "Mrs. Wilcox"—senses an even more comprehensive incarnation.

> "I feel that you [Helen] and I and Henry are only fragments of that woman's mind. She knows everything. She is everything. She is the

house, and the tree that leans over it. People have their own deaths as well as their own lives, and even if there is nothing beyond death, we shall differ in our nothingness. I cannot believe that knowledge such as hers will perish with knowledge such as mine. She knew about realities. She knew when people were in love [Helen and Paul], though she was not in the room. I don't doubt that she knew when Henry deceived her."

"Good night, Mrs. Wilcox," called a voice.

"Oh, good night, Miss Avery." (pp. 313–14)

The oracular, disembodied voice of Miss Avery, who also "knows everything," emphasizes the interpenetration of Margaret and Ruth Wilcox, but she is included. In fact, the vagueness of the antecedents in Margaret's sentences gestures toward her.

By the end of the book, Margaret even acts and speaks like Ruth Wilcox, settling disputes and muddles with instinctive, atavistic generosity rather than with her earlier Schlegel liberalism, which tends to victimize its legatees. On being praised for this by Helen, she says, sitting amidst the hay: "'Things that I can't phrase have helped me'" (p. 339). "The wisdom the past alone can bestow" has descended on her, through Mrs. Wilcox. But Miss Avery too is a reincarnation; she appears in the book only after Mrs. Wilcox dies, and gradually we learn of an extraordinary bond between the two, who outwardly have been almost mistress and servant. The country people credit Miss Avery with "prophetic powers," and she foretells the futures of all the key characters and of Howards End. So she carries on the "spirit" of Ruth Wilcox in the ordinary sense, but also becomes the *genius loci*, though the male Wilcoxes insist on treating her as a simple charwoman. Whereas the "inattentive" Aunt Juley can never get straight the name of Howards End, she knows every inch of the place as if it were her skin, knows that the Schlegels are fated to oust the obtuse Wilcoxes, and knows just what the latter are good for: "'Wilcoxes are better than nothing, as I see you've found,'" she says dryly to Margaret (p. 274).

Miss Avery is not only sibylline and a *genius loci*, but also embodies the idea of "folk" wisdom. Forster does little with the folk except for one memorable scene, the aftermath of Ruth Wilcox's funeral. Without telling us that she had died or even that she was ill — indeed the immediately preceding chapter has her "'fit as a

fiddle,'" by her own account (p. 87)—Forster begins Chapter 11
with "The funeral was over." Here the "virtual" narrative consciousness (though not the voice) is that of the country people, and
eventually one of them in particular, a young woodcutter who
pollards elms while the funeral takes place beneath him. For him
and the other villagers the ritual is a sensual experience, not a
mock-solemn mummery. "The funeral of a rich person was to them
what the funeral of Alcestis, of Ophelia, is to the educated. It was
Art; though remote from life, it enhanced life's values, and they
witnessed it avidly" (p. 88). For the Wilcoxes, in contrast, the
woodcutter and his ilk are merely nuisances; blind to the values of
communal ritual, they think of the funeral as their property, which
others may mar or mishandle.[17] Through the woodcutter Forster
underlines all the previously established connections between fatality and fertility, death and rebirth, which are such regular features
of autochthonic ideology.

> The young wood-cutter stayed a little longer, poised above the silence
> and swaying rhythmically. At last the bough fell beneath his saw. [The
> very pollarding of the elms emblematizes the ritualistic, sacrificial sense
> that death is necessary to make way for new life.] With a grunt, he
> descended, his thoughts dwelling no longer on death, but on love, for
> he was mating. He stopped as he passed the new grave; a sheaf of
> tawny chrysanthemums had caught his eye. "They didn't ought to have
> coloured flowers at buryings," he reflected. Trudging on a few steps,
> he stopped again, looked furtively at the dusk, turned back, wrenched
> a chrysanthemum from the sheaf, and hid it in his pocket. (pp. 88–89)

Later we find it was Margaret who had the instinct to send the
chrysanthemums; her act would no doubt have pleased Mrs. Wilcox, but it annoys the conventional-minded family. In the same
spirit, Margaret herself attended the funeral but "stood far back
among the [village] women" (p. 101)—another instinctively correct
gesture, but not because of the implied deference for which the
Wilcoxes approve it.

Forster has been accused, with some justice, of romanticizing
his yeomen; indeed, this aspect of his autochthonic thinking might

---

17. Compare p. 219: "Henry treated a marriage like a funeral, item by item."
Naturally the Wilcoxes are unaware of the fructifying power of Leonard's death,
which is manifested in the hay harvest of the last pages.

be called Tory apologetics. The Wilcoxes are certainly representative of Whiggery: they are climbing, grasping, snobbish without right, vulgarly "modern," and shallow — in short, self-righteous *arrivistes* in their worst form.[18] They have no sense of the land, of the people, of the culture; they care only for commercial success, social appearances, and the rights of property construed suspiciously and legalistically. Forster does not trouble to subtilize their offensiveness: "When Mr. Wilcox said that one sound man of business did more good to the world than a dozen of your social reformers, [Helen, in what can only be called a moral rape-fantasy] had swallowed the curious assertion without a gasp, and had leant back luxuriously among the cushions of his motor-car" (p. 24). The motorcar is a fine touch, for it symbolizes their rootless, thoughtlessly destructive way of life. For Forster, entrepreneurial and imperialist drives are simply rationalized spoliation of the earth. Against these activities he sets a complex of almost feudal values: landedness against mercantilism, instinct against calculation, atavism against sophistication.

Forster's latent Toryism shows up most gracelessly in the unsatisfying treatment of Leonard Bast. In spite of his tepid Bloomsbury leanings, Forster was capable of uttering such disclaimers as this: "We are not concerned with the very poor. They are unthinkable, and only to be approached by the statistician or the poet. This story deals with gentlefolk, or with those who are obliged to pretend that they are gentlefolk" (p. 45). Even his most fervent admirers must squirm at that one. This is by no means the only passage that implies that men were better off when all knew their places: when Wilcoxes treat the lower classes rudely, this is meant to contrast with the noblesse oblige of true aristocracy, under which all ranks prosper amicably. But Forster's political views are not as troublesome as their consequence, which is the inability to make the Basts materialize for us. Leonard remains precisely the theoretical pauper of the women's-club debate that leads the Schlegels to try to help him: the novel patronizes him as remorselessly as the ladies do.[19]

However, Forster's social views are well adapted to engender

18. Malcolm Bradbury makes the connection with Whiggery in his essay on *Howards End* in *Forster: A Collection of Critical Essays* (Prentice-Hall, 1966), p. 132.

19. See the later comparison of Leonard with Fitzgerald's *Gatsby*.

another important pattern of imagery in the novel. Throughout, the thrusting, exploitative Whiggery of the Wilcoxes is characterized by restless, aimless movements from place to place, house to house; they cannot alight anywhere; unsurprisingly, they approve of developers' demolitions of huge blocks of flats in London, in order to throw up more flats, as "good for trade," whereas Margaret finds the "continual flux" deeply unsettling: "us at our worst — eternal formlessness" and loss of differences (p. 182).

> The feudal ownership of land did bring dignity, whereas the modern ownership of movables is reducing us again to a nomadic horde. We are reverting to the civilization of luggage, and historians of the future will take note how the middle classes accreted possessions without taking root in the earth, and may find in this the secret of their imaginative poverty. [N.B. the implied warning to readers.] The Schlegels were certainly the poorer for the loss of Wickham Place. It had helped to balance their lives, and almost to counsel them. Nor is their ground-landlord spiritually the richer. He has built flats on its site, his motor-cars grow swifter, his exposures of Socialism more trenchant. But he has spilt the precious distillation of the years, and no chemistry of his can give it back to society again. (pp. 149–50)

Much of the book is occupied with searches for new houses, as leases expire and other modern barbarisms take effect. Margaret sees the tides of the Thames as emblematic of the condition and of the forgetfulness it brings (p. 137). London in this book always stands for an unsatisfactory blur of hurry and construction, an aimless tide washing this way and that, a pointless aggrandizement (Howards End is small). London engenders a "red rust" creeping out into the country in the form of Suburbia (pp. 15, 167, etc.). Looking at this glow of supposed energy but real decay, Helen mourns: "And London is only part of something else, I'm afraid. Life's going to be melted down, all over the world." To which Margaret can only reply, "This craze for motion has only set in during the last hundred years. It may be followed by a civilization that won't be a movement, because it will rest on the earth" (p. 339). They speak at Howards End — itself a survival, a time capsule of the real England sealed against Suburbia and such threatening forces manifest in Wilcox values. The house itself has maneuvered the Schlegels to victory over the Wilcoxes in order to ensure its own preservation.

The pattern of rest versus movement is admirably expressed in the opposition of house to motorcar: as mentioned earlier, the car represents the unseeing, uncaring, destructive oscillation of Wilcoxes careering back and forth. Every time car journeys are described or mentioned, the danger to children and animals is dwelt on. In the most distasteful incident, Charles Wilcox leads a convoy of cars, one of which runs over a cat; instead of stopping, Charles drives on, and Margaret jumps out of the car.

> No doubt she had disgraced herself. But she felt their whole journey from London had been unreal. They had no part with the earth and its emotions. They were dust, and a stink, and cosmopolitan chatter, and the girl whose cat had been killed had lived more deeply than they. (p. 214)

Even when not so stupidly lethal, cars rob their occupants of the sense of space — which, given the importance of land and geography, is severe loss. Wilcoxes never notice this, of course, but Margaret does: "She looked at the scenery. It heaved and merged like porridge. Presently it congealed. They had arrived" (p. 198). This journey takes them smack up to the entrance to Howards End, but she cannot grasp this because the car has deprived her of spatial orientation. "A little porch was close up against her face. 'Are we there already?'" (p. 199)

This quality of motor journeys is also used metaphorically, in a passage that contrasts Mrs. Wilcox's slowminded nobility to the mercurial dartings of a representative set of Bright Young People (among whom, interestingly, is a Miss Quested): "Clever talk alarmed [Mrs. Wilcox], and withered her delicate imaginings; it was the social counterpart of a motor-car, all jerks, and she was a wisp of hay, a flower" (p. 74). She says to Margaret, "You younger people move so quickly that it dazes me" (p. 78). Margaret has the wisdom to feel this as a reproof from a spiritual agency she cannot comprehend, "a personality that transcended their own and dwarfed their activities" (p. 76). Mrs. Wilcox's transcendence lies of course in her merger with the earth — literally so at her funeral, after which even her smallminded husband has a glimmer of insight: "Ruth knew no more of worldly wickedness and wisdom than did the flowers in her garden, or the grass in her field" (p. 89). The Biblical imagery joins together the associations of her first name, plus Keats's line about the "alien corn," with the Demeter motif. But Henry's metaphorical thought is ironic — and far more accurate than he realizes — because, as we later learn, behind his reverence for her innocence there is a self-congratulatory smugness; he thinks she never suspected his affair with the improbable Jacky. (Later Margaret and Helen intuit that she knew, but her transcendence must have entailed untroubled acceptance of all things brought to her by atavistic wisdom.) Henry's flash of insight dissipates among his hypocrisies. His world is business and motorcars: even the furniture he likes consists of "chairs of maroon leather. It was as if a motor-car had spawned" (p. 163). Margaret, at this point about to marry Henry under the delusion that he deserves "connecting" with, sinks into such a chair, just as Helen earlier leaned back in his car when yielding to his preposterous views. The most offensive of all the Wilcoxes, Charles, whose corrosive suspicions twist every act and motive into caricatures, persistently drives or attends to cars throughout the book. No wonder that when Helen most keenly grasps how the Schlegels and Wilcoxes have unwittingly combined to ruin Leonard Bast, she has a vision of him being crushed by a "Juggernaut car" (p. 316).

The automobile imagery is linked to yet another pattern: whereas men in the story are associated with cars and restless proprietorship, women are the vessels of true possession, permanence, and rest. In acquiring property, women react instinctively to places and houses themselves, endowing them with feelings and lives in cheerful acceptance of the pathetic fallacy. Thus feminine discourse provides Forster his opportunities to embed autochthonous figures of speech that provide the thematic backbone of the book. The female Schlegels keep up a drumfire of proleptic remarks about the importance of place and their own dependence on it, even before they see the point of their own understanding. Long before she ever sees Howards End, Margaret says "I quite expect to end my life caring most for a place" (p. 130). The implausibility of the sisters' interest in Leonard Bast is sketchily concealed by giving him a role in this pattern. His pitiable attempts to acquire culture have entailed shallow reading of some of the English travel writers and historians of place, from Ruskin to Stevenson and George Borrow; hence his failure to transcend these writings can become the occasion for remarks by Margaret: "Haven't we all to struggle against life's daily greyness, against pettiness, against mechanical cheerfulness, against suspicion? I struggle by remembering my friends; others I have known by remembering some place — some beloved place or tree — we thought you one of these" (p. 143).

Even Evie Wilcox, otherwise a hardminded and conventional girl with all the Wilcox suspicion and concern for appearances, responds to places with feminine instinct. She it was who induced her father to buy Oniton Grange, another house that Margaret quickly learns to love, only to have her new husband rent it out from under her. Of Evie and Oniton, Henry says: "Poor little girl! She was so keen on it all, and wouldn't even wait to make proper inquiries about the shooting. Afraid it would get snapped up — just like all of your sex" (p. 260–61). Whereas his own approach, naturally, is businesslike and unsentimental, all calculation and hardnosed beating down of others, with few thoughts about the house itself. "One bit of advice: fix your district, then fix your price, and then don't budge. That's how I got both Ducie Street and Oniton. I said to myself, 'I mean to be exactly here,' and I was, and Oniton's a place in a thousand" (p. 155). As usual, Henry's accounts of the acquisition contradict themselves, but his sense of the difference in the masculine and feminine approaches to house buying is ironically accurate. For him no house will really "do," because of his placeless instincts; he is ingenious in finding reasons for moving. Since the act of acquisition is for him more important than the property itself, he gets his satisfaction from the negotiations, which he no doubt conducts on the model of his rebukes to servants and inferiors. Without bothering to tell his new wife, who had "determined to create new sanctities" there (p. 222), he disposes of Oniton because it is "damp" (p. 260), although Forster lets us understand that in reality the house has purposefully repelled him as an intruder, just as Howards End later does. Indeed, while Evie is getting married from Oniton, Margaret feels that the ceremony is somehow unreal and that "the Norman church had been intent all the time on other business" (p. 222).

We find that the whole pattern of rest and movement, with cars and houses, is sexually polarized, and that the shadowy struggle between Schlegels and Wilcoxes is really between atavistically sensitive females and no-nonsense males. Unsurprisingly, the book brings itself to this question: "Are the sexes really races, each with its own code of morality, and their mutual love a mere device of Nature to keep things going?" (p. 240) This thought occurs to Margaret; she thrusts it down, but it recurs later in unanswerable form when she shuts herself up in Howards End with her fugitive and pregnant sister. "A new feeling came over her; she was fighting for women against men. She did not care about rights, but if men came into Howards End, it should be over her body" (p. 290). Here at last the metaphors coalesce, and the struggle that seemed between families is revealed as sex war, full of overtones of race war. Howards End is not to be the possession of any family — the "ancestors" are ultimately generalized — but a home for refugee women and their nameless, almost parthenogenetic offspring. Women deserve it; while males have striven to dominate the earth and to inherit it in a legalistic sense, the females have been half-consciously serving as guardians and stewards.

Forster was not much of a feminist, but he did see that such devices as chivalry are at best patronizing. Margaret knows this, but pretends not to in deference to Henry: a deference she is obliged to repeat again and again until goaded beyond it by what she sees as Henry's attack on her sister, in his refusal to let the two women spend one night with their ancestral *lares* at Howards End. Men are equally objectionable, whether patronizing or suppressing women. Henry has done his best — fortunately that's not much — to denature Howards End with his improvement projects, undertaken to "please" his first wife: the result is a "series of mistakes," a house disfigured internally by rooms "that men have spoilt through trying to make it nice for women" (pp. 297–98). Always men will rationalize their spoliations with cant about doing it all for wives and families, but they make no effort to grasp female points of view, nor would they be caught dead understanding women. The book is unrelieved by the presence of males who can take even a step beyond themselves to try the female side of any issue. Even Tibby Schlegel is an outsider who can silence feminine play (p. 65), although in her early infatuation with Wilcox maleness Helen compares him unfavorably with them, grumbling that he's not a "real boy" and calling him "Auntie Tibby" (p. 43). In a distracted way men sometimes aid women's projects, to keep them quiet, but underneath the sexes are at eternal cross-purposes.

This view of life has enough truth in it to carry the plot over some gross implausibilities, though it is no profound contribution to the theory of sexual warfare. Forster's males, except for the unconvincing Leonard Bast and the inert Tibby Schlegel, are simply projections of his enemy, the arrogant bullying public-schoolboy, or "Red-blood." And his females, for all their sensitivity, are only vaguely women. They are theoretical in every sense, whether idealized or caricatured. Forster had, after all, only a limited ability to imagine himself in other identities, and just as his portrayal of a clerk on the lowest rungs of gentility lacks all *effet du réel*, his women are substantial only from a distance. They are "Mollycoddles," the opposite of "Red-bloods," in dresses.

Forster's characters serve well enough on a first quick reading, but the trouble is that his quasi-impressionist techniques of accreting images are best savored on rereading, and such scrutiny provokes embarrassing questions not only about the characters but also about the plot. Many critics have found Forster's plots in general, and that of *Howards End* in particular, to depend far too heavily on unlikely coincidences, improbable impulses, strained connections. Given the nature of the Wilcoxes, why would the Schlegels ever have anything to do with them? Forster can get away with asserting that for a brief period Helen was perversely attracted by their "manliness," but the plot requires continued contact, so they have to turn up literally across the street from the Schlegel's London house: a shameless device. Then comes the celebrated problem of the attraction between Margaret and Henry Wilcox — equally unlikely for either one, given what is established of their characters.[20] Forster does labor to suggest that the motive force of their union is Margaret's desire to "connect the prose with the passion" (p. 186). Henry is certainly prosaic, so Margaret's deference to his supposed strengths and forgiveness of his weaknesses is just barely plausible as an extremely deluded form of generosity. But even if that problem is put aside, many more improbabilities intrude. The Basts have to be dragged in repeatedly, by the handle

20. As Frederick C. Crews puts it: "Both Margaret and Forster struggle unconvincingly to remind themselves of the Wilcox virtues." *E. M. Forster: The Perils of Humanism* (Princeton University Press, 1962), p. 108. F. R. Leavis, remarking that "nothing in the exhibition of Margaret's or Henry Wilcox's character makes the marriage credible or acceptable," discusses the problem helpfully: see his essay in Bradbury, *Critical Essays*, pp. 40–41.

of Leonard's umbrella. Leonard's overpowering urge to discuss books is the barest contrivance, but not worse than Jacky's unimaginable liaison with Henry in an unlikely past, or Helen's ridiculous invasion of Evie's wedding party with them. Most contrived of all is Leonard's supposed desire to confess to "ruining" a woman of higher station. This brings him on a pre-dawn train ride to Howards End, there to be "thrashed" by the bully Charles Wilcox and to die, most conveniently, of heart disease. Although Forster tries to imply that this trip is a kind of Grail quest for Leonard, it is the last term of an absurd series.

As one reads through the book to see what happens next and why, to see a "story" turn into a "plot" in Forster's own terms, one credits these events provisionally, always hoping for further explanation or insight. On rereading, one finds little more than chatty rationalizations by the narrator or the characters. Yet sometimes Forster can make one problem mask another: for instance, he knew better than to attempt direct transcription of the impossible scene in which Leonard impregnates Helen. No amount of insistence on Helen's sexual impulsiveness or deranged state can make us believe this, and Leonard's acceptance is even more unthinkable (Katherine Mansfield said the umbrella did it).[21] However, we don't learn of this intercourse until the crescendo of final events is already in motion, when Margaret and Henry are pursuing what they suppose to be a "mad" Helen, and the revelation of the pregnancy comes as a nice touch. Then our attention is diverted from the impossible by the merely implausible: Leonard's fatherhood is almost forgotten in the impressionist handling of the death scene.

The thread showing that all the implausibilities are linked together is sexual evasiveness, and this is not surprising given Forster's astonishing ignorance, at the age of thirty, of the physical facts of sexual intercourse.[22] Even the unlucky Jacky's sex life, though several times asserted, is portrayed by no more than half-hearted hints. But Forster's reticence achieves more than conformity with Victorian standards, for it forces us to look elsewhere,

21. Quoted in Francis King, *E. M. Forster and His World* (Thames & Hudson, 1978), p. 49.
22. See P. N. Furbank, *E. M. Forster: A Life* (Secker & Warburg, 1977), vol. 1, p. 37.

to see if sexual energy shows up in deflected forms. And though the sexual lacunae mar the book novelistically, they contribute to the theme of autochthony a sense of ominous and telling silence. Sex becomes an indescribable mystery at the heart of human existence, as fertility is for tribal societies: it is sex that is truly "the unseen" in *Howards End*.

In autochthonous cultures, not only is fertility the great mystery but intercourse also is the model of human relationships with the world of nature and animals, much to the distress of missionaries. On cave walls in France and Spain, on rocks in Australia and Polynesia and America, representations of animals survive that are clearly emblems of power, including sexual power. In some instances the intercourse with humans is portrayed, or mimed in ritual. Totemism is an ideology that is inconceivable without animal ancestors, and the proliferation in mythology of hybrid creatures—Centaurs, satyrs, and the like—is evidence of the ubiquity of this kind of thinking. Western writers cannot touch the theme explicitly, though Lawrence comes close and Faulkner gives us glimpses: one Snopes falls in love with a cow, several characters achieve reverence for a totemic bear, and so on. Forster does little with animals—even later with Hinduism to help him—and presumably would have been horrified by "bestiality," but he preserves the sense of sanctified yet obscene mystery and overpowering curiosity that a child's approach to sex can embody, and which figures in autochthonic art.[23]

There is, however, one exception to the rule of loveless coupling in *Howards End*, one tender and intimate scene, at the end of Chapter 40.

> The peace of the country was entering into her. It has no commerce with memory, and little with hope. Least of all is it concerned with the hopes of the next five minutes. It is the peace of the present, which passes understanding. Its murmur came "now," and "now" once more as they trod the gravel, and "now," as the moonlight fell upon their father's sword. They passed upstairs, kissed, and amidst the endless iterations fell asleep. The house had enshadowed the tree at first, but as the moon rose higher the two disentangled, and were clear for a few

23. See again my *Sacred Discontent*, pp. 60–62, 92–93. The one touch in which Forster shows some awareness of this motif is having young Tom, of Miss Avery's lineage, charmingly confuse humans and rabbits (p. 300).

moments at midnight. Margaret awoke and looked into the garden.
How incomprehensible that Leonard Bast should have won her this
night of peace! Was he also part of Mrs. Wilcox's mind? (p. 315)

Out of context, the only element that would prevent reading "this
night of peace" to refer to postcoital languor is the fateful and
phallic "father's sword," which is unobtrusive here though manifest
later. Notice the images of house and tree, already given as both
vital and personal on the first page: while the house pervades the
book, even the wych-elm recurs insistently. It has pigs' teeth set in
its bark, to cure "toothache." When Margaret first sees it, she
identifies it as "a comrade." "Neither warrior, nor lover, nor god,"
it is beyond "any simile of sex" and yet suggests earthy relationships
(p. 206). Now, in the night which she spends alone with Helen in
the house, against her husband's express prohibition and with all
males barricaded outside, the house–tree relation embodies that of
the "comrades" Margaret and Helen. As we read the paragraph,
we look over the preceding chapters and realize that, as Wilfred
Stone says, this reunion is the "only convincing love-scene" in the
book.[24] Hence the surprisingly ambiguous phrase "as the moon
rose higher the two disentangled." Checking ourselves and the text,
we find that no, Forster has not written a scene of lesbian incest,
but in one way it would certainly seem fitting if he had, and we
pass on with relief or disappointment. Forster was good at these
tricky situations: what really happened in the Marabar cave? That
in both cases the ambiguities are intentional is not to be doubted.
When Margaret and Henry finally trap the "truant" Helen in the
house, Margaret has only time to "whisper: 'Oh, my darling—'"
before she has to shoo all the males away (289). Then a chapter
later, she returns and says "'Oh, my darling!'" and "'My darling,
forgive me,'" bolting the door from the inside (p. 292). Forster
goes far enough, during the ensuing conversation, to establish that
Helen has been living with one Monica, a "crude feminist of the
South," that is, Italy (pp. 293–94). Much of "dear," "dearest,"
"dear old lady," recurs in the sister's talk, along with the earlier
noted rhetoric about war between the sexes. Then this:

And the triviality faded from their faces, though it left something behind—the knowledge that they never could be parted because their love

24. *The Cave and the Mountain: A Study of E. M. Forster* (Stanford University
Press, 1966), p. 265.

was rooted in common things. . . . Helen, still smiling, came up to her
sister. She said: "It is always Meg." They looked into each other's eyes.
The inner life had paid. (p. 299)

With "the past sanctifying the present," the house is their "salva-
tion" because, among other things, it furnishes a redoubt against
males. Finally: "'But it would give me so much pleasure to have
one night here with you. It will be something to look back on.
Oh, Meg lovey, do let's! . . . Why not? It's a moon'" (p. 301).
Presumably Helen means a lark, but also a honeymoon. (This
theme could then be entitled "Come Back to the House Again,
Meg Lovey.") Before the scene of embracing and falling asleep
"amidst the endless iterations"—of the murmur of "now," of
course, but do we not also think automatically of lovers' protestations?—Helen asks Margaret to flee with her, to leave her husband
for life in Germany (in spite of a Monica with whom she would
not "get on" [p. 314]) in a most unconventional ménage. Though
this flight is obviated by the death of Leonard, the imprisonment
of Charles, and the breakdown of Henry, the two sisters in the
final chapter are living in the house, in full control of it and of the
situation. Helen's unnamed baby who is to become legal heir plays
in the hay field, Henry is defeated and so "eternally tired" that he
can no longer career about, the Wilcoxes are dismissed, Leonard
can barely be remembered, and the sisters are as contented a couple
as appears in Forster's work. No more is said about Monica.

Forster had the grace to recognize the greatness of Proust, whose
Albertine was really Albert, and whose example suggests that the
insights of homosexuals into love can be especially keen. Critics
have, it appears, been looking for love in all the wrong places in
Howards End, just as they have caught the autochthonic theme
only fitfully. Forster's transposition of sexes, turning homosexual
lovers into sisters, has the effect of making his characters vague as
women, but it allows him to treat "passion" with some knowledge.
Moreover, he can use it as a screening device: as with Hardy's
image of the stiffening corpse, readers were disposed to deny what
they saw, even to themselves. But, as with the autochthonic motifs,
we have only to read what the text says without Wilcox assumptions. Indeed, the themes are intertwined; it seems likely that the
tenderness of the love scene owes something to Forster's imagination of the reunion of Demeter and Persephone. This maiden is
with child, a child with no real father—so much the better mytho-

logically. The homosexual's point of view opens up possibilities to
Forster that he might otherwise not have explored: knowing that
sexual desire cannot always be made to behave in approved ways,
he becomes excruciatingly aware of blindnesses of all sorts. "'Oh,
Meg, the little that is known about these things!'" (p. 313) If we
insist on reducing the novel to a "believable" bourgeois drama,
we do violence to the imaginative structure and reveal our own
conventionality, in sexual as in spiritual matters.

Given the book's opportunities for *méconnaissance*, its history
of misreadings is predictable. Some have been more revealing than
others. D. H. Lawrence wrote to Forster that he had made "a
nearly deadly mistake in glorifying those *business* people in *Howards End*. Business is no good."[25] What can he have been thinking
of? To be sure, Forster makes some efforts to persuade us that
Margaret's love for Henry is not hopelessly inconceivable, and
Margaret is made to give a few rationalizations of modern capitalism. More to the point, Forster makes Schlegel liberalism boomer-
ang: every time Margaret and especially Helen try to help the Basts,
they pauperize or degrade them a little more, from the umbrella
business to the unpaid hotel bill at Oniton. Helen's ultimate gift,
of herself, leads directly to Leonard's death, in a reversal of the
myth of Zeus and Semele (so much for heterosexual love). Yet
these touches of grim comedy don't really balance the treatment of
the Wilcoxes, which is surely a caricature and not a glorification.
In Lawrence we should probably diagnose a case of willful blindness, along the lines that Harold Bloom and the late Paul de Man
have sketched out. Lawrence's own interest in autochthonic themes
was already developed—his fondness for the Pluto–Persephone
myth, with a dark male from underground carrying off a pale
virgin, has been remarked—and was to grow obsessive.[26] Perhaps
he could not see *Howards End* because similar ideas were consuming him, in other forms. But whereas he, like Hardy, embraced
primitivistic emphases, neither used autochthony as an actual plot
element as Forster does. Nor, on the other hand, does either offer
a brittle comic surface over which casual readers can skate, avoid-

---

25. *Letters of D. H. Lawrence*, ed. Aldous Huxley (Viking, 1932), p. 558.

26. See George H. Ford, "The 'S' Curve: Persephone to Pluto," in Julian Moynahan, ed., *Sons and Lovers: Text, Background, and Criticism* (Viking, 1968; originally published, 1913), pp. 577–96.

ing the deeper reverberations as "some mystic stuff." Hence *Howards End* can be read without the mythological meanings, whereas Lawrence's work can hardly be mistaken for bourgeois drama.

Some critics, feeling the tension between readings, have argued that *Howards End* is seriously flawed by a confusion between the realistic conventions of the traditional novel and the "mystic" or "fabular" elements.[27] This seems imprecise, for the convention is not the book's problem. *Howards End* is a realistic novel but with certain premises that the modern mind is not disposed to accept; in fact it could be said that the book dramatizes just this weakness, as Forster sees it. Wilcox offensive behavior is a consequence of spiritual poverty. But with the autochthonic premises accepted — or at least disbelief suspended, for after all this is fiction — the book makes quite good sense in its own terms. Its problems arise not from its convention but from Forster's limitations as a novelist. As I have argued, these problems catch up with the book when it is reread; yet the rereading is necessary to savor the themes fully. The difficulties are there, but do not prevent the book from being a significant novel, and at least a timid precursor of Modernist developments.

Aside from its place in relation to the Modernist concern with mythology, there are interrelations of *Howards End* with texts by other writers, in ways not easily discerned and almost surely indirect. Two curious examples can be taken from T. S. Eliot and F. Scott Fitzgerald. Forster was well acquainted with Eliot, as they had met at Bloomsbury salons and on Garsington weekends. Forster declined however to contribute to a volume of appreciations of Eliot on grounds of insufficient sympathy.[28] Possibly he felt Eliot's churchiness to be a problem, and certainly Eliot could not

27. For example, Peter Widdowson, *E. M. Forster's* Howards End: *Fiction as History* (Sussex University Press, 1977), pp. 14–15, 55, 97–98. Forster's chapters on "Fantasy" and "Prophecy" in *Aspects of the Novel* (Harcourt Brace, 1954) are apropos here, especially the latter. The world of *The Brothers Karamazov* or *Moby Dick*, Forster says, "is not a veil, it is not an allegory. It is the ordinary world of fiction, but it reaches back" (p. 134). The oracular phrase is clear if we remember what the Past means to Forster. He does not claim a place for his own work with that of Dostoevsky, Melville, D. H. Lawrence, and Emily Bronte, yet his discussions of them strongly suggest that he aspired, if wistfully, to this status.

28. King, *Forster and His World*, p. 52. See also Forster's essay on Eliot in *Abinger Harvest*.

have liked the dismissal of "poor little talkative Christianity" in *A Passage to India*. But consider this section from *Howards End*, one of several in which Forster sets Nature against London:

> Nature, with all her cruelty, comes nearer to us than do these crowds of men. A friend explains himself: the earth is explicable — from her we came, and we must return to her. But who can explain Westminster Bridge Road or Liverpool Street in the morning — the city inhaling; or the same thoroughfares in the evening — the city exhaling her exhausted air? (p. 108)

Westminster Bridge naturally suggests Wordsworth, who found the city beautiful when asleep and uncrowded, and his sonnet's currency made it easy for Forster to play with the image of the city as sleeping giant. A natural progression leads to some of the most unforgettable lines of *The Waste Land*:

> A crowd flowed over London Bridge, so many,
> I had not thought death had undone so many.
> Sighs, short and infrequent, were exhaled,
> And each man fixed his eyes before his feet. (ll. 62–65)

The exhalation is displaced into the crowd of clerks, of Leonard Basts, but the force is the same. The clock delivers its "dead" sound, and Stetson is queried about the corpse planted in his garden — a touch of English murder-mystery macabre that opens into an autochthonic motif. Eliot of course put the Cambridge anthropologists to the most vigorous use of any Modernist. He covered over his poem's heteroclite origins in prophetic rhetoric ("voices singing out of empty cisterns and exhausted wells" is from a very old layer, and "I John saw these things, and heard them" was excised) with a "mythical method."[29] The passage on London Bridge reads as if Eliot had been badly depressed while watching early newsreels: the crowds move spectrally and jerkily. But in the light of the *Howards End* passage, several possible points of contact show up, starting with the image of exhalation. Eliot returned to it in the third section of *Burnt Norton*:

> Men and bits of paper, whirled by the cold wind
> That blows before and after time,

29. See Valerie Eliot, ed., *The Waste Land: A Facsimile and Transcript of the Original Drafts* (Harcourt Brace Jovanovich, 1971), pp. 9, 75.

Wind in and out of unwholesome lungs
Time before and time after.
Eructation of unhealthy souls
Into the faded air, the torpid
Driven on the wind that sweeps the gloomy hills of London. . . .

Another displacement, but the same Dantesque adaptation as in *The Waste Land*: the crowds are dead souls, blown aimlessly over a hellish landscape. Even if these lines do not derive directly from Forster's passage, they certainly show a similarity of vision. The mythology of earth and place is after all the organizing principle of the *Four Quartets*. Especially at the beginning of *East Coker* ("Mirth of those long since under earth/ Nourishing the corn") and at the end of *The Dry Salvages*, Eliot acknowledges "The life of significant soil"; but Frazer and Jane Harrison and even Jessie Weston are implicit throughout.[30] If *Howards End* served as mediator, it added several chips to the mosaic of intertextuality in Eliot's work.

The resonance of Forster with Fitzgerald is of a different order, less spiritual and more mechanical, in several senses. *The Great Gatsby* can be read as an American piracy of *Howards End*, in the vein of San Simeon or London Bridge in Arizona. But the autochthonous themes are transmuted beyond recognition; the house of the novel, no longer small and sacred, has hypertrophied into Gatsby's garish mansion, "a factual imitation of some Hotel de Ville in Normandy"—the book mocks what it enacts.[31] Geography is vital in *Gatsby* but not in Forster's way, although the dialectic of country versus London reappears in the theme of "Westerners" who are "subtly unadaptable to Eastern life" (p. 177).[32] Eastern life is flashy, impersonal, pseudosophisticated, like the Wilcoxes transplanted. It is in pursuit of a "vast, vulgar, and meretricious beauty" (p. 99), in contrast to more earthy Western ways. The towns beyond the Ohio are "bored, sprawling," and smallminded (p. 177), but they are at least free of the specious glitter of New York and its satellite communities. The problem with this geo-

30. On Eliot's debt to the Cambridge anthropologists, see Chapter 5 of this book.
31. *The Great Gatsby* (Scribner, 1953; originally published, 1925), p. 5.
32. Fitzgerald deliberately has Gatsby place San Francisco in the Middle West (p. 65) as part of his Family Romance, but the operational moral geography of the novel can be described by adapting the remark attributed to John Barrymore: Outside New York, every place is Bridgeport.

graphical pattern is that Fitzgerald confuses it by mixing in his own obviously cherished memories of New York's "meretricious beauty" and its romantic appeal to his permanently adolescent sensibility. He remained entranced with the "incomparable milk of wonder" that leads us to pursue "the green light, the orgastic future" long after he knew he should have outgrown it (pp. 112, 182).[33]

Paradoxically, it is the transparent, innocent quality of his own breathless wonder at riches and success that makes Fitzgerald ultimately palatable. Like Gatsby, he is admirable because, not in spite of, the "colossal vitality of his illusion." As Hugh Kenner has remarked, the story of Gatsby is Fitzgerald's attempt at the theme of metaphysical ambitions "to be as gods," which were reborn in our cultural tradition with the grandiose promises of the Renaissance, and which America both lives out and symbolizes: the land is the "fresh, green breast of the new world [that] had once pandered in whispers to the last and greatest of all human dreams," the last goal — he did not think of space — "commensurate to [man's] capacity for wonder" (p. 182).[34] The novel, like Gatsby's project, is only a partial success, but as such serves all the better as a parable of the American fetishization of illimitable ambition.

The means that Gatsby uses to achieve his ends are as vague as those in a Horatio Alger novel, or as Heathcliff's in *Wuthering Heights*. But the enabling act is the creation of a new identity, sprung "from his own Platonic conception of himself," that makes him a "son of God" instead of a product of his "shiftless and unsuccessful" parents (p. 99). In unrooted America, especially the West, the Family Romance becomes as valid as any other genealogy. Indeed, parents themselves nurture the Family Romance by planting fantasies that their offspring will emerge as *wunderkinden*, cancelling their own ordinariness (cf. Mr. Gatz). We Americans are under an unspoken command to succeed, to prove ourselves, and the usual mark of success is to outdo our parents spectacularly. Hence Walker Percy suggests, "Imagine that you

33. Fitzgerald insisted on "orgastic," as he believed it to be "the adjective for orgasm." See Jennifer E. Atkinson, "Fitzgerald's Marked Copy of *The Great Gatsby*" in Matthew J. Bruccoli and C. E. Frazer Clark, Jr., eds., *Fitzgerald/Hemingway Annual 1970* (NCR Microcard Editions [Washington, D.C.], 1970), pp. 30–31.

34. See Hugh Kenner, *A Homemade World: The American Modernist Writers* (Knopf, 1975), pp. 26–31.

have lived your entire life in the house where you were born. For an American, an uncanny, even an unsettling fantasy."[35] Gatsby is the antithesis of Ruth Wilcox.

Gatsby also has no access to the simple homebound pleasures that Ruth's life at Howards End affords. Indeed, his own fetishization of ambition turns him into a typical American anhedonist, unable to enjoy what he's worked so hard for. He could never have enjoyed Daisy; so much is evident from his wistful attitude toward his car, his speedboat, his pool, his shirts, his house ("I have been glancing into some of the rooms," he says absently in reply to Nick's wonder at its illuminated splendor). The watchful sobriety that keeps him from enjoying his own parties — fittingly, since their only purpose is to serve as lure for the Buchanans — characterizes him. Throughout, he watches over others, but his voyeurism has no hint of the sensual. (Americans like to think that they have a powerful streak of sensuality, but this is merely a Puritan self-accusation: they are far more inhibited, in spite of their eroticized environments, than those of other behavioral traditions, and frank, luxuriant hedonism is much rarer than the confusion between needs and desires, means and ends, that leads to acquisitiveness.) A torrid affair with Daisy would have satisfied him were desire his motive force, but he must acquire and possess, and therefore lose. At least he got a swim in.

Living the life of a socialite partygoer himself, Fitzgerald imagined what happens to poor sons of God/bitches (the transformation is accomplished in the words that were Gatsby's and his own eulogy) who don't get rich enough to marry their Ginevras or Zeldas until too late. Although he had acquired both money and princess, Fitzgerald remained haunted by the fear of failure — naturally enough, since he couldn't see why he had earned them. So he sympathized as Nick Carraway does with those who futilely chase success in New York, such as "poor young clerks who loitered in front of windows waiting until it was time for a solitary restaurant dinner — young clerks in the dusk, wasting the most poignant moments of night and life" (p. 57). This pseudopathos about America's Leonards betrays a juvenile romanticism that obtrudes every-

35. Walker Percy, *Lost in the Cosmos: The Last Self-Help Book* (Pocket Books, 1983), pp. 146–47.

where, in raptures about the "racy, adventurous feel" of New York, and of course in the building up of Gatsby.

If Gatsby is an Americanized Leonard Bast, devoted to self-improvement, Tom and Daisy Buchanan have a full measure of Wilcox nomadism and exploitiveness. They "drifted here and there unrestfully wherever people played polo and were rich together. . . . I felt that Tom would drift on forever seeking, a little wistfully, for the dramatic turbulence of some irrecoverable football game" (p. 6). They also have the Wilcox attitude toward servants and inferiors; Tom is concerned to preserve the "Nordic" race against "the colored" and all immigrants and *arrivistes*. Like Charles Wilcox he is often found in automobiles, though he affects horsiness as a form of defiant nostalgia: "'I'm the first man who ever made a stable out of a garage'" (p. 119). Fitzgerald adopts Forster's vision of the "Juggernaut car," but for him it does not signify merely the onrush of Philistinism. He sees it as a glamorous but lethal weapon, destroying not only our geographical mooring and orientations but very often life itself, and raising grave questions of responsibility. The key question in the book is: Who was driving?

Several critics have commented on the patterns of movement and drift in *Gatsby*, but the elaborate structure of "driving" imagery that holds the book together is not often noticed, although Nick's head is full of it.[36] On his thirtieth birthday he thinks, "Before me stretched the portentous, menacing road of a new decade" (p. 136). He gets involved with the "incurably dishonest" Jordan Baker, and his first insight into her coincides with finding that she was a "rotten driver." Chastised about this, she gives a Wilcox retort. "'They'll keep out of my way,' she insisted. 'It takes two to make an accident.'" This mentality augurs trouble, although it will come from Daisy rather than Jordan. Nick muses further: "Her gray, sun-strained eyes stared straight ahead, but she had deliberately shifted our relations, and for a moment I thought I loved

36. Compare Gale H. Carrithers, Jr., "Fitzgerald's Triumph," in Frederick J. Hoffman, ed., *The Great Gatsby: A Study* (Scribner, 1962), p. 316: he observes that "images of drift, flutter, or rush, the figure of purposeless action" run through the novel. This aligns even the billowing skirts of Daisy and Jordan (p. 8) with the driving imagery.

her. But I am slow-thinking and full of interior rules that act as brakes on my desires . . . " (p. 59). Fitzgerald sensed as early as anyone that American was becoming a culture in which the locus of romance and sexual initiation is likely to be a car: the earliest recorded tryst of Gatsby and Daisy is in her "white roadster" (p. 75). Fittingly, on his honeymoon with Daisy, Tom has an injurious, adulterous auto accident in Santa Barbara, breaking the arm of the girl with him, a chambermaid (like Henry Wilcox, Tom likes his liaisons with the lower classes).

The climax of *Gatsby* comes not with a runover cat but with a hideous accident to Tom's most recent mistress. The preposterously energetic "Myrtle Wilson, her life violently extinguished, knelt in the road and mingled her thick dark blood with the dust." This near-Homeric simile degenerates into a gross evocation of an Aztec sacrifice: "Her left breast was swinging loose like a flap, and there was no need to listen for the heart beneath" (p. 138). Daisy was the driver, we finally learn, although Gatsby with foolish chivalry takes the responsibility and literally dies for her, in a shooting that is as grotesque a mistake as is Charles Wilcox's "murder" of Leonard Bast. But there is a poetic justice in the verdict against Charles, for Wilcoxes bear collective guilt, whereas in *Gatsby* the unpunished real culprit is the callous Wilcox-like indifference of both Buchanans: "They were careless people, Tom and Daisy — they smashed up things and creatures and then retreated back into their money or their vast carelessness, or whatever it was that kept them together, and let other people clean up the mess they had made" (pp. 180–81).

Not many readers observe that Fitzgerald has prepared for the climactic accident by inserting a parodic anticipation of it, in a "bizarre and tumultuous scene" created by the drunken guests leaving a Gatsby party. In a ditch next to the road rests a coupe, "violently shorn of one wheel." Out steps a man in a long duster, who says to spectators:

> "I know very little about driving — next to nothing. It happened, and that's all I know."
> "Well, if you're a poor driver you oughtn't to try driving at night."
> "But I wasn't even trying," he explained indignantly, "I wasn't even trying."
> An awed hush fell upon the bystanders.

"Do you want to commit suicide?"

"You're lucky it was just a wheel! A bad driver and not even *trying*!"

"You don't understand," explained the criminal. "I wasn't driving. There's another man in the car."

The real driver appears, much drunker than his passenger: "'Wha's matter?' he inquired calmly. 'Did we run outa gas?'" When the "amputated" wheel is pointed out to him, he remarks:

"At first I din' notice we'd stopped."

A pause. Then, taking a long breath and straightening his shoulders, he remarked in a determined voice:

"Wonder'ff tell me where there's a gas'line station?"

At least a dozen men, some of them a little better off than he was, explained to him that the wheel and car were no longer joined by any physical bond.

"Back out," he suggested after a moment. "Put her in reverse."

"But the *wheel's* off!"

He hesitated.

"No harm in trying," he said. (pp. 55–56)

This driver's inability to see reality proleptically parodies Gatsby and his intoxicated dream: "'Can't repeat the past?' he cried incredulously. 'Why of course you can!'" (p. 111). And the confusion over apparent and real drivers grotesquely foreshadows Daisy's repellent irresponsibility. With this scene in mind, we can more fully appreciate observations contained in the famous catalog of Gatsby's guests, that Miss Claudia Hip came "with a man reputed to be her chauffeur" and that Ripley Snell "was there three days before he went to the penitentiary, so drunk out on the gravel drive that Mrs. Ulysses Swett's automobile ran over his right hand" (pp. 62–63). That right hand had long forgotten its cunning, probably. Fitzgerald sees us as alternately obsessed with and maimed by our cars, endlessly led on; so the green light at the end of the Buchanan dock that stands for "the orgastic future" appears as a transcendent traffic signal, beckoning treacherously. It links the "boats against the current" of the book's very last image with the careening automobiles that have replaced war as our way of eliminating surplus young men. The car is linked to us by unbreakable bonds of desire, however, so we can't get rid of it. Fitzgerald shrewdly links the "Dutch sailors'" fateful vision of the New World with the romantic intoxication of the world seen from cars: "The city seen from the

Queensboro Bridge is always the city seen for the first time, in its first wild promise of all the mystery and beauty in the world" (p. 69). Hart Crane saw the American myth in bridges, Fitzgerald in the vehicles upon them.

Musing on American self-contradictions, Walker Percy wonders "whether it is a coincidence that this country is not only the most Christian and most eroticized of all societies but also the most technologically transformed and the most violent."[37] *Gatsby* articulates a vision in which Americans combine "romantic readiness" with violence — especially if it can be produced by technology — in the service of projects not only to repeat the past but also to correct and purge it, to pursue a future that is really a retreat: we are "borne back ceaselessly into the past" (p. 182). Fitzgerald's vision marks him as the product of a culture that is haunted, even for its Catholics, by an ambivalent Calvinism that distrusts great cities, great desires, great projects, and yet feeds on them at the same time.

This makes him very different from Forster, whose Biblical thinking is much less obvious. Indeed, Forster's very classicism represents among other things an embarrassment with "Hebraism," which in England means Dissent, not Jews, and with the evangelism of his forebears. In his day, Greek and Latin, gentility, public school education, and the Established Church were the marks of privilege; to be a scion of evangelistic traditions was (at least latently) socially precarious. No wonder Forster's autochthonous ideology smacks of Tory apologetics. He borrows, however, the rhetoric of the prophets of Israel against all human pride and pretension, against all imperialism and massive power structures, in indirect and disguised ways. Surely his denunciations of Wilcoxery owe something to the prophets' assurances that all great works, rich cities, and mighty armies will end where we all began: in the dust.

Forster sometimes invoked this idea as a Mephistophelean spirit of Denial. It appears in *Howards End* as "goblin footfalls" emanating from Beethoven's Fifth Symphony, or at least from Helen's synesthetic fantasy about it. "[The goblins] were not aggressive creatures; it was that that made them so terrible to Helen. They merely observed in passing that there was no such thing as splendour or heroism in the world" (p. 33). For Helen this represents a

---

37. Percy, *Lost in the Cosmos*, p. 177.

sudden collapse of ideals, connected to her disillusionment about
the Wilcoxes. Later she arrives at a more engaging paradox, in
which the goblins of Denial become the force of mortality itself.
"'Death destroys a man; the idea of Death saves him.'" The idea
of Death, undercutting all human ambitions but especially those
swollen with pride, triumphs because it

> shows me the emptiness of Money. . . . men like the Wilcoxes are
> deeper in the mist than any. Sane, sound Englishmen! Building up
> empires, levelling all the world into what they call common sense. But
> mention Death to them and they're offended, because Death's really
> Imperial, and He cries out against them for ever. (pp. 238–39)

This rhetoric is not however totally compatible with autochthonic premises, which may be why *A Passage to India* embodies a
harsher vision. The earth of India transcends and precedes even
the mythical powers invested in it. "The high places of Dravidia
have been land since land began. . . . They are older than anything
in the world, [they are] flesh of the sun's flesh."[38] As such "they are
older than all spirit" (pp. 116–17). The Marabar caves are not holy,
have no particular powers; they are so primal that they precede all
attributes. "Nothing, nothing attaches to them" (p. 117). Their
smooth polished surfaces have no carvings, paintings, not even
bats' or bees' nests, and their famous echo wipes out all distinctions, reduces all words to "ou-boum." "A Marabar cave can hear
no sound but its own" (pp. 145–46). For Mrs. Moore the echo
destroys Christianity—"All its divine words from 'Let there be
light' to 'It is finished' only amounted to 'boum'" (p. 141)—and all
Western certainties. In this landscape the incursions of all conquerors—Hindu, Muslim, or English—are fatuous illusions. The English invasion is comically symbolized by the right-angled streets,
mentioned in the first pages, that fit so poorly in the landscape of
Chandrapore, "symbolic of the net Great Britain had thrown over
India" (p. 11). But the earth of India mocks such ludicrous imposi-
tions. "How can the mind take hold of such a country? Generations
of invaders have tried, but they remain in exile. The important
towns they build are only retreats, their quarrels the malaise of
men who cannot find their way home" (p. 128). The lives of plants
and animals are almost undisturbed. "It matters so little to the

---

38. *A Passage to India*, ed. Oliver Stallybrass (Arnold, 1978; originally published, 1924); subsequent page references are to this text.

majority of living beings what the minority, that calls itself human, desires or decides. Most of the inhabitants of India do not mind how India is governed" (p. 105). The heat, beginning in April, produces in men "irritability and lust" (p. 201) and spreads infectious, impersonal evil among them, but it awakens life in the very rocks. Thus Adela, climbing up to her cave, feels the sun quickening the soil under her feet: "The temperature rose and rose, the boulders said, 'I am alive,' the small stones answered, 'I am almost alive'" (p. 142).

But there are comparatively few metaphors for the animate earth in the novel, compared to *Howards End*. This time what interests Forster is not life, but death. In the cave is "something very old and very small . . . the undying worm itself" (p. 198). Like the goblins it mocks all large ideas, all heroism, all generosity, all achievement, even our ideas of "Heaven, Hell, Annihilation": "No one could romanticize the Marabar, because it robbed infinity and eternity of their vastness, the only quality that accommodates them to mankind" (p. 141). Thus the echo that can reduce even "the tongues of angels" to a meaningless reverberation tells Mrs. Moore: "Pathos, piety, courage—they exist, but are identical, and so is filth. Everything exists, nothing has value" (p. 140). This is true levelling. Indian earth is purposive, but not in the services of Eros: at the end it thrusts itself between the horses of Aziz and Fielding in spite of their desire, just as the mirrored surface of the cave prevents the struck match and its image from uniting. "The two flames approach and strive to unite, but cannot, because one of them breathes air, the other stone. A mirror inlaid with lovely colours divides the lovers" (pp. 117–18). (Forster's vision of human love varies that of Aristophanes in Plato's *Symposium*.) So the ideology of *A Passage* cannot be called autochthonous; nevertheless, here as in *Howards End* geography is destiny, a point that several of the characters apprehend but in ironic or misleading forms, usually racist.

There are no houses of importance in the later novel, for even the most magnificent buildings are mocked by the Indian landscape, and the bungalows of the conquerors seem pathetic. The land is deeply and essentially jungle, absorptive and proteiform; its boundaries flow, and forms of life spring up and fall back, escaping human classification: "Nothing in India is identifiable, the mere asking of a question causes it to disappear or to merge in something else" (p. 78). Adela, as her last name indicates, is always searching and asking; this is why she seems a prig to Fielding, as if always taking notes, and why she cannot grasp India. To the inhabitants of the jungle, other than human, a house is simply "a normal growth of the eternal jungle, which alternately produces houses trees, houses trees" (p. 29). Mrs. Moore's wasp is found inside, having "no sense of an interior."

There is autochthony in India, as in the cult of "Esmiss Esmoor" that springs up at her death, and in Hinduism and related ideologies it goes far toward grasping the essence of things, but it remains a posteriori to what is in the cave. Though it cannot answer final questions, it gives Indians clear spiritual advantages. One of the most important is their sensitivity to poetry:

> Of the company, only Hamidullah had any comprehension of poetry. The minds of the others were inferior and rough. Yet they listened with pleasure, because literature had not been divorced from their civilization. The police inspector, for instance, did not feel that Aziz had degraded himself by reciting, nor break into the cheery guffaw with which an Englishman averts the infection of beauty. (p. 97)

In *Howards End* the role of India is played by Germany. The German characters and material are trivial and forgettable, and seem to represent some unassimilated personal experiences of Forster's (he lived in Germany for a few months), although he is able to get off a few sadly prophetic remarks about the looming conflict of the countries. But if we start from the clue given by the Schlegels' name — relating them to the propounders of Romantic, organicist aesthetics — the major pattern becomes clear. A German does

> take poetry seriously. . . . He may miss it through stupidity, or misinterpret it, but he is always asking beauty to enter his life, and I [Margaret] believe that in the end it will come. At Heidelberg I met a fat veterinary surgeon whose voice broke with sobs as he repeated some mawkish poetry. So easy for me to laugh — I, who never repeat poetry, good or bad, and cannot remember one fragment of verse to thrill myself with. (p. 73)[39]

39. That Germans are the mediums of poetry here relates to the Germanic wordplay on his own name. The Schlegels are half German, and this spirit in them is part of the reason that they are the true heirs of Howards End. Thus the complex of meanings that inhere in the house in the novel — based on Forster's own childhood in a house named Rooksnest — seems also to include his own interlude in Germany as a tutor in a castle. Only the name is then unexplained; on that, no one seems to

Forster is here rebuking the English more than praising the Germans—he had a deeper admiration for Indians—and the issue concealed an important facet of his own sense of alienation from his culture. Indeed, he put himself into the novel under a German name—just as Shakespeare hid himself among puns on "will" in his sonnets and plays. One of the book's most ironic passages concerns Helen, who had a proposal from a German that seemed to her merely comical; he was "Herr Forstmeister" (literally, "forest master") who "lived in a wood" (p. 105).

> "It is sad to suppose that places may ever be more important than people," continued Margaret.
> "Why, Meg? They're so much nicer generally. I'd rather think of that forester's house in Pomerania than of the fat Herr Forstmeister who lived in it." (p. 130)

"Fat" was a sufficient disguise, but the play with "forester" leaves little doubt about what is going on—in fact the passage suggests, appropriately, that Forster is the house, not the character. This self-exile places Forster himself in the milieu, here Germany, where "literature and art have what one might call the kink of the unseen about them" (pp. 77).

Even before Wilcoxes and other imperialists went about their business of trying to crush venerable civilizations, there was a spirit of pragmatism in the English heritage that Forster identifies as the root of his own self-estrangement.

> Why has not England a great mythology? Our folklore has never advanced beyond daintiness, and the greater melodies about our countryside have all issued through the pipes of Greece. Deep and true as the native imagination can be, it seems to have failed here. It has stopped with the witches and the fairies. It cannot vivify one fraction of a summer field, or give names to half a dozen stars. England still waits for the supreme moment of her literature—for the great poet who shall voice her, or, better still, for the thousand little poets whose voices shall pass into our common talk. (p. 267)

Plaintive hopefulness is evident, but Forster also knows that even

---

have noticed that there is a tiny place called Howletts End not far from Cambridge.

On Forster's view of poetry, see his remark in *Aspects of the Novel*, p. 93: "Hardy seems to me essentially a poet," even in his novels. This relates to the discussion in Chapter 1 of this book.

if he becomes one of the "little poets" he will still be a "Mollycoddle" to most of his countrymen. One must keep this poignant passage in mind to know how Forster felt personally about the theme of autochthony; it was not mere scaffolding for him. In some earlier passages, we might be tempted to underestimate the irony:

> To speak against London is no longer fashionable. The earth as an artistic cult has had its day, and the literature of the near future will probably ignore the country and seek inspiration from the town. One can understand the reaction. Of Pan and the elemental forces the public has heard a little too much—they seem Victorian, while London is Georgian—and those who care for the earth with sincerity may wait long ere the pendulum swings back to her again. (p. 108)

This is related to the dismissals of "Borrow, Thoreau, and sorrow," and also serves to forestall criticism of the more labored mythology of his earlier work. "Pan" was truly too arty, too colorful, too decorative. Houses that can seem to live are a far more appropriate motif. Any Englishman can be made to respond, even against his instincts for real-estate development if necessary, to Ruth Wilcox's plaint about being allowed to die in the room where one was born. Gatsby would never want that, but even Leonard might have found it a comfort. For those who understand autochthony, it becomes a mighty theme, expressive not merely of *pietas* and continuity, but also of "only connecting" to those spirits of place that can give our lives wholeness. Henry's frustration of his wife's dying wish is the lowest of his mean tricks.

Forster plants the phrase "safe as houses" several times on Henry Wilcox's lips, and it encompasses the book's irony: Henry means it of course in the most reprehensible sense, turning spirits into investments. If he had only tried to understand why his wife wanted to die in her house, he would have had a glimpse into a world in which houses offer safety of a kind that mocks the rise and fall of fortunes and empires. His lack of a sense of the past, and of its religious insights into earth's tenure of us, does him in. For Forster, the past can transform our ineffectual liberalisms into social harmonies, redeem our greedy commercialism, and so on. Had he had more of Lawrence's ruthlessness, Forster might like his friend have been drawn closer to an atavistic vision that is hard to distinguish from an idealized Fascism.

3

The Primal Scene in *The Secret Agent*: Sex and Violence in the Nightmare Universe

> Unhappy Europe! Thou shalt perish by the moral insanity of thy children!
>
> BARON STOTT-WARTENHEIM

The Secret Agent is an apocalyptic work in more than one sense. Composing it at a time of financial strain and worry about his children's health, Joseph Conrad took a calculated risk in approaching the topic of anarchist bombing and the threat to the public therefrom. He risked public disapproval, and thus low sales, "on the ground of sordid surroundings and the moral squalor of the tale," yet he hoped to capitalize on the thirst of the reading public for exposé treatment of such "outrages."[1] He knew perfectly well that one of the cheaper thrills for the public in such a book — even more satisfying than safe indignation at the "criminal futility" of anarchist acts — would be indulgence in the fatuously apocalyptic sententiousness illustrated by Baron Stott-Wartenheim's deathbed speech (p. 36).

But something drew him deeper, further into the potentialities of the "simple tale," so that it now appears as the most harrowing of his works, and no more a potboiler than Faulkner's *Sanctuary*. Many critics have analyzed its unsettling reverberations. J. Hillis

---

1. For convenience, page references will be to the most accessible edition: Joseph Conrad, *The Secret Agent: A Simple Tale* (Doubleday, 1953; originally published, 1907). This quotation is from p. [7], "Author's Note," dated 1920.

Miller has drawn out its nihilistic exposure of the forms and institutions of the social order, observing that they appear not only arbitrary but also tied together in a sinister web of complicity: criminals with police, anarchists with society matrons.[2] Avrom Fleishman has discerned in the book a masterpiece of a twentieth-century genre, the "landscape of hysteria."[3] All recent critics testify to the book's uncanny power. Of the several sources for this, one is the sustained irony that Conrad chose for the mode of narration. The irony is so pervasive that it forces the reader to wonder how far it can go, and thus to contemplate the very alarmisms that the book so ruthlessly undercuts: what if the collapse of the social order, or even the annihilation of the human race, were serious possibilities instead of rumors mongered for manipulative purposes by press and police?

In this light the book's most haunting character is the Professor, a scruffy zealot who has given up ordinary life in the service of death, devoting himself to the production of explosives for "the destruction of what is" (p. 249). He awaits the advent of a "perfect detonator," trusting that the sciences that invented dynamite will not fail him. He is however somewhat daunted by the "unattackable stolidity of [the] great multitude" (p. 88), the numbers and numbness of mass man, swarming in the streets of London like a noisome breed of insect. "What if nothing could move them?" (p. 77) By which he means, suppose he cannot find a destructive force great enough to kill many and terrify the rest, cowing them so that they will acquiesce in the end to the present order? "Madness and despair! Give me that for a lever, and I'll move the world" (p. 251).

The question leads naturally to our own times, for we have furnished all the Professor could want in the way of lethal devices, and our very governments are the "perfect detonators." Society has put itself into the position so ardently desired by the old-time anarchists, holding the threat of destruction over all our heads— an evolution that Conrad would have noted with mordant satisfac-

2. Miller, *Poets of Reality: Six Twentieth-Century Writers* (Harvard University Press, 1966), pp. 40, 41.

3. Fleishman, "The Landscape of Hysteria in *The Secret Agent*," in Ross C. Murfin, ed., *Conrad Revisited: Essays for the Eighties* (University of Alabama Press, 1985), pp. 89–105. See also Miller's essay on apocalypse in this same volume.

tion. If today we voice most noisily our fears of fanatic groups, still we know in our hearts that the grimmest menace comes from what our governments would be tempted to do if faced with threats to themselves. A state terrorism that would have excited the imaginations of the worst despots of history is simply taken for granted these days. No doubt Conrad would have relished the paradox of our morbid dilemma, for his book forecasts what we have created in the name of exterminating the exterminators. *The Secret Agent* implies that governments will be fatally drawn into such ironic predicaments, since they cannot stamp out terrorism without resorting to equally sinister measures. And our effort to keep ahead of enemies has resulted in unimaginable weapons. The Professor would not now have to worry about the sheer numbers of people; thus the Baron's humbuggery has taken on a new, realistic tone.

The book is apocalyptic in a more basic way, however, in the sense of an unveiling, a revelation, but what is revealed seems at first to be only a void. Like a cynical illusionist, Conrad delights in showing us that there is nothing behind the veil. Later we find that what is revealed is unveiling itself, in the sense of the forbidden scene, but the emptiness has its own resonances. The book projects a vision that may have lured Conrad deeper into his own tale, helplessly drawn on by the very horror he sees, like Kurtz or like Decoud driven to suicide: a nightmare of meaninglessness, related to those discussed in the previous chapter and no doubt endemically recurrent in a civilization that inherits the drive to expose all myths without fear or favor. This vision overwhelmed and subsumed Conrad's original purpose of merely entertaining the public with a satire upon anarchists as a lazy, futile lot who, in this story, can be swept aside by the outraged instincts of a housewife.

To see this clearly we must trace the book's genesis: Conrad says he gleaned the images around which it coalesced from laconic conversations with Ford Madox Ford, who was in fact related to some would-be anarchists, and from some memoirs of police work, including those concerning the Greenwich bomb plot of 1894.[4] He determined to think it out as a tawdrily commonplace domestic

4. "Author's Note," pp. 9–10; see Ian Watt, ed., *Conrad: The Secret Agent: A Casebook* (Macmillan, 1973), esp. Norman Sherry, "The Greenwich Bomb Outrage and *The Secret Agent*" (pp. 202–228); and Watt, "The Political and Social Background of *The Secret Agent*" (pp. 229–251).

drama masquerading as a thriller, in which a married couple who
had lived for years in close proximity but near-total misapprehension of each other — so constantly at antipodean cross-purposes
that they were not even aware of it — clash in a way that overshad-
ows the machinations of dynamitards, *agents provocateurs*, and
secret police. The sensational intrigue would turn out to be dominated by utterly bourgeois motives. But the ironic reduction at
some point acquired a momentum of its own, and the domestic
angle grew more intriguing. Conrad began to see a revelation of
the nihilistic potential in every household, and in the societies of
which they form the backbone. He saw, with Gauguin, that a parlor is as full of dangers as the darkest jungle. Beginning by painting
in the manner of Millet a scene emphasizing the humbleness of real
life, he let his irony lead to something more comparable to Picasso's *Demoiselles d'Avignon*, a work of the same year (1907–
1908). Picasso's picture, famous for the annunciatory violence with
which it opened the way to Cubism and to the appropriation of the
primitive in modern art, embodied a savagery that mocked Western
art's classical motifs: the nude idealized female figure decomposes
into a parade of blank-faced whores, and every element in the
picture becomes unnerving in some way, even the sharp weaponlike
edges of the innocent piece of fruit. The work suggests, as does
Conrad's novel, an atavistic return of supposedly long-buried and
disturbing forces. By the end of the book, atavism is an insidious
question, with several ramifications.

Conrad surely never saw Picasso's painting and would have disliked it if he had, as his tastes in art were quite reactionary.[5] But he
possessed a "negative capability" that allowed him to transcend his
own biases, in art as in politics. Indeed, this was a crucial element
in the novel's crystallization:

> I have no doubt . . . that there had been moments during the writing
> of the book when I was an extreme revolutionist, I won't say more
> convinced than they but certainly cherishing a more concentrated pur-
> pose than any of them had ever done in the whole course of his life. I
> don't say this to boast. I was simply attending to my business. In the
> matter of all my books I have always attended to my business. I have

5. Ian Watt, *Conrad in the Nineteenth Century* (University of California Press,
1979), p. 173.

attended to it with complete self-surrender. And this statement, too, is not a boast. I could not have done otherwise. It would have bored me too much to make-believe. (pp. 12–13)

Here Conrad declares not only his ability to take the anarchist's view, but also his impatience with aestheticism's "taste for the unreal" and its rhapsodies about the creative imagination — the same impatience that led Ford, Hardy, Joyce, and Pound to repudiate or deform the premises of fiction and of genteel amateurism, and that made Conrad into one of J. Hillis Miller's "poets of reality."[6] For these writers, realism was not merely a method of treatment but a dismissal of all that is implied in the term *make-believe*.

And just as Conrad was able to participate in the revolutionary mindset for the book's purposes, so his work suggests strange affinities with artists he would have consciously ignored, like Picasso. Of course the *Demoiselles* is more obviously a gauntlet flung in the face of humanistic conventions, but *The Secret Agent* poses as severe if more backhanded a challenge. Among those who saw this were early negative reviewers of the novel. One, anonymous, drew himself up in disdain:

> Unless the creations of an author's brain seize the attention and exercise the mind of his readers they are not worth considering at all; but a less amusing set of people never filled the imaginary world of a novelist than have been chosen for the pages of *The Secret Agent*. . . . Mr Conrad, in this book, is naughty without being at all nice.[7]

This writer had very little insight into the story, but he could sense that some of his most cherished beliefs were being insidiously attacked. Even the favorable reviews registered similar kinds of uneasiness. So when Conrad wrote an Author's Note for a later edition, he returned worriedly to objections of this sort. He admitted that "it seems ungracious to remember so little reproof amongst so much intelligent and sympathetic appreciation" (p. 7); yet he could not let go of it, and sought in several ways to excuse himself for writing so disturbing a work: "There was no perverse intention, no

6. Miller, *Poets*, esp. pp. 5–7, 36–37. Miller traces a different aetiology for Conrad's "realism," but the vector of literary history drawn here leads to many of the characteristics he points out.

7. "A Book of the Week," *Country Life*, September 21, 1907; quoted in Watt, *Casebook*, pp. 27–28.

secret scorn for the natural sensibilities of mankind at the bottom of my impulses" (p. 8). One has to wonder at this self-defense. The Author's Note ends with a similar protestation: "But still I will submit that telling Winnie Verloc's story to its anarchistic end of utter desolation, madness and despair, and telling it as I have told it here, I have not intended to commit a gratuitous outrage on the feelings of mankind" (p. 13). Of all the ironies in the book, none is greater than this sentence. Conrad must have seen on rereading just how harrowing the book was, but wanted to deny even to himself that he had been nihilist enough to perpetrate "outrages."

The offenses against mankind's feelings begin immediately. What respectable novel would open with a description of Verloc's "French-letter" shop? Of course the fact that the shop sold condoms is only hinted at, but the hints are very broad:

> The window contained photographs of more or less undressed dancing girls; nondescript packages in wrappers like patent medicines; closed yellow paper envelopes, very flimsy, and marked two-and-six in heavy black figures; a few numbers of ancient French comic publications hung across a string as if to dry; a dingy blue china bowl, a casket of black wood, bottles of marking ink, and rubber stamps; a few books, with titles hinting at impropriety; a few apparently old copies of obscure newspapers, badly printed, with titles like *The Torch, The Gong* — rousing titles. (p. 17)

The paragraph is admirable in its suggestive economy, and also in its foreshadowing: even the marking ink comes back to play a key part, when Winnie uses it to write Stevie's address in his coat and this tag becomes the only part of him that survives the bomb blast. But the insidious effect of the paragraph comes from its maintenance of imperturbable domesticity amid the ambiguous sleaziness of the goods purveyed, and its characterization of Verloc's function as pornographer of revolutionary tracts. For *The Torch* and *The Gong*, in spite of their "rousing titles," were not erotic; they were anarchist sheets.[8] This is the first appearance of the pattern of motifs implying that revolutionary propaganda is a particularly loathesome variety of pornography, pandering to deprived and idle minds, offering a voyeurism of lurid revanchist fantasies. When the anarchists meet at the shop, the retarded Stevie overhears the "terrorist" Karl Yundt, aged and impotent, denouncing society's

---

8. Watt, *Casebook*, pp. 241, 248.

exploitation of the poor with passionate clichés about cannibalism. In Stevie's mind metaphors are real, and he is incited to vengefulness. But Stevie is only an extreme example of the inflammable audience Yundt habitually aims at:

> The famous terrorist had never in his life raised personally as much as his little finger against the social edifice. He was no man of action; he was not even an orator of torrential eloquence, sweeping the masses along in the rushing noise and foam of a great enthusiasm. With a more subtle intention, he took the part of an insolent and venomous evoker of sinister impulses which lurk in the blind envy and exasperated vanity of ignorance, in the suffering and misery of poverty, in all the hopeful and noble illusions of righteous anger, pity, and revolt. (p. 51)

With shrewd insights into what might elsewhere be called *ressentiment*, Conrad creates in Stevie a figure for the strange but inextricable connections between pity and violence. "In the face of anything which affected directly or indirectly his morbid dread of pain, Stevie ended by turning vicious" (p. 144). In the first chapter, we learn that one of Stevie's abortive efforts to hold a job came to an end when he stampeded his employer's offices by "letting off fireworks on the staircase. . . . It seems that two other office-boys had worked upon his feelings by tales of injustice and oppression till they had wrought his compassion to the pitch of that frenzy" (p. 22). This comic incident is of course the plot of the novel in little. In another proleptic scene, Stevie reads about German officers tearing off recruits' ears, and Winnie has to restrain him. "'I had to take the carving knife from the boy,'" says Winnie. "'He was shouting and stamping and sobbing. He can't stand the notion of any cruelty. He would have stuck that officer like a pig if he had seen him then'" (p. 61). The carving knife will reappear in the lethal hand of Winnie, Stevie's sibling and (as Ossipon sees, to his horror) also his reincarnation when he dies. The comedy here is bitterly sharpened when Winnie rounds off her thoughts by musing that "'some people don't deserve much mercy'" and by asking the insomniac Verloc whether she should put out the light: "'Yes. Put it out,' he said at last in a hollow tone." The whole scene is a bizarre, anticipatory parody of *Othello*, and Winnie is a submissive Desdemona who turns into a Clytemnestra; her feelings for the dead Stevie turn to violence in the way foreshadowed by his own easily inflamed sense of injustice.

The "raging, implacable pity" that makes Stevie want to take the poor cabman and cabhorse to bed with him, and to cadge money for the charwoman's "little 'uns" (which she spends on drink), is easily channeled by Verloc into his project for having Stevie plant the bomb at the Observatory. Thus does Conrad caricature vengeful destruction fantasized by impotent terrorists and inert agents, but carried out by innocent yet violent women and children. All of the revolutionaries are portrayed as sponging idlers — "the enemies of discipline and fatigue mostly" (p. 56) — but Verloc's indolence is special. There is no obvious practical reason why Verloc doesn't carry the bomb himself, except for his hope that Stevie's inarticulateness would be useful if the police were to catch him, yet he considers action beneath his dignity: his job is to provoke. Goaded by Vladimir's insults and threats, he has searched among his terrorist friends for one who can be stirred up to an "outrage," but of course they are all talk. Michaelis is a vapid idealist, Ossipon a pseudoscientific gigolo, Yundt a parody of Milton's Satan; even the Professor fanatically restricts himself to supplying the dynamite. After agonies of desperation and insomnia, Verloc has the idea of Stevie put into his mind by, of all people, Winnie: she wants to insinuate a father–son bond between them, and propagandizes for it with fatal results. "'You could do anything with that boy, Adolf. . . . He would go through fire for you'" (p. 155). Her concern is, naturally, for Stevie, knowing that Verloc could any day object to keeping him, but just as the sewing of Stevie's address tag in his coat becomes disastrous, so also this apparently harmless bit of bourgeois caretaking ends with all three of them its victims. (She has also taught Stevie that Verloc is "good" and must be obeyed, thus tightening the net.) One of the book's most chilling ironies is her sentiment on seeing Verloc and Stevie go off together. "'Might be father and son,' she said to herself" (p. 157). If so, they caricature Abraham and Isaac, but instead of a divine intercessor, they have only a calmly deluded woman who sends them all into the "damned hole" of eternity.

Verloc's inertia demands still more comment, however. It dominates the book's imagery in many places: "His eyes were naturally heavy; he had an air of having wallowed, fully dressed, all day on an unmade bed" (p. 18). Even winking is strenuous for him. In the retrospective account of how he and Winnie came to be married, we learn of his habit of breakfasting in bed and "wallowing there with an air of quiet enjoyment till noon every day" — days he ends posing as a good anarchist at meetings. Thus he courts Winnie, bringer of his breakfast tray, from the bed

> with jocular, exhausted civility, in the hoarse, failing tones of a man who had been talking vehemently for many hours together. His prominent, heavy-lidded eyes rolled sideways amorously and languidly, the bedclothes were pulled up to his chin, and his dark smooth moustache covered his thick lips capable of much honeyed banter. (p. 20)

Verloc spends his evenings lying to revolutionaries and his mornings lying to Winnie (in between he fabricates reports for his employers exaggerating terrorist threats, so as to stay on the payroll). His image in the bed summarizes these activities.[9] He loves repose; Vladimir's threats work on him because he feels "menaced in what is dearest to him — his repose and his security" (p. 54). His position in society, poised between the terrorist and the policeman, is a carefully chosen immobility.

Clearly Conrad is trying to evoke something more than pathological laziness. Verloc, in his "fanatical inertness," is an energy sink, a black hole absorbing activity around him, swallowing it up as London, "a cruel devourer of the world's light" (p. 11), swallows lives and as the "damned hole" of eternity engulfs humankind. (In return, his fatness is contagious; it infects many other characters and renders them nearly immobile.)[10] Although he is the agent of the title, the root sense of the word is violently ironic applied to him. The activeness of Stevie and Winnie contrasts with the torpor of all the revolutionists, but most obviously with Verloc.

Yet Verloc represents bourgeois premises taken all too seriously; he is in fact a grotesque paterfamilias. What drives him into the arms of the demon he dreads most, that of sleeplessness, is that he cannot afford to lose his job; he must provide for his wife and family. Although his life is a multifold lie — he is an unreliable

---

9. Cf. Daniel R. Schwarz, *Conrad: Almayer's Folly to Under Western Eyes* (Cornell University Press, 1980), p. 158, on this image: "It is as if Verloc's death had already occurred, as indeed it had for the retrospective narrator." For me the "narrator" is simply the voice of a disembodied irony, and thus retrospectivity is irrelevant, but the linkage of bed and death is perceptive.

10. Cf. Miller, *Poets*, pp. 50–52.

agent pretending to be an anarchist who pretends to be a pornographer pretending to be a shopkeeper — he is sincerely "responsible," and never thinks seriously about absconding with his hoarded pay. After being exposed, he thinks first of his wife and of the business: "The shop was an asset. Though Mr. Verloc's fatalism accepted his undoing as a secret agent, he had no mind to be utterly ruined, mostly, it must be owned, from regard for his wife" (p. 195). Like many employees, he finds himself imperilled by a change among his superiors, and suddenly discovers that "there is no occupation that fails a man more completely than that of a secret agent of police" (p. 58). The delicious irony of this careerist reflection never occurs to him.

Even in the very last seconds of his life, when Winnie stabs him, he preserves the amiable illusions of a good husband; he thinks she's gone mad. His marriage, though frankly conceived as a device for continuing comfortable indolence (its image is Winnie with the breakfast tray), is not simply one of convenience: "Mr. Verloc loved his wife as a wife should be loved — that is, maritally, with the regard one has for one's chief possession" (p. 152). The marriage thus conforms to society's demands for respectability; it is neither cynical nor impulsive but is practical to a fault. "'Of course we'll take over your furniture, Mother,' Winnie had remarked" (p. 20). Verloc's youthful misadventure with French army secrets, which cost him five years in prison, had been motivated by amorous adventure, "a fatal infatuation" for a woman who sold him out, or so he says. But like a good bourgeois scion, he has disseminated these wild oats and won't make that mistake again: Winnie is chosen not for her full figure but for her "steadiness." She too eschews passion and adventure in favor of a marriage that provides stable support for a mother and feebleminded brother. Such "commonplace sacrifices" (as Joyce calls them in "Eveline")[11] are the stuff of middle-class existence, the glue that keeps families together in spite of gulfs of misapprehension and disharmony. These are the templates of supposedly adult "real life," contrasted to immature self-indulgence and childish dreams.

In this book such self-sacrifice opens a way not only for duplic-

---

11. James Joyce, *Dubliners: Text, Criticism, and Notes*, ed. Robert Scholes and A. Walton Litz (Penguin, 1976; originally published, 1914), p. 40.

ity, anger, and recrimination, but also for a terrible "freedom," the free fall of Winnie once the revelation of Stevie's death has broken her delusions of family loyalty. Having made marriage to protect Stevie, by his death she is suddenly alienated from it and from her whole past life: she drops into a moral void, and can live only long enough to hunt out its physical equivalent, the sea. The bonds of marriage, once she sees them as arbitrary, become as counterfeit as Verloc's pretenses to his various roles, and like these they come to appear as shackles to be escaped, with violent revenge to be taken against her captor.

Sexual relations in the Verloc marriage also conform to bourgeois expectations, dutiful but not exploratory or intimate. In seven years in a shared bedroom Verloc never catches a glimpse of Winnie's pragmatic, opportunistic motives; his insensitivity and staunch middle-class assumptions pander to his illusion that he is desirable, "loved for his own sake" (p. 207). Indeed, for him Winnie's desirability is linked to the "provocation of her unfathomable reserve" (p. 19) — she is as much a *provocateur* as he, and her stone-faced silence kindles his last, fatally miscalculated erotic summons to her. All the anarchists except the Professor are parasitically dependent on women — Michaelis on his lady patroness, Yundt on an old virago, Ossipon on "silly girls with savings-bank books" — but Verloc feels superior to them precisely in the conformist nature of his role. He congratulates himself on being a good provider, and this helps sustains his sexual illusions about himself. Moreover, he precipitates the final act of his domestic tragedy with an attempt at "communication" — "for the first time in his life he was taking that incurious woman into his confidence" (p. 198). Conrad offers no easy criticisms of bourgeois marriage. Rather he holds out the prospect of an abyss of meaninglessness at the base of the institution.

Sexuality provides a consistent subtext throughout the novel, in forms that are either unprepossessing in themselves or repellent precisely because they replicate bourgeois ideals too accurately. Even Stevie's patterns of mind are based on stunted sexuality: he wants to take the cabman and horse to bed because Winnie used to do this for him; and he was used to hiding from their father's wrath "behind the short skirts of his sister Winnie" (p. 21). Winnie reciprocates, unconsciously: her desires are fixed on Stevie, and she avenges his death on her aging husband just as if he had murdered her lover. The warmer family relations get, the more they parody incest, the ultimate bourgeois horror.

The subtext continues: the terrorists live off women and off their own pornography of violence. Even the Professor, though womanless, pleasures himself with bombing fantasies, and has taken dynamite as a substitute phallus to masturbate and display.[12] The rigged-up bomb he carries in his pockets to prevent arrest is a prosthesis for his personality, rubber tubes ready to channel the lethal ejaculation that he can produce by squeezing the bulb. The apparatus enables him to transcend his sickly appearance and to exhibit himself in face-offs of machismo with Ossipon and with Inspector Heat. As a "moral agent," his force of character comes from his willingness to blow himself up, along with a host of bystanders and any police foolish enough to seize him. Thus he encapsulates all the infantile hostility that lies at the bottom of war as well as terrorism, and that draws its power from erotically tinged fantasies of vigilantism. In addition, Conrad makes sure to include the morbid curiosity of the public in his unappetizing register of perverse pleasures: he notes in passing that Stevie was often overexcited by dramas of the streets, particularly by "fallen horses, whose pathos and violence induced him sometimes to shriek piercingly in a crowd, which disliked to be disturbed by sounds of distress in its quiet enjoyment of the national spectacle" (p. 21). Such notations belong to the theme of the pornographic morbidity and violence in everyday life—the very pleasure that provides readers for "shilling shockers." How can anyone, after writing the sentence above, say that he does not cherish a secret scorn for the "natural sensibilities of mankind?"

All the moments of grimmest comedy in the book are manifestations of similarly ambiguous intertwining of violence and sex. The great classics of black humor all use this; perhaps the genre was invented by Euripides, when he has *The Bacchae* open with smoke curling up from the tomb of Semele, mother of Dionysus.[13] Twenty

12. See Joseph I. Fradin and Jean W. Creighton, "The Language of *The Secret Agent*: The Art of Non-Life," *Conradiana* 1 (1968): 23–33. The authors point out that in the manuscript and serial versions the hints at masturbation are very obvious.

13. *The Bacchae*, ll. 1–8.

years earlier she had been impregnated by Zeus in a coupling that entailed her violent death, because Hera tricked her into making Zeus promise to make love to her "in all his glory" — in other words, in approximately the condition, for nearby humans, of an explosion. (Cf. Yahweh hiding Moses in the rock while he displays his glory, Exod. 33:18–23.) *The Secret Agent* is full of the glory of dynamite, and other ironies in this vein, but the last scenes between Winnie and Verloc, and then Winnie and Ossipon, are the bravura triumph of the black humor of sex and violence, and especially the way in which the erotic potential of violence and the aggression implicit in sexuality become interinvolved, or even indistinct from each other.

On the night in which he betrays himself, Verloc receives an amorous gesture from Winnie, who, knowing nothing of the bomb and thinking that Stevie is still alive, wants to forestall his muttered talk of emigration. Her mode is to give him a glance "half arch, half cruel," of which she would have been incapable in her virgin days (p. 165). And his response is to approach her with an agitated expression that "made it appear uncertain whether he meant to strangle or to embrace his wife." But they are interrupted by the Assistant Commissioner, who has determined to extract from Verloc a confession that will implicate Vladimir and the Embassy, spare Michaelis, and thus avoid trouble with his wife's friend, the great lady who is Michaelis' patroness (even detective work has a domestic, conjugal motivation). For this purpose he takes Verloc to "a house of bad repute called the Continental Hotel" (p. 182), sometime refuge and meeting point of assassins and dynamitards, but now the site of a parodic assignation. (Heat later tells Verloc: "I know too well whom you have been giving yourself away to," p. 174). During this unsavory tryst between the spy and the policeman, Heat comes to the shop seeking his own intercourse with Verloc; from him Winnie gets the first hint of Stevie's death. Thus when Verloc returns and tries to rally her, typically not noticing her state of shock, he alienates her painfully in his very attempt to reassert connubial bonds. As he expostulates, twice mentioning the possibility of being stabbed by "infuriated revolutionists," his appetites waken; first hunger, and he cuts with the carving knife a piece of cold roast, a "funereal baked meat" (p. 208) like those that

in *Hamlet* "did coldly furnish forth the marriage tables."[14] As in
the earlier allusions to *Othello*, Conrad finds in Shakespeare those
motifs in which love and death are interlinked.

Verloc is provoked by Winnie's silence — "You have a devilish
way of holding your tongue sometimes" (p. 212) — a remark that is
funny enough in itself, given husbands' traditional complaints, but
here is ironized when it becomes clear that Verloc is aroused, as
usual, by her "unfathomable reserve." Her silence is like the aphro-
disiac blistering of Spanish fly. "A man isn't made of stone," he
thinks, and then rationalizes his lust:

> He had been unanswerable in his vindication. He was loved for himself.
> The present phase of her silence he interpreted favorably. This was the
> time to make it up with her. . . . "Come here," he said in a peculiar
> tone, which might have been the tone of brutality, but was intimately
> known to Mrs. Verloc as the note of wooing[!]
>
> She started forward at once, as if she were still a loyal woman bound
> to that man by an unbroken contract. Her right hand skimmed slightly
> the end of the table, and when she had passed on towards the sofa the
> carving knife had vanished without the slightest sound from the side of
> the dish. Mr. Verloc heard the creaky plank in the floor, and was
> content. He waited. Mrs. Verloc was coming. (pp. 214-15)

He never rises from that fatal recumbency on the sofa, does not
even manage to stir hand or foot while he sees the knife descend.
He is the passive victim, she the penetrator: the killing reverses the
complicit rape of which their sex life has consisted.

Once absolutely free, she stumbles out into the "black abyss" of
London, trying to get to the river so she can throw herself in and
avoid hanging, which she dreads. As luck would have it, she meets
Comrade Ossipon, coming to heed the Professor's sardonic advice
to "fasten yourself upon the woman for all she's worth" (p. 75). He
is able to insinuate himself into her confidence because he had been
the object of her one extramarital fantasy, with his "shameless and
inviting eyes." However, he is misled by her garbled confession (he
believes it was Verloc who died in the explosion) into thinking that
Verloc was some kind of sexual sadist, whose last perverse act was
to commit suicide with the bomb. Then, when they return to the
shop, he sees the victim of her wrath on the sofa and grasps that

14. *Hamlet*, I, ii, 180-81.

Stevie, whose defectiveness he used to analyze by Lombroso's methods, was the one blown up: "He exclaimed scientifically, in the extremity of his astonishment: 'The degenerate–by heavens!'" (p. 237) Luckily for him, Winnie thinks he's referring to Verloc's last flare of ill-timed lust. Whoever cannot laugh at the death of Little Nell can never appreciate this touch.

Suddenly she is the Gorgon, cum Lamia: "He positively saw snakes now. He saw the woman twined round him like a snake, not to be shaken off. She was not deadly. She was death itself — the companion of life." While Ossipon muses fearfully on her likeness to her "degenerate" brother, concluding scientifically that he can read in their physiognomies the "type" of the murderer, she says "'You took a lot of notice of [Stevie], Tom. I loved you for it'" (p. 242). The cross-purposes that characterized her life with Verloc, and eventuated in his murder, are now hilariously compounded. Ossipon is right, for the wrong reasons, to perceive in her "a murdering type." Conrad discerns behind the warmth of maternal and connubial affections, even behind the nurturing instinct of woman, a harrowing and lethal force.[15] By violence she had once quelled their father, and now she has killed her husband to avenge her brother. Love can enlist death in its service, and vice versa.

As J. Hillis Miller says, following Thomas Moser, Conrad associates sex with the jungle, with loss of lucidity; but in *The Secret Agent* he goes further, almost as if foreseeing Freud's speculations about Eros and Thanatos.[16] (No doubt he would have repudiated Freud.) Ossipon sees in Winnie "death and life" intertwined snakily, an insight that blinds him to its own power. Like all the other supposedly opposing forces in the book, emblematized in the criminal and the policeman, life and death are in sinister complicity. Manifested as the forces of sex and violence, desire and destructiveness, they interinanimate each other. Conrad's strength as a writer is in registering this duplicity of emotions, this symbiosis of rival

---

15. Cf. Walter J. Ong, *Fighting for Life: Contest, Sexuality, and Consciousness* (Cornell University Press, 1981), esp. p. 61: "Evolutionary development has consequently equipped females generally with fewer of the controls that normally turn off intraspecific male ceremonial combat at a certain threshold." In other words, women are reluctant to fight, but if, say, their offspring are threatened, they will fight to the death; they will not like males be satisfied by submission.

16. Miller, *Poets*, p. 30.

forces. He would have been pleased by the research showing that many emotions that we classify as opposites are not physiologically distinguishable; their bodily effects are the same, because the nervous system does not make our bourgeois distinctions.[17] Surely he noticed that one of the staples of pornography is "moans of pleasure."

The likeness or intertwining of love and death has of course been a resonant artistic motif from the cavemen to Woody Allen. In the art of the Ice Age there are many manifestations of a perceived kinship between fertility and fatality; the horn held by the so-called Venus of Laussel is very probably a symbol of life-giving as well as of lethal power, and the parallelism of weapon and phallus has multiple variants in later eras.[18] The great and problematic ritual of sacrifice—in which the death of the victim gives new life to the community—implies a similar form of linkage. In the age from Homer to Shakespeare, favored motifs involved likeness in the arts of love and combat. The points of semblance are many: the irrationality of the passions involved, the goal of penetrating the body of another with a rigid instrument, and so on. Even the homoerotic comradeship of warriors is suggestive: when Hotspur promises to embrace Hal "with a soldier's arm," he evokes an image that recalls David and Jonathan, Achilles and Patroclus, perhaps Gilgamesh and Enkidu (a bonding on which Spartan and other warrior societies were built), although he means that such loving entails fighting.[19] Shakespeare's histories contain an elaborate series of figures playing on the intermixture of war and sexuality.

The seventeenth-century puns on "die" (meaning orgasm) signal a new interest in the metaphysical resemblance of the erotic and the nirvanic, eventuating in such diverse forms as Wagner's *Liebestod* and Whitman's listening for the "low and delicious word death" in the sea's ebb.[20] To be half in love with easeful death is almost a Romantic duty; the *topos* reveals the erosion of the classical

17. See Walter B. Cannon, *Bodily Changes in Pain, Hunger, Fear and Rage* (Appleton, 1929), esp. p. 352.

18. See my *Sacred Discontent: The Bible and Western Tradition* (Louisiana State University Press, 1976), p. 98.

19. *1 Henry IV*, V, ii, 73.

20. Wagner, *Tristan und Isolde*, act 3; Whitman, "Out of the Cradle Endlessly Rocking," l. 168.

comparison which, in the continuum of values between Stoicism and Western Christianity, tended to deplore the irrationality of emotion and its self-destructive effects. After Romanticism, irrationality loses its bad reputation and becomes an opening to new perceptions; or, in a writer like Conrad, becomes a given for his portrayal of the self-deluded nature of human strivings. In *The Secret Agent*, all of the grotesque posturing and maneuvering of the characters manifests rationalization of the irrational, the infantile, the stunted and frustrated, and all of it reveals itself as so much dancing on the edge of the abyss of meaninglessness, the "damned hole" of eternity.

Nowhere is this kind of activity better epitomized than in the supremely irrational, paradoxical character of Winnie's last hours: she wants to commit suicide because she fears death. Yet this is the most realistic, convincing touch of all, because that is just how Winnie would feel in her situation. Specifically she fears hanging, mesmerized by the newspaper phrase "the drop given was fourteen feet," but drowning also repels her, even though she rushes toward it: she flounders out of the shop "like a person falling over the parapet of a bridge. This entrance into the open air had a foretaste of drowning: a slimy dampness enveloped her, entered her nostrils, clung to her hair" (pp. 220–21). The book has established London as an environment of sooty, liquid darkness, a black wet hole, and here it materializes in a form that drowns Winnie's spirit, even before the Channel drowns her body. Yet although her fear of hanging drives her to suicide, she desperately wants to live. After Ossipon betrays her and steals her money, and is turned into a walking corpse by his guilt for this crime, he recalls her as the symbol of the ultimate human desire: "Mankind wants to live — to live," he tells the Professor, thinking painfully of Winnie's "vigour of vitality, a love of life that could resist the furious anguish which drives to murder and the fear, the blind, mad fear of the gallows" (pp. 248, 250).

The narrative of Winnie's last hours is one of Conrad's most unforgettable passages because of the richness with which he invests this theme of the irreducible doubleness of human emotion: as it fulfills all the implications of the motifs of intertwined sex and violence, the chapter forms the keystone in the arch of the book's structure. He has prepared us in great and small ways for

it, from the suggestiveness radiating from the equation of propaganda and pornography to such innocent-looking notations of
emotional duality as the "few tears in sign of rejoicing" shed by
Winnie's mother (p. 132). These preparations flow into one another, and their confluence crests in the love-and-death scenes between Winnie and Verloc, to which the scenes with Ossipon serve
as jeering reprise. For Ossipon approaches Winnie as another silly
girl he intends to relieve of her savings, only to find himself terrified by her ferocious resolve and adamantine appearance. The
would-be predator finds himself to be the prey; like Actaeon he
has seen a forbidden sight that reverses his role as aggressor in the
amatory wars. Both men, even though they set in motion the events
that drive Winnie to suicide, are as nothing in the face of her rage
and anguish, which destroys them in passing. She destroys Ossipon
only in a sense, however: he lives on, a kind of caged sibyl, to bear
witness to the final paradox of the life–death theme. Just as Stevie
causes so much to happen after his death, Winnie has more power
over Ossipon in death than she could ever have had in life. Not only
are the women and children in this story effective and lethal compared to the futile and immobile men; they survive in ways that dwarf
their earthly powers. Ossipon becomes a candidate for Skid Row,
demoralized and unmanned by the ghostly hold of Winnie.

> "I am seriously ill," he muttered to himself with scientific insight.
> Already his robust form, with an Embassy's secret-service money (in-
> herited from Mr. Verloc) in his pockets, was marching in the gutter as
> if in training for the task of an inevitable future [but not the Future of
> the Proletariat]. Already he bowed his broad shoulders, his head of
> ambrosial locks, as if ready to receive the leather yoke of the sandwich
> board. (p. 252)

The "ambrosial locks" remind us of his kinship to Greek heroes
who see Artemis, the Gorgon, or other forbidden sights. In a way,
Ossipon has committed suicide: his apathy and despair leave him
in a death-in-life state, both turned to stone and pursued by Furies.
Indeed, several of the main characters commit suicide in one or
another sense; self-destruction has many forms.

Conrad was fascinated by suicide: he made one attempt himself,
and it abounds in his works — he is the antithesis of Hardy.[21] But

---

21. Watt, *Conrad in the Nineteenth Century*, pp. 11–14. See Chapter 1 of this
book and also Miller, *Poets*, pp. 21, 33–34.

whereas in Hemingway, say, one is driven toward suicide by fears and anxieties and insomniac horrors, in Conrad the act is always the result of looking too deeply into the abyss of meaninglessness, seeing the truth that cannot be borne. The "freedom" that comes with the disappearance of illusions, such as Winnie's, is so shocking that one loses hold on life, even if the will to live remains. Benign lies are necessary to life; the truth is usually hidden — "luckily, luckily," as Marlow says. Decoud in *Nostromo* is another example; a few days alone on a barren island reveal to him the nothingness of ambitions, the vanity of life itself. The insidious placidity of the Golfo makes the water an emblem of the blankness of things; he looks in vain for meaning. The metaphor of looking into things always has suicidal implications for Conrad, as in Winnie's case: she thinks "things don't bear looking into very much" (p. 153), but at the end she, "who always refrained from looking deep into things, was compelled to look into the very bottom of this thing" (p. 219). One must immerse oneself in the destructive element, as Stein says in *Lord Jim*, but not try to climb out — nor look into it. The same "surface-truth" keeps Marlow from sinking into the Congo; seamanship is not only "deliciously real" compared to the rapacious fantasies of the "pilgrims," but it keeps the steamer afloat and occupies the mind. The various motifs of whiteness that occur in *Heart of Darkness*, including the white lead that Marlow uses to patch the steamer, are all associated with reflective surfaces that prevent insight. Often these are symbolic of hypocrisy — the incongruous white faces in the jungle, the accountant's collars and cuffs, the "whited sepulchre" that is Brussels — but always they are vanities that cover profound emptiness. In Melville whiteness masks the inscrutable malignity of the universe, but in Conrad it offers serviceable superficiality, that which keeps us from looking into things and away from despair.[22]

What makes the primal scene — the forbidden sight of parents coupling — so threatening is that the child cannot distinguish sexual acts from aggressive ones. The forbidden scene is always just out of sight in Conrad's works, and manifestly here, where the motifs of sex and violence are mixed with such grim hilarity. The many mythic analogues — the blindness of Tiresias, the punishments of Actaeon and of Orpheus (for looking back, as with Lot's wife),

22. *Moby Dick*, chaps. 36, 42.

and others — find the ultimate exemplar in the myth of the Fall, of guilty knowledge. What paralyzes Ossipon is a newspaper clipping he carries with him, telling of Winnie's death. His torment is not the "impenetrable mystery," in the notice's jargon, that hangs over the affair, for he knows too well what happened. But what "if he alone of all men could never get rid of the cursed knowledge" (p. 250)? "All men" are fallen into knowledge, indeed; they can bear this curse and get through life only if they avert their gazes. But Ossipon's guilt is also Conrad's and the reason for his defensiveness in the Author's Note: the ever-present irony of the narration, which both disguises and reveals the book's secrets, is not only the equivalent of Picasso's iconoclasm, but also a self-*méconnaissance*. It is the weapon of someone telling what he's not supposed to tell, and evading his own awareness of his strategy.

Looking at death, and at dead bodies, becomes the most pervasive form of the fascinating but petrifying sight in *The Secret Agent*. Conrad enriches its effect by exploiting all kinds of blackly comic aspects. When Winnie looks on Verloc's corpse, the high irony of their domesticity and his chronic immobility is invoked:

> Mrs. Verloc, who thought in images, was not troubled now by visions, because she did not think at all. And she did not move. She was a woman enjoying her complete irresponsibility and endless leisure, almost in the manner of a corpse. She did not move, she did not think. Neither did the mortal envelope of the late Mr. Verloc reposing on the sofa. Except for the fact that Mrs. Verloc breathed these two would have been perfectly in accord: that accord of prudent reserve without superfluous words, and sparing of signs, which had been the foundation of their respectable home life. . . . Mrs. Verloc lowered her gaze deliberately on her husband's body. Its attitude of repose was so homelike and familiar that she could do so without feeling embarrassed by any pronounced novelty in the phenomena of her home life. Mr. Verloc was taking his habitual ease. He looked comfortable. (pp. 216–17)

The deaths of Winnie and Stevie are offstage, but their effects on Ossipon and Heat, respectively, are mined for comedy. Heat's discomfort at the sight of Stevie's remains is mostly in the stomach regions. Having breakfasted only on a "good deal of raw, unwholesome fog in the park," he sees a body that resembles "an accumulation of raw material for a cannibal feast" (this brings back Yundt's cannibalistic metaphors and their effect on Stevie: pp. 81, 53).

Carnality in its most repellent forms dominates the images, reminding us of what we strive to forget in bourgeois life, the dependencies and contingencies of our bodies.[23] The constable who gathered the remains repeats mindlessly his phrase "as fast as my legs could carry me," as if compelled to recognize that human bodies can consist of detachable parts. Although the scattered limbs suggest Osiris or Orpheus, the true mythic analogue appropriate to Heat's feelings is a parodic version of the loaves and fishes gathered into baskets. Heat has to fight down "an unpleasant sensation in his throat," and the reader remembers another of Conrad's offensive foreshadowings, the earlier remark in which the narrative summarizes the worries of Winnie and her mother about how Stevie may be settled in life and provided for: "For he was difficult to dispose of, that boy" (p. 21). Whoever reads the novel attentively finds that it has been sown with gallows humor.

Some critics dig in their heels at the nihilistic implications of such emphases, and want us to stop at this point (or much earlier) to remember the constructive purposes of Conrad's political and social satire. It is easy to find in Conrad's letters and other writings comparatively forward-looking observations, and the usual methods of historiographic criticism would want to gloss the novel with these. But the more compelling point is that Conrad had to protect himself from the consequences of his own relentless demythologizing of the forms of culture, and thus any affirmative statements are subject to that qualification. In *The Secret Agent* the temptation is to contrast British common sense and libertarian tradition with Continental reactionary obscurantism, as represented by the Assistant Commissioner and Vladimir. Up to a point this is valid, but as has already been noted, the Commissioner's aplomb and competence are undercut by his obsession with the Great Lady, who might turn against him if Michaelis were to be implicated, and cause no end of trouble with his wife. Moreover, this good civil servant is miffed by Vladimir's success in the salons, and his deepest satisfaction comes when he forces Vladimir to understand that further appearances at the Explorers' Club might prove embarrassing. Even his success in solving the crime comes from a frustrated

---

23. See Miller's important discussion of the fatness that is endemic to the characters, in *Poets*, pp. 50–52.

detective instinct turned onto Heat instead of a suspect (p. 105), and he stumbles across the Verloc connection as fortuitously as Heat stumbled on the address label. Above all he fears irregularity, and desires that his wife's favorite salon be as undisturbed as his daily whist game.

Nor do the other political figures suggest England as a model. Sir Ethelred, whose name appears to imply "the Unready," pushes his "revolutionary" Fisheries Bill in a way that mocks the impotent terrorists, but he and "Toodles" can hardly be taken seriously. To be sure, English tolerance comes off better than post-Metternich Europe's habituated repression, but Conrad is more surreal than political here. Some critics assume from Vladimir's name that "the Embassy" is Russian, and Conrad no doubt hated Czarism. But we may forget that Baron Stott-Wartenheim preceded Vladimir, who also is advised by Privy Councillor Wurmt, so that it seems that Conrad wanted to suggest an unholy alliance of Russia, Austria, and Prussia, the traditional dismemberers of Poland (and as diplomats they sometimes speak French). The Embassy is a surrealistic caricature of Europe, and one could easily contrast England without imputing to it excessive political virtue. The British government at the time was itself heavily involved with double agents, *provocateurs* and police informers, especially in repressing Ireland and discrediting Parnell, and Conrad had read about this in the memoirs he used for writing the novel.[24] So, although Marlow in *Heart of Darkness* prefers the "red" places on the map (British colonies) because "real work" is done there, in contrast to what happens in the cynically corrupt imitation-empires of Belgium and Germany, we should be wary of concluding that Conrad was blind to the sins of British imperialism. In the nihilistic black light of Verloc's London, efficiency and toleration are minor virtues at best.

The Great Lady herself represents the governing classes of England, and her fatuous ideas almost make the other characters seem wise. She has befriended Michaelis because "she was such a complete stranger to [human miseries]" that his plight satisfies her abstract notions of suffering (p. 97). Then she develops a weird case of radical chic:

24. Watt, *Casebook*, pp. 232ff.

> She had not only felt him to be inoffensive, but she had said so, which last by a confusion of her absolutist mind became a sort of incontrovertible demonstration. It was as if the monstrosity of the man, with his candid infant's eyes and a fat angelic smile, had fascinated her. She had come to believe almost his theory of the future, since it was not repugnant to her prejudices. She disliked the new element of plutocracy in the social compound. . . . The humanitarian hopes of the mild Michaelis tended not towards utter destruction, but merely towards the complete economic ruin of the system. And she did not really see where was the moral harm of it. It would do away with all the multitude of the "parvenus." . . . The disappearance of the last piece of money could not affect people of position. (pp. 99–100)

In short she epitomizes the vacuous rigidity of British upper-class mentality, and the Assistant Commissioner's obligation to placate her illustrates the comical liabilities of that system of deferences.

To suppose that England is a peculiar repository of political virtues is to ignore the theme of complicity, the web of connections that links all strands of society even when they seem hostile to one another. Conrad goes to great lengths to expose the mutual parasitism; even the Professor declares that "the terrorist and the policeman both come from the same basket. Revolution, legality—counter moves in the same game; forms of idleness at bottom identical" (p. 68). The novel's plot proceeds on the principle that it takes a thief to catch a thief—"the mind and instincts of a burglar are of the same kind as the mind and instincts of a police officer" (p. 85)—so that they are not only in complicity, as in police use of agents, but together form the phenomenon René Girard would call "the enemy twins." From such myths as Jacob and Esau, Romulus and Remus, and the like, we can derive the pattern that in social structures (even animal ones) likeness, not difference, is what engenders conflict, because it prevents hierarchization. It is "not the differences but the loss of them that gives rise to violence and chaos," as Girard puts it.[25] Not only will beings that are too much alike inevitably fight; opponents in a fight will soon come to resemble each other uncannily—"the *mimetic* attributes of violence are extraordinary"—a phenomenon that can be as easily observed in people's arguments as in modern ethological research: most argu-

---

25. Girard, *Violence and the Sacred*, trans. Patrick Gregory (Johns Hopkins University Press, 1977), p. 51 (cf. pp. 2, 31).

ments quickly reduce themselves to *tu quoque*. But humans also have an amazing knack of freezing the principle into a mode of life. The role of revenge and the feud in tribal cultures is telling, but even more chilling is the example of those who hate their enemies so much that they eventually become exactly like them, especially when these enemies are their parents. That childbeating and molesting run in families does not indicate defective genes; it shows that hate imprints patterns of behavior even better than love. There really is a repetition-compulsion, and it makes nonsense of the pleasure principle. One more of the heavy effects of the Bible on our culture comes from the instances when "a man's enemies shall be those of his own house" (Micah 7:6); from Cain and Abel to David and Absalom, we see the potential for rending, heartbreaking conflict. Girard reads the Bible, and myth, as a series of parables testifying to the force of this point.

In the world of *The Secret Agent*, the strongest oppositions reveal the most uncanny resemblances underneath. The Professor, who fancies himself a lone wolf opposed to everybody else, supposes that he is an exception to his own rule that the terrorist and the policeman are "at bottom identical." Yet Conrad makes sure that his traits are mirrored in several other characters. Vladimir, who like him aspires to the status of unmoved mover, unknowingly mimics his vocabulary about a "clean sweep of the whole social creation" (pp. 39, 71). The Assistant Commissioner shares his devotion to efficiency, Sir Ethelred his lofty contempt for the details of how things shall happen. Thus the novel appeals to our sense of how we unconsciously come to imitate our most despised opponents. The Professor is himself an example of how easily society's radical enemies can be produced from its most conservative households: he was the son of "an itinerant and rousing preacher of some obscure but rigid Christian sect" (p. 76). He replicates his family piety in the "ascetic purity of his thought," and in the violent apocalypticism of his imagination, so that the more he changes, the more he stays the same.

But Verloc is truly the one who envelopes Girard's principle in his considerable self: playing both ends against his middle, he has no "true" identity except to be an intrinsically double man (one more reason for his fatness). If he had had real revolutionary convictions, or none at all, it would have made no difference in the end. He has just a glimpse of this, though without grasping the constitutive duplicity of his own role, when he decides that "anarchists and diplomats were all one to him" and that his revenge on Vladimir could consist of turning against the Embassy his professional practice of "betraying the secret and unlawful proceedings of his fellow-men" (p. 202). He is, in a very literal sense, his own worst enemy (twin), and a symbol of the underlying law of the book that makes revolutionaries who preach violence, and authorities determined to punish them, look very much alike. Conrad could not be surprised that our respectable societies have put themselves in the place of the old terrorists.

These patterns — indistinguishable antagonists, guilty complicities, intertwined desire and destructiveness — all make the factitious nature of social institutions painfully clear. Human culture is an artificial construct imposed on a recalcitrant world: London is an "enormous town slumbering monstrously on a carpet of mud under a veil of raw mist" (p. 244). As in *Heart of Darkness*, Conrad labors to make it clear that London like Africa is "one of the dark places" (naturally so, if the parlor is as danger-filled as the jungle): the "carpet of mud" suggests the very primeval slime of the Congo. Like Forster in *Passage to India*, Conrad shows that in domesticating landscapes we have mostly deluded ourselves, as did Sinbad: we sit on islands that may reveal themselves to be sleeping dragons. The "carpets" and "veils" of the sentence above indicate wishful anthropomorphism, as do the geometric patterns of straight streets that result from our feeble attempts to throw a net over forces that sooner or later will dwarf us. Ossipon, after robbing and abandoning Winnie on the Channel train, walks for hours through "interminable straight perspectives of shadowy houses bordering empty roadways lined by strings of gas-lamps. He walked through Squares, Places, Ovals, Commons, through monotonous streets with unknown names where the dust of humanity settles inert and hopeless out of the stream of life" (p. 245). After thus seeing the city of self-centered delusions and dead hopes through Conrad's eyes, how can we believe his protestation that "I have not intended to commit a gratuitous outrage on the feelings of mankind"?

The progress of the book has effected a defamiliarization of London, showing it as a sinister comic rigamarole propped up by streetlamps and policemen, the indispensable regularities that support our illusions of purposefulness and rationality. On Verloc's walk in chapter 2, a critic's favorite because of its ambiguous images, a "thick" police constable, who looks like "part of inorganic nature," surges "apparently out of a lamp-post" (p. 25). Society wants us to think that its guardians are so spawned, that they are "given" in our world, part of the order of things, necessary rather than contingent. Hence, after the explosion in Greenwich Park, "there's a constable stuck by every lamp-post" (p. 126). But a lamp-post casts a sinister shadow, which may look like a gibbet, and when Winnie leans on one for support after staggering out of the house containing Verloc's body, she is sickeningly reminded of the fearsome newspaper phrase "the drop given was fourteen feet" (p. 221). Her insight here is foreshadowed in her surprised self-revelation, induced by having to explain poverty to Stevie, that the police "are there so that them as have nothing shouldn't take anything away from them who have" (p. 147). Police and lampposts can reveal themselves as threats, despite their supposed role as protectors, and symbolize the always hypocritical and often malicious pretences of society.

Verloc, with his impressive though empty voice, can make constables spin round as if they were mechanisms, which in a sense they are (p. 33). The image of Verloc making the policeman jump is a link to a favorite Conrad motif, voice and lies. In a well-known paragraph of *Heart of Darkness*, Marlow reduces the dreamlike experience he is trying to convey to a babble of voices: "like a dying vibration of one immense jabber, silly, atrocious, sordid, savage, or simply mean, without any kind of sense." The words derive from combining the images of Kurtz's hollow, meretricious voice with the repulsively exploitative rhetoric of the colonialist "pilgrims." Kurtz's voice stands for lying, just as does Verloc's. At this point Marlow (who is only a voice, in the dark) is trying to provoke his listeners: "Here you all are, each moored with two good addresses, like a hulk with two anchors, a butcher round one corner, a policeman round another, excellent appetites, and temperature normal — you hear — normal from year's end to year's end." They cannot understand the fever dreams brought on by the atavistic power of the wilderness, because they live like Winnie before her last hours, "stepping delicately between the butcher and the policeman, in the holy terror of scandal and gallows and lunatic asylums." The trip up the Congo has been a journey to the "earliest beginnings of the world," into prehistory. Marlow continues:

> How can you imagine what particular region of the first ages a man's untrammeled feet may take him into by the way of solitude — utter solitude without a policeman — by the way of silence — utter silence, where no warning voice of a kind neighbor can be heard whispering of public opinion?

Policemen and voices together symbolize the conventional fictions of civilization, which we see through at our peril. Silent solitude can release the self-deifying or self-destructive forces within us, as with Kurtz and Decoud, because in it we don't hear the lies that keep us on the surface of things — lies like those Winnie tells Stevie about the "goodness" of Verloc, or of policemen, which she finally recants so bitterly and so violently. All lies, says Marlow, have a "flavour of mortality," like rotten hippo meat.[26] The mortality is of those who look into them too closely.

Conrad's Congo experience was as revelatory for him as was the discovery of African masks for Picasso. Even the fever he contracted there was decisive in settling him into a writing career. For both men, Africa meant a recognition that savagery (not the noble kind) was hidden within self-protective civilization with its dangerous police and conventional neighbors — not only because imperialists revealed their rapacity in exploiting the colonized lands and their peoples, but also because the barbarous energies of primitive life and art could evoke thrills or shudders of self-recognition in the souls of those who imagined that they had long since outgrown these impulses and their meanings. *Heart of Darkness* is full of the Victorian fear of atavism and of "degeneration," in the form of "going native," but it faces and surmounts these fears and reveals the experience to be purgative, as well as revelatory. Marlow grasps that men are "capable of anything" — all is permitted — because their minds contain "all the past." He is chastened and disillusioned in suffering the wilderness's revenge for the "fantastic invasion" of the white men; he becomes an Ancient Mariner who must tell his surreal and unnerving tale to captive audiences forever. Conrad is

26. *Heart of Darkness* (Norton, 1971; originally published, 1902), pp. 48–50, 34, 27.

surely the most ambivalent of all the proto-Modernists in accepting atavism — after all he experienced it in its rawest form — but he clearly means to show that we cannot believe that "progress," or evolutionary bromides, will carry us beyond the powerful attractions and repulsions that savage life reveals as constitutive of human possibilities at all times.

In *The Secret Agent*, Conrad uses Ossipon's scientific interest in Lombroso to stand for the preposterous theories of degeneration that abounded in his day: criminals were all throwbacks to certain "types," whose physiognomies would give them away: "It's enough to glance at the lobes of his ears," Ossipon pontificates of Stevie (p. 50). Such theories are merely the most twisted form of self-congratulatory delusion, as Ossipon's fatuous embrace of them proclaims. But Conrad's purposes for these ideas are multiply ironic. At the climax of the action in the novel, when Winnie is crossing the room to stab Verloc, a startling atavistic unveiling occurs:

> Mr. Verloc heard the creaky plank in the floor, and was content. He waited. Mrs. Verloc was coming. As if the homeless soul of Stevie had flown for shelter straight to the breast of his sister, guardian, and protector, the resemblance of her face with that of her brother grew at every step, even to the droop of the lower lip, even to the slight divergence of the eyes. But Mr. Verloc did not see that. He was lying on his back and staring upwards. He saw partly on the ceiling and partly on the wall the moving shadow of an arm with a clenched hand holding a carving knife. It flickered up and down. Its movements were leisurely. They were leisurely enough for Mr. Verloc to recognize the limb and the weapon.
>
> They were leisurely enough for him to take in the full meaning of the portent, and to taste the flavour of death rising in his gorge. . . . But they were not leisurely enough to allow Mr. Verloc the time to move either hand or foot. The knife was already planted in his breast. It met no resistance on its way. Hazard has such accuracies. Into that plunging blow, delivered over the side of the couch, Mrs. Verloc had put all the inheritance of her immemorial and obscure descent, the simple ferocity of the age of caverns, and the unbalanced nervous fury of the age of bar-rooms. (pp. 215–16)

Winnie in her lethal fury reincarnates Stevie, and all their numberless ancestors as well: atavism in its most dramatic form. Lombroso, like his disciple Ossipon, is right for the wrong reasons: there is a murderer in Winnie, but also in every loving woman. The irony is compounded in her victim. Verloc, whose chronic immobility is his undoing at the last as at the first, represents the Victorian paterfamilias who can never, not for his life, rise up to face the forces implicit in his household; if he sees these forces, he can accept their appearance only in the form of madness or "degeneracy." But it can be fatal, as well as absurdly tendentious, to believe that the age of barrooms has transcended the age of caverns. Those who propose positivistic interpretations of evolution ignore the evidence all around them of surviving primitive energies. If Verloc had been able to understand such powers, he would have had a chance to save himself. But marriage and bourgeois life have brought him only regularity, not understanding. He cannot see that Winnie's love for Stevie represents primeval forces as well as motherhood and family piety, and that the combination turns these bourgeois virtues into whirlwinds that can sweep all before them. Indeed, her recapitulation of her ancestors not only involves the recurrence of archaic aggression, but also invokes all those pictures of heaven in which we meet again with those whom we have lost. Reunion with earlier generations is still one of the most moving images with which we try to grasp the meaning of human life, but even it develops a lethal, black-humorous aspect in Conrad's ambivalent and ironic presentation of atavism.

The very phrase "age of bar-rooms" refers to the Silenus Restaurant, where Ossipon meets the Professor; its name and decorations embody the human need to misrecognize the past. There, frescoes show "scenes of the chase and of outdoor revelry in medieval costumes. Varlets in green jerkins brandished hunting knives and raised on high tankards of foaming beer" (p. 61). The knives irresistibly recall Winnie's roast-beef knife (though she doesn't carve Verloc as a dish fit for the gods), just as the tankards are found in the hands of the ineffectual terrorists who meet there. Whether we see high-spirited refreshment or drunken violence in these images, they persuasively imply that we cannot tolerate the unvarnished past; we inevitably glamorize or trivialize our history and our ancestors. The same hypocrisies and pretensions that falsify everyday life show up in our fantasies of the past, and the Great Lady's conception of family parodically appears in the form of Winnie's link to her ancestors. As the existentialists were later to say, our notions of the past are nothing but excuses.

The necessity of distorting the past and of refusing to recognize the fateful appearances of atavism is only a special case, for Conrad, of humans' intrinsic self-evasions. Believing this as he does, for him it must follow that a writer is either a voice mouthing society's lies, or one crying in the wilderness. Obviously he thinks of himself as the latter, yet his constant implication that we cannot look straight at truth without being paralyzed in despair qualifies his own sense of his role, and his own plain inability to face what he has written in this book testifies to the painfulness of his own insight. In this light the novel's images of writing are the bleakest of all. The connection of revolutionary propaganda to pornography is only the first of many such images, and it has reverberations that continue on to the end. Every kind of writing, even when vatic or prophetic, must share properties with these two loathesome species, and its readers in turn must reveal their own weaknesses in their reactions. Ossipon, for instance, writes pamphlets for the Future of the Proletariat, and also a "medical (and improper) pamphlet" (p. 242) on syphilis; he is a failed medical student. Not only is there a sinister connection among the genres here, but also a link to Verloc's purveying of his "shady wares," the condoms that are "poor expedients devised by a mediocre mankind for preserving an imperfect society from the dangers of moral and physical corruption" (p. 212). In turn, syphilis points toward the last image of the book, in which the Professor walks onward fanatically: his masturbatory "thoughts caressed the images of ruin and destruction. . . . He passed on unsuspected and deadly, like a pest in the street full of men." Of the incipient plagues that spread over this world, those spread through writing are the most dangerous, and the Professor's walk emblematizes these.

One of the most harrowing images of writing accompanies Ossipon's exit from the Silenus Restaurant:

> In front of the great doorway a dismal row of newspaper sellers standing clear of the pavement dealt out their wares from the gutter. It was a raw, gloomy day of the early spring; and the grimy sky, the mud of the streets, the rags of the dirty men harmonized excellently with the eruption of the damp, rubbishy sheets of paper soiled with printers' ink. The posters, maculated with filth, garnished like tapestry the sweep of

the curbstone. The trade in afternoon papers was brisk, yet, in comparison with the swift, constant march of foot traffic, the effect was of
indifference, of a disregarded distribution. (pp. 75–76)

These images enhance one another by a kind of demoralizing syn-
ergy: newspapers are merely transformed rags sold in muddy gut-
ters; yet the ink is capable of further soiling them; what then must
be said of what is signified by the letters graven in the ink? Do they
multiply the foulness? What dirty insinuations and slimy gossip do
they purvey?

Then we must remember what is in the papers for this day: the
news of the bomb, from which a powerful story could be deduced — which is, of course, the book itself. Needless to say, no
one grasps the point; wisdom cries out in the street, but no man
regards it.[27] No wonder T. S. Eliot admired Conrad so much and
chose the words of Kurtz's death scene for epigraphs: the image of
the dispirited city crowd, blind to the sibylline news that could spell
out its own fate, has its ancestry in Conrad as well as in Forster
and Dante.[28] (The scene even suggests Melville's notation, at the
end of "Bartleby," that the scrivener had served a blighting apprenticeship in a Dead-Letter Office: "On errands of life, these letters
speed to death," observes the narrator in an image that aligns Melville's years of silence with Bartleby's "I would prefer not to.")[29]
The hurrying crowd around the Silenus Restaurant is seeing and
not perceiving, hearing and not understanding; it is the multitude
of Isaiah 6:10 and Mark 4:12. What is written could save them —
even if its writers' intentions be trivial or corrupt! — but it cannot
be received. "What if nothing could move them?" worries the Professor, but also the author. A profound sense of frustration characterizes all references to writing.

There is a book within the book, as telling in its way as Hamlet's
play within the play: "Michaelis was writing night and day in a
shaky, slanting hand that 'Autobiography of a Prisoner' which was
to be like a Book of Revelation in the history of mankind" (p.
107). But his writing, vapid to begin with, becomes more enervated
and ineffectual than ever through his futile efforts to lose weight.

27. *1 Henry IV*, I, ii, 83–84; see Proverbs 1:20–27.
28. See Chapter 3 of this book.
29. See the last page of "Bartleby."

Though he lives on "a diet of raw carrots and a little milk," he cannot lose an ounce; only his writing grows thinner. "'The poverty of reasoning is astonishing. He has no logic. He can't think consecutively'" (p. 246). This book of softheaded millenarian fantasies recalls the endless circles drawn by Stevie earlier, "a confusion of intersecting lines suggest[ing] a rendering of cosmic chaos, the symbolism of a mad art attempting the inconceivable" (p. 49). How aware was Conrad of the self-reflexive possibilities in these images? How much did the fear that nothing connects with nothing suffuse his anxieties about his own work?

Like the motif of the interview, which in this novel expresses not the possibility of communication but its failure, writing provides one more instance of the grotesque dance on the edge of the abyss of meaninglessness.[30] Writing's irreducibly contingent status is emblematized in the last dialogue of Winnie and Verloc, where she looks fixedly at the wall behind him, so intently that Verloc turns; but "the excellent husband of Winnie Verloc saw no writing on the wall" (p. 198). Only Winnie sees the message that is not there, one that foretells her short future; she sees "a blankness to run at and dash your head against" (p. 202). Many writings must seem to be inciting us to suicide, given the nature of our need for surface-truth and the danger of revelation. But their potentialities for nightmare do not stop there. For what dreams may come when we have shuffled off this mortal coil? The Assistant Commissioner compares Verloc with "an impulsive man who, after committing suicide with the notion that it would end all his troubles, had discovered that it did nothing of the kind" (p. 183). Not even despair is an adequate response to the potentialities of this universe; the blankness of the writing on the wall makes suicide seem here merely one more pointless and ineffectual act — even presumptuous and self-indulgent, as it would have been for Verloc — or for Michaelis (p. 48). But here we can only remember the book's grim humor. The bemused tone of the Commissioner's observation reminds us that this nightmare universe, like that of Beckett or Kafka, is after all a comic spectacle. As Walker Percy provocatively asks: "Why was it that when Franz Kafka would read aloud to his friends stories about the sadness and alienation of life in the twentieth century everyone

30. Miller, *Poets*, p. 56.

would laugh until tears came?"[31] The tears of laughter are also fitting responses here. The release of the emotional duality at the core of Conrad's novel enables us to see even humanity's plight under the bomb, the new sword of Damocles, as merely one more irony of the universe. Human pretensions are so ruthlessly unveiled and exposed under this threat that really there is nothing to fear, no reason to despair: if we experience those feelings, we must remember that they are as baseless and transitory as our joys. Like Winnie, and the rest of us, Conrad could look at this vision only intermittently; hence his apologies. But his creative power and joy too came from the effort to transcribe it.

31. Percy, *The Message in the Bottle: How Queer Man Is, How Queer Language Is, and What One Has to Do with the Other* (Farrar, Straus & Giroux, 1975), p. 5.

4

The Personal Past Recaptured: Anderson & Sons

> Into my heart an air that kills
> From yon far country blows:
> What are those blue remembered hills,
> What spires, what farms are those?
>
> That is the land of lost content,
> I see it shining plain,
> The happy highways where I went
> And cannot come again.
>
> A. E. HOUSMAN

> It was in one of Barrie's early books that I first read the remark, which other people have also made, that genius is the ability to prolong one's childhood.
>
> Early reviewer of *Winesburg, Ohio*

> Men do not exist in facts. They exist in dreams.
>
> SHERWOOD ANDERSON[1]

In the early decades of the twentieth century, one form of literature in English underwent unprecedented development: the apparently

---

1. Epigraphs: Housman, poem 40 of *A Shropshire Lad* (1896). Reviewer, quoted in Sherwood Anderson, *Winesburg, Ohio: Text and Criticism*, ed. John Ferres (Penguin, 1977; originally published, 1919), p. 225 (cited hereafter as Ferres). Anderson, quoted in William A. Sutton, *The Road to Winesburg: A Mosaic of the Imaginative Life of Sherwood Anderson* (Scarecrow, 1972), p. 59 (cited hereafter as Sutton).

autobiographical *Bildungsroman*, the novel of formation or education, exemplified by D. H. Lawrence's *Sons and Lovers* and James
Joyce's *A Portrait of the Artist as a Young Man*. Though this
development owes something to Dickens and even to Mark Twain,
the twentieth-century works are different from all predecessors in
the value they place on childhood experience as a form of revelation — appropriately, in the age of Freud.[2] In both works, the most
ambiguously poignant moments of childhood and adolescence are
highlighted with luminous detail, so as to create an implication
that infinite significance could be spelled out from the recapture of
these primal joys and fears.

   In the early discussions of both books, attention centered on the
frankness of the sexual implications, and indeed they drew on the
older genre of the confession, as in Augustine or Rousseau. But
the skillfully evoked sexual awakenings were used by both authors
simply as means to delineate the shape of a strenuous *heldenleben*,
which their protagonists live out. The struggle for independence,
against the domination of parents or comrades or bourgeois codes,
was the real story. Thus the works appealed most directly to young
people of a Shelleyan turn of mind, hostile to tyrannies both obvious and insidious. This attitude was prevalent in the early twentieth
century, as a holdover from the nineteenth. Ezra Pound included
several rather callow poems among his early works that illustrate
how strong a hold it had: in one, he urges his poems to

> Speak against unconscious oppression,
> Speak against the tyranny of the unimaginative,
> Speak against bonds.
> . . . . . .
> Go to the adolescent who are smothered in family —
> Oh how hideous it is
> To see three generations of one house gathered
> together!
> . . . . . .
> Be against all sorts of mortmain.[3]

2. See Jerome H. Buckley, *Season of Youth: The Bildungsroman from Dickens
to Golding* (Harvard University Press, 1974), esp. pp. 226 ff. on Joyce. Note also
the parallel development in France of Alain-Fournier and Proust.
   3. "Commission."

As earlier noted, the fear of mortmain appears powerfully in Joyce's early works. Thus, when Joyce had Stephen Dedalus cobble together a fierce miscreed with the ringing motto "Non serviam!" out of Ibsen, Nietzsche, and like heroes, he won such instant acceptance from Pound and others that the ironies in his portrait of Stephen were long overlooked. For Pound, the feeling was so strong that he even read Henry James by these lights: he surprisingly dismissed talk of James's style in his 1918 essay, because it obscured "the major James, the hater of tyranny." He celebrated instead "book after early book against oppression, against all the sordid petty personal crushing oppression, the domination of modern life."[4]

Now that the need for such protestations has passed, we can see that the real power and luminosity of both *Sons and Lovers* and *Portrait* is in the recreation of early memories. The first chapter of the *Portrait* is unforgettably vivid; the precise rendering of the sensitive child's hesitant awakening to language, violence, authority, punishment, sex, sin, and death – all of them prefigured in the "overture" on the first page – has never been equalled. The confused shames and pleasures of the little cosmos at Clongowes lead up to unforgettable scenes throughout the book: the passions exposed at the Christmas dinner, the sordid revelations and embarrassing reminiscences of the trip to Cork, the discovery of the "swoon of shame" available in Nighttown, and the repulsively calculated, manipulative rhetoric of the sermon on Hell. The petty tyrannies of puritanical yet worldly Irish Catholicism, and of its attendant milieu of bullying schoolmates and narrowminded companions, are alembicated through the childish imagination, interacting mysteriously with the covert politics of the family. As in "The Sisters," the first of the *Dubliners* stories, the mysteries of the Church contrast with its seedy realities, but they still promise revelations of awesome powers, at once dangerous and seductive, recalling the encounters with gods or the ordeals set before quester-heroes in myths. This motif intertwines with that of the need to clarify an obscured parentage, to identify spiritual fathers and authority figures, and together these quests bind all Joyce's works into unity (although in *Ulysses* and *Finnegans*

4. *Literary Essays of Ezra Pound*, ed. T. S. Eliot (New Directions, 1954), p. 296.

Wake the mothers are seen as truly constitutive, and have the last word).

Sons and Lovers has an even greater power to evoke the terrifying assault of adult passions on the feelings of the child: the parents' mutual brutalization forces Paul Morel to undergo the torture of an extended primal scene. The secrets of the linkage between love and pain, sex and cruelty, compel his guilty witness, luring him on into agonizing but fascinating knowledge. Though these passages are overburdened with Lawrence's tendentious philosophy of the life-force, they are magnificent in spite of it. In the most vivid and painful, which occurs even before Paul's birth, Walter Morel thrusts his hectoring wife out into the garden "while the child boiled within her"; a harrowing parody of Joseph and Mary is enacted. When we hear that policemen are more afraid to intervene in marital quarrels than in those of hardened criminals, we know that the forces implicit in this scene, as in the domestic violence in *The Secret Agent*, are truly lethal. The unborn child is seared, or so the book implies, with these moments, and the compulsion to repeat them appears in him as it does in the actual participants. Mrs. Morel, locked out in the garden, relives each moment helplessly as the child is later to do: "For a while she could not control her consciousness; mechanically she went over the last scene, then over it again, certain phrases, certain moments coming each time like a brand red-hot down on her soul." In familial life we must all have that burning sensation. But the child grows into an artist, and turns his repetition-compulsions into the novel: such are the unpredictable matrices of art.[5]

Sons and Lovers grows distorted, however, once the representation of childhood memory is left behind. The life-force idea becomes more and more programmatic, and so does the tendency that alienated Jessie Chambers ("Miriam") from Lawrence: the insistence that the mother must dominate all, with the consequent need to downgrade all others. Actually this latter force eats at the novel from the early pages on: thus, the vigorous sensuality that was so appealing in the father as young miner is eroded by his

---

5. Julian Moynahan, ed., *Sons and Lovers: Text, Background, and Criticism* (Viking, 1968; originally published, 1913), p. 23. Subsequent page references are to this edition.

wife's puritanical rigidity, but the novel manages to blame him for it: "He had denied the God in him" (p. 63). His "face the flower of his body, ruddy," makes him like the young David, but his "wavy black hair" and "red, moist mouth" somehow turn into "the collier's small, mean head" (pp. 10, 62). Morel's vitality is beaten down by his wife's outraged disapproval of his harmless recreational drinking and his easygoing attitude toward money: full of the most hardbitten form of Protestant ethic, she regards her husband's debts as offenses to her soul. And when he conceals them to spare her worry, she damns this as cowardly subterfuge: he can't win.

But whenever Lawrence is able to get out from under his need to glorify his mother, the memories of the father are the most lyrical in the book:

> He went downstairs in his shirt and then struggled into his pit-trousers, which were left on the hearth to warm all night. There was always a fire, because Mrs. Morel raked. And the first sound in the house was the bang, bang of the poker against the raker, as Morel smashed the remainder of the coal to make the kettle, which was filled and left on the hob, finally boil. His cup and knife and fork, all he wanted except just the food, was laid ready on the table on a newspaper. Then he got his breakfast, made the tea, packed the bottoms of the doors with rugs to shut out the draught, piled a big fire, and sat down to an hour of joy. He toasted his bacon on a fork and caught the drops of fat on his bread; then he put the rasher on his thick slice of bread, and cut off chunks with a clasp-knife, poured his tea into his saucer, and was happy. With his family about, meals were never so pleasant. (p. 27)

The clarity of this is like a Fra Angelico painting, all the more remarkable because it describes a recurrent, habitual scene as if it were a single vivid occurrence. The paragraph is, as it were, in the imperfect tense, yet has the sharp immediacy of a unique action, seen in all its freshness and individuality. The most important feature of narratives in general is that they possess the power to bring experiences suddenly to us, even to make us feel part of the scene, although they are typically given in a past time grammatically; and here a daily, quotidian past.

Narratives can make even remote events more vivid to us than our ambient reality, while we are reading. If we wonder why some characters and acts in fiction are more "real" to us than our neigh-

bors and their lives, we may hypothesize that our very consciousness is a narrative mode, our means of navigating through the
universe by irreducibly verbal means. We weave a latent, submerged story, a controlled fantasy that enables us to work through
all that impinges on us. To paraphrase much post-Freudian
thought, we consist of the stories we tell to ourselves. Lawrence
like other writers grasped this, and his own gift for recalling the
most poignant moments out of childhood consciousness, with its
succession of imprinted scenes, became the source of his best work.

The gift shows in his poems as well as in *Sons and Lovers*. When
I. A. Richards selected a Lawrence poem as one of the set with
which to test his students' unguided reactions, he chose "Piano," in
which the adult speaker is carried back to childhood years in a
Proustian mode:

> Softly, in the dusk, a woman is singing to me;
> Taking me back down the vista of years, till I see
> A child sitting under the piano, in the boom of the tingling strings
> And pressing the small, poised feet of a mother who smiles as she sings.
> . . . .
>   The glamour
> Of childish days is upon me, my manhood is cast
> Down in the flood of remembrance, I weep like a child for the past.

The Cambridge students resisted the poem because they saw in it
an invitation to sentimentality. Richards, who had the advantage
of knowing the poem was in the canon, dismissed their various
objections to its supposed flaws and commented on the "vividity"
of the poet's memory. Such vividity is a key to Lawrence's whole
oeuvre.[6]

One can only regret that in the second half of *Sons and Lovers*
Lawrence deliberately blurred the early clarity: after the childhood
pages, the life-force idea takes over as an urge to represent innerness by forsaking clear outlines. Paul explains to Miriam that one
must paint not the outer shape of a flower, which is a mere "dead
crust," but rather "the shimmering protoplasm in the leaves and
everywhere. . . . the shimmer is inside really" (p. 152). After this,
the book turns into one form after another of literary *sfumato*.

---

6. *Practical Criticism: A Study of Literary Judgment* (New York: Harcourt
Brace, 1929), pp. 99–112, esp. p. 101.

Throwing off Blake's insistence on the "distinct and wirey bound-
ing line," Lawrence pours himself into a vitalistic program that has
to be self-defeating. Clarity is replaced by much repetitive rhetoric;
heavy melodramatic portentousness, "peewits screaming in the
field" while lovers couple, dominates the action as Lawrence struggles to convey the power of suprapersonal urges.

Indeed, in all his later novels Lawrence never regained the luminosity of childhood memory in such passages as Walter Morel's
breakfast. *Women in Love*, for instance, loses this entirely and
almost chokes itself in the infinite regress of the characters' arguments about which of them is most spontaneous. We feel hectored,
and by other passages too. When Gerald forces his mare to face
the clanking train, we are beaten over the head with the lesson of
his destructive sexuality. The scene is a patent allegory of brutal
intercourse, a favorite Lawrentian motif (in *Sons and Lovers* it
appears when Paul pushes Miriam in a swing). But in the later
book both the images and the rhetoric have a hysterical, ranting
quality, as of the mother's Dissenting heritage gone wild, turned
into a nightmare of all that Swift feared in "enthusiasm."[7] Finally
the urge to "paint the protoplasm" results in passages that turn
back on themselves into pure grotesquerie, as where Ursula on her
knees is holding on to Birkin's loins:

> Unconsciously, with her sensitive finger-tips, she was tracing the back
> of his thighs, following some mysterious life-flow there. She had dis-
> covered something, something more than wonderful, more wonderful
> than life itself. It was the strange mystery of his life-motion, there, at
> the back of his thighs, down the flanks. It was a strange reality of his
> being, the very stuff of being, there in the straight downflow of the
> thighs. . . . After a lapse of stillness, after the rivers of strange dark
> fluid richness had passed over her, flooding, carrying away her mind
> and flooding down her spine and down her knees, past her feet, a
> strange flood, sweeping away everything and leaving her an essential
> new being, she was left quite free, she was free in complete ease, her
> complete self. . . . There were strange fountains of his body, more
> mysterious and potent than any she had imagined or known, more
> satisfying, ah, finally, mystically–physically satisfying. She had thought
> there was no source deeper than the phallic source. And now, behold,
> from the smitten rock of the man's body, from the strange marvellous

7. *Sons and Lovers*, p. 10.

flanks and thighs, deeper, further in mystery than the phallic source, came the floods of ineffable darkness and ineffable riches.[8]

To call this self-parody is too easy. What's wrong here is not that it's an unconscious confession of homosexual desire for anal intercourse, as some think, but rather that Lawrence has obviously lost all sense of how his repetitive, pseudomantric word chains must for the reader slip over into comically unintentional scatology. With the aid of Norman O. Brown we could point to the psychic needs that led to an apocalypticizing of the "dark riches" flowing from the "split rock of the man's body," but for the present a comparison with almost any page of the first half of *Sons and Lovers* will suffice to make the point that the problem is as much rhetorical as anatomical.

The early clarity that contrasts so vividly with the later self-indulgence had been achieved partly by Flaubertian restraint, eschewal of comment, learned by both Lawrence and Ezra Pound at the feet of Ford Madox Ford. Though the two pupils disliked each other, Pound's review of Lawrence's early poems registers unfeigned admiration for the adaptations of "*le mot juste* and living language" that Pound wanted to cross-pollinate from French prose into modern poetry. He wrote that Lawrence had "brought poetry up to the level of prose," a key phrase in his concept of the "prose tradition" transmitted by Ford.[9] In the first half of *Sons and Lovers*, the Flaubertian discipline combined synergetically with recall of childhood memory to achieve lambent passages. Later the rhetoric became "mystically–physically satisfying" in the worst sense.

Perhaps Lawrence anticipated our regrets. He was as ruthless as Hemingway in putting his friends and lovers into books, and as callous in betraying their trust. The point is not to belabor personal failings, but to suggest that in both men there was a certain desperation in their uses of people and of memories, as if they had to sacrifice personal relations in order to recapture some visionary gleam — and in both cases their treatments of childhood corroborate this.

The ghost of Wordsworth lurks behind this whole topic, indeed.

---

8. David Farmer, Lindeth Vasey, and John Worthen, eds., *Women in Love* (Cambridge University Press, 1987; originally published, 1920), pp. 313–14.

9. *Literary Essays of Ezra Pound*, p. 388.

The mighty poet was not merely pandering to sentimental taste or recycling the old Platonic theory of recollection when he portrayed the child's world as lit by a mysterious light, with maturation as loss and forgetting, in the Immortality Ode. We all accept this in one way or another, if only in the Freudian way in which the power of childhood is that of atavistic recurrence. Though the Biblical Eden has nothing to do with childhood, we can see how as a myth it comes to reinforce idealization of a time before we were habituated to doubt, guilt, and grief. Especially in America — because we don't send our children to work or to boarding schools? — we place great faith in childhood. We all know that sudden access to childhood memories can unleash complicated and forceful emotions, and we are always replaying these inner stories of ours, sometimes desperately striving to amend them, sometimes simply playing out their poignant echoes. A clever, though heartless, cinematic adaptation was *Citizen Kane*'s appropriation of "Rosebud," Hearst's name for Marion Davies' genitalia, for the remembered sled of childhood — compare the genuine recovery of joy in Ingmar Bergman's *Wild Strawberries*.[10]

Critics often surmise that the best moments of Sherwood Anderson's highly uneven writing involve such evocations of a personal past. Although he could not write a genuine *Bildungsroman*, partly because he distrusted the factitious unity of the novel form, Anderson seems to have grasped the power of the art of memory at about the same time as Joyce and Lawrence did. Curiously enough, apparently it cannot be determined if he had read either writer when he began *Winesburg, Ohio*, his most memorable work and most usefully transmuted autobiography. Though he later boasted that *Dark Laughter* was an adaptation of the methods of *Ulysses*, there is no certainty that he had read *Dubliners* or *Portrait* in the 1915-16 period when he wrote the first of the Winesburg stories.[11] Similarly, Anderson scholars agree that Lawrence was a powerful influence, but only on the later works. Yet if direct influence is dubious, there must have been an uncanny telepathic communication, possibly abetted by talk of Joyce and Lawrence in the circles

10. See Barbara Leaming, *Orson Welles: A Biography* (Viking, 1985), p. 205.
11. Sister Martha Curry, "Sherwood Anderson and James Joyce," *American Literature* 52 (1980): 236-49.

of the "Chicago Renaissance." If, as he later said, Anderson's "first connection [*sic*] of literature was through Margaret Anderson [no relation] who started the *Little Review* in Chicago," he surely was stimulated by her awareness of European developments.[12] Moreover, his own early work was published by the John Lane Company and by B. W. Huebsch, both of whom had had dealings with Joyce. Huebsch published *Dubliners* and *Portrait* in America, and some of Lawrence's work as well. Thus if Anderson did not read these works, he was strangely neglectful. Nor would it be surprising that he did not record any debts. Like Hemingway and Faulkner, to whom he may have taught the trick, he had a habit of covering his tracks: when influences were uncomfortably powerful or obvious, he denied or evaded. Most notoriously, he led his publishers to believe that he had not read Edgar Lee Masters' *Spoon River Anthology* before writing *Winesburg*, no doubt to avoid an undeserved charge of being derivative. He also denied having read Freud, although he clearly had absorbed many of the ideas from his Chicago friends.[13]

On the other hand, the possibility remains that he arrived at Joycean–Lawrentian conceptions simply by intuition. Just as William Carlos Williams was not consciously imitating the *Cantos* or *Finnegans Wake*, despite the similarities of many features of *Paterson*, so Anderson may have been subconsciously embodying the principles of American "homemade" Modernism, to use Hugh Kenner's term. The whole problem would be easier if we believed in spiritualism or fate; it is unsettling to learn that Anderson died just two months after Joyce, from a very similar cause (peritonitis).

The three writers clearly shared an intensity of feeling for what Lawrence called "the spirit of place." Anderson's creation of Winesburg (he said he found out only later that there was a town in Ohio with that name) not only parallels Joyce's evocation of Dublin and Lawrence's of the Midlands, but also embodies childhood memories in similar ways. For instance, Anderson's hometown Clyde served his family mainly as a fixed point in a history of vagabondage — like the Joyce family, they moved often but circled

---

12. *Letters of Sherwood Anderson*, ed. Howard Mumford Jones and Walter Rideout (Little, Brown, 1953), pp. 274–75.

13. Frederick J. Hoffman, in Ferres, pp. 314–320; Sutton, p. 181.

around one place. Anderson's parents were almost itinerant in his earliest years, and young Sherwood explored his environment in much the same way as Stephen Dedalus in the second chapter of *Portrait*.[14] In all three writers, the home base became a hermetic island, enchanted in memory, unaffected by time or by unrestful self-exile in cosmopolitan locales: Joyce in Trieste and Zurich and Paris, Lawrence in the Mediterranean and the New World, Anderson in Chicago and New Orleans and finally rural Virginia. These travels were not sentimental attempts to relocate or re-create "home," but they provide evidence of the hold of that idea. Joyce, most obsessive of the three, revenged himself on Irish *passéisme* by adopting it as artistic strategy, and frankly concentrated all his powers on the remembered material of his early years, even taking as the scaffolding of his last work the relationships of the family unit, at once archetypal and everyday. Lawrence, on the other hand, delved wherever he went into the local "spirit of place," trying to connect cultural with chthonic roots. All the quests imply, in different ways, that what we restlessly seek is somehow right under our noses, yet interred in a past of one kind or another. The buried giant in the dream landscape of *Finnegans Wake*, as noted earlier, stands for Joyce's adaptation of Irish *passéisme* to recover a world. He wrote about Dublin, he said, "because if I can get to the heart of Dublin I can get to the heart of all the cities of the world. In the particular is contained the universal."[15] But it was not the living, ongoing Dublin that fascinated him, nor some essence of *civitas*. Joyce's Dublin was an imaginary place, preserved in memory like a mammoth in the ice of Siberia. It was so self-contained that his adepts are often surprised to find how much he left out — the whole Anglo-Irish social world into which Yeats and Beckett were born, for instance. For him, the threadbare urbanity of a declining Catholic milieu was enough to consume the imagination; it became a grain of sand in which to reflect the cosmos prismatically.

Both Lawrence and Anderson tried writing on other subjects, but with mixed results. In Anderson's case the variation in quality between the work for which Clyde was the source and the more

14. Sutton, pp. 512 ff.
15. See William Noon, S.J., *Joyce and Aquinas* (Yale University Press, 1957), p. 60.

ambitious ventures is especially marked. Though he did not begin his artistic career until middle age, the memories of childhood and youth, transmuted and projected onto other figures, were its vital force: he had little capacity to absorb new environments or material. His later life was eventful enough, but never inspired successful writing. He learned nothing from several wives (cf. Joyce who turned Nora into yet another source of access to the undiscovered country of the past). The truth is that Anderson was not just self-absorbed; he lived an existence so subjective that without artistic control and expression he would have qualified for a mental ward. Although he frequently proclaimed a passionate desire to tell the stories of the persons he encountered, he would use phrases like "behind every face there is a story."[16] But one does not tell the stories of transient faces except by projecting free-form "lives" onto them, out of a fantasy-embroidered past. His imagination battened on strangers, *tabulae rasae* onto which he could inscribe the invented lives of childhood acquaintances. The limitations of this habit of perception were well put by Lionel Trilling:

> In Anderson's world there are many emotions, or rather many instances of a few emotions, but there are very few sights, sounds, and smells, very little of the stuff of actuality. The very things to which he gives moral value because they are living and real and opposed in their organic nature to the insensate abstractions of an industrial culture become, as he writes about them, themselves abstract and without life. His praise of the racehorses he said he loved gives us no sense of a horse; his Mississippi does not flow; his tall corn grows out of the soil of his dominating subjectivity.[17]

To see the justice of Trilling's observation, we have only to look at the story "Sophistication" in *Winesburg*, in which Anderson awkwardly attempts Breughel-like scenes:

> In the main street of Winesburg crowds filled the stores and the sidewalks. Night came on, horses whinnied, the clerks in the stores ran madly about, children became lost and cried lustily, an American town worked terribly at the task of amusing itself. . . .

---

16. Malcolm Cowley in Ferres, pp. 361–63. See also Sutton, pp. 16 and esp. p. 325: "I often see, being what I am, the whole life of some individual met, in a few seconds."

17. Ferres, pp. 461–62.

> . . . In Winesburg the crowded day had run itself out into the long night of the late fall. Farm horses jogged away along lonely country roads pulling their portion of weary people. Clerks began to bring samples of goods in off the sidewalks and lock the doors of stores. In the Opera House a crowd had gathered to see a show and further down Main Street the fiddlers, their instruments tuned, sweated and worked to keep the feet of youth flying over a dance floor.[18]

These might be displays of toy figures in a cheap diorama. The empty rhetoric and useless specification ("their instruments tuned") show clearly that Anderson's attention was elsewhere. Where? The key passage, though so clumsy that it makes us wince, tells it all:

> There is something memorable in the experience to be had by going into a fair ground that stands at the edge of a Middle Western town on a night after the annual fair has been held. The sensation is one never to be forgotten. On all sides are ghosts, not of the dead, but of living people. Here, during the day just passed, have come the people pouring in from the town and the country around. Farmers with their wives and children and all the people from the hundreds of little frame houses have gathered within these board walls. Young girls have laughed and men with beards have talked of the affairs of their lives. The place has been filled to overflowing with life. It has itched and squirmed with life and now it is night and the life has all gone away. The silence is almost terrifying. One conceals oneself standing silently beside the trunk of a tree and what there is of a reflective tendency in his nature is intensified. One shudders at the thought of the meaninglessness of life while at the same instant, and if the people of the town are his people, one loves life so intensely that tears come into the eyes. (pp. 240–41)

For Anderson, like Hardy, the living people are ephemeral: what seizes his imagination are the ghostly traces of their passage. The true subject is himself, passionately reminiscing over the remains of presence, always apart. The consciousness here is worked up from that of the solitary Wordsworthian boy, who would be essentially lonely even knocking about with his chums (which in *Winesburg* he never does), revelling in the observer's unconstrained freedom to remember and fantasize. As Trilling says, this subjectivity annihilates the external world, and sets Anderson far apart as a writer from both Lawrence and Joyce, with their clearly realized worlds.

18. Ferres, pp. 233, 241.

Walter Rideout notices that the crisis scenes in the large majority of the stories in *Winesburg* occur in the evening, so as to set the "night world" of imagination against the daylight of dispensable facts. And "many of the tales end with the characters in total darkness. Such a device not only links the tales but in itself implies meaning. . . . the briefness of the insight is emphasized by the shutting down of the dark."[19] If we knew that Anderson had read Joyce's "Araby," we could argue that it had spread its suffused darkness over the whole town of Winesburg. In Joyce's story, the myopic boy-narrator prefers to keep all dim ("I was thankful I could see so little") in order to indulge his quest-romance visions. Even the street of the opening sentence is "blind," and the narrator deliberately keeps his heroine "Mangan's sister" (never even named, a metonymy of hair and dress and "the white border of a petticoat") obscurely backlit by winter twilight and lampglow, so as to cast her as a fairy-tale being for whom he can walk the "flaring streets" in search of an enchanted gift.[20] The effect recurs in some of the other stories of *Dubliners*, but in *Winesburg* it is compulsive and endemic, and makes Trilling's point in another way.

"Araby" might well have been a key to Anderson's book. Pound's description of it highlights an Andersonian point: "Much better than a 'story,' it is a vivid waiting."[21] So Anderson also wanted to cast off the shapes and restrictions of story and novel form in search of a "new looseness": "There are no plot stories in life."[22] And the epiphany of emptiness with which "Araby" ends could easily have led to much in *Winesburg*: Malcolm Cowley and other critics have called attention to the epiphanic structuring of Anderson's stories around lyric moments. The ending of "An Awakening," for instance, recalls Joyce's "An Encounter" and "A Painful Case" as well as "Araby." (In fact this story also reenacts a crucial scene in *Sons and Lovers*, in which an older man beats a younger one who has temporarily become the lover of his estranged wife — or in Anderson's version, future wife.)[23]

19. Ferres, pp. 292–93.

20. Robert Scholes and A. Walton Litz, eds., *Dubliners: Text, Criticism, and Notes* (Penguin, 1976; originally published, 1914), pp. 29–35.

21. *Literary Essays of Ezra Pound*, p. 400.

22. Ferres, p. 14.

23. *Sons and Lovers*, pp. 365–66.

The interconnections between the *Dubliners* stories could also have given Anderson hints for his own collection. No named character like Anderson's George Willard unifies Joyce's stories by continual reappearance, but the narrators and protagonists are often linked to one another, and Anderson probably would have read them as essentially autobiographical; hence his creation of a young Stephen Dedalus figure. George Willard the young dreamer is Anderson's tribute to his own "dominating subjectivity." The point of view is that of an impersonal narrator rather than his, but this is a technicality, like the use of third-person viewpoint on the first page of *Portrait* where the child's consciousness is being manifested, or the semblance of an imperfect tense in the scene of Morel's breakfast. In fact, the *Winesburg* stories are projections of childhood wonder onto remembered faces and details, and George Willard is the dreamer as well as the character. That so many of the "grotesques" tell their stories to him is no coincidence. As Trilling's analysis implies, Anderson's figures are not really characters at all, compared to those of most good writers: they are stick figures, cartoonish wraiths. Anderson had no gift for "rounded" characters, and so like some modern painters made use of his own lack of facility; this allowed him to reach another realm, that of the child's imagination in which persons are more forces than characters. They are dream figures comparable to those in myth, not really "human" at all, nor possessed of well-formed aetiological backgrounds. They appear and disappear swiftly and inexplicably, tell — or more precisely confess, in *Winesburg* — mysterious stories that are like messages from some chthonic realm, some land of spirits and powers. To compare them with other writers' characters somewhat misses the point. In the book's last sentence, George Willard sits in the train that will take him away: "When he aroused himself and again looked out of the car window the town of Winesburg had disappeared and his life there had become but a background on which to paint the dreams of his manhood" (p. 247). But the dreams of the man were always about childhood; they were obsessive fantasies linked to the strange adults he could not really understand, but to whom he could attach explanatory stories as children do with their toy soldiers and dolls. *Dream* was Anderson's favorite and most revealing word; there, he thought, was where people lived, and his stories proceed by a dream logic as strange, ultimately, as that of *Finnegans Wake*.[24] Freud would have recognized it easily. Anderson wrote dream visions, as Chaucer did, and so to look for realism is to make a category mistake.

Anderson was as discontented as Lawrence was with "the old stable ego of character"; he resented its essentialism. In "The Book of the Grotesque," the matrix story of *Winesburg* (and its original title), the old writer does not create characters. Rather, "something" drives a procession of "grotesques" before his half-sleeping eyes; in spite of his age he is like a child, with a succession of play figures. Still more revelatory on this point is the story "Loneliness." In this self- confession, Anderson portrays a painter, Enoch Robinson, as an eternal child whose real happiness is to stay in his room without family or friends, with only imaginary companions.

> The mild, blue-eyed young Ohio boy was a complete egotist, as all children are egotists. He did not want friends for the quite simple reason that no child wants friends. He wanted most of all the people of his own mind, people with whom he could really talk, people he could harangue and scold by the hour, servants, you see, to his fancy. Among these people he was always self-confident and bold. They might talk, to be sure, and even have opinions of their own, but always he talked last and best. He was like a writer busy among the figures of his brain. . . .
>   . . . They were an odd lot, Enoch's people. They were made, I suppose, out of real people he had seen and who for some obscure reason made an appeal to him. . . . There must have been two dozen of the shadow people, invented by the child-mind of Enoch Robinson, who lived in the room with him. (pp. 171–73)

This passage shows Anderson's awareness of where his own characters came from. He lacked interest in more polished concepts of character, just as he did in that of the conventional form of story or novel. In these feelings he was strengthened by the example of Gertrude Stein as well as Joyce and Lawrence. When he read Stein, he felt validated also in his monotonous repetition of monosyllabic words, rudimentary sentence structure, and other forms of verbal primitivism. And he no doubt thought of himself as she did, as a Modernist painter among writers: his figures were flat, like those of Matisse; caricatures, like those of Miró. So, as had Cézanne, Hardy, William Carlos Williams, and Stein herself, he discovered

---

24. Sutton, pp. 59–60; cf. pp. 207, 539.

his own lack of fluency and polish to be a precious asset.[25] The appearance of clumsiness did not put him off; he feared far more the appearance of facility, for he had learned in his advertising career to mistrust those who were adroit with words. "I have had a great fear of phrase-making. . . . [Words] are very tricky things. Look, for example, how that man Mencken can rattle words like dice in a box."[26] He knew he would be easily bested by other writers in competitions of fluency, so made a strength of his weaknesses.

Both flattened syntax and unrounded characters suited Anderson's pervasive lack of interest in human and linguistic variation, his preference for a kind of tranced musing over people and words. Here he also would have been influenced by potent memories of the laconism and parataxis of Biblical style, reinforced according to one anecdote by a habit of tearing pages out of Gideon Bibles in hotels and poring over them.[27] Bible reading was still one of the recreations of the poor in his youth, and he intensified the habit in middle age, continually absorbing stylistic patterns. Parataxis in the Bible, as in other ancient works, was a concomitant of scribal conditions: the earliest manuscripts had no punctuation (or even separations between words), and no obvious ways to mark transitions and linkages: the "and" phrases were thus useful. However, as Erich Auerbach has shown, parataxis became the sign of protest against classical hypotaxis, which was linked to a social stratification that the Bible opposes.[28] Parataxis then became part of our idea of a sacred text, and its connectives, rhythms, and itemizations have come to be the markers of magisterial style, especially in American literature. Hemingway's strings of "and" clauses derive from his having "learned to write" by reading the Bible, particularly the Old Testament.[29]

"A Testamental accent and vision modulate every page of Ander-

---

25. See Chapter 1 of this book; William Phillips in Ferres, p. 279; Sutton, p. 298.

26. *Letters of Sherwood Anderson*, p. 79.

27. Ferres, pp. 336, 409.

28. *Mimesis: The Representation of Reality in Western Literature*, trans. Willard Trask (Princeton University Press, 1968), pp. 71–72. Cf. Roger Asselineau in Ferres, p. 350.

29. Charles A. Fenton, *The Apprenticeship of Ernest Hemingway: The Early Years* (Farrar, Straus & Young, 1954), p. 5.

son's [*Winesburg*]," observed Waldo Frank.[30] The effect was not only on style; some of the stories are adaptations of folk typology, as in the four-part story called "Godliness." Thought to be leftover inserts from another, abortive novel, these parts are not situated in Winesburg but belong to another project, which perhaps aimed to show the hold of half-digested and overliteralized Biblical archetypes on the rural imagination.[31] But their typological character provides a hint of the way the stories in *Winesburg* are linked, a way that would have reinforced the *Dubliners*-derived connections.

The four parts of "Godliness" tell of the dynastic ambitions of a farmer named Jesse. Apparently in an early draft he was called Joseph, but the change was appropriate. He is a fanatical latter-day prophet whose zeal—plus the fact that his four older brothers are killed in the Civil War—drives him in good Calvinist fashion to multiply his patrimony. He sees signs from God everywhere, especially in his brothers' deaths and his own prosperity. Thus he believes he must be doing "God's work." His desire for an heir becomes combined with his sense of providential destiny, and he pleads with "Jehovah of Hosts" for "a son to be called David." (As with the original Jesse, the mother is occulted.) The first story ends here: in the second we learn that he was granted instead a daughter named Louise, but eventually she bears the son to be named David. The story tells that Louise was petulant and discontented in motherhood for no obvious reason, but the significance of this comes out only later. David is finally sent to Jesse's farm, reawakening the old man's thirst for a sign of approval from God. He takes the child out into the woods to await a theophany, but succeeds only in frightening him into running away; in his flight, the boy falls and hurts his head on a rock—another empty epiphany. The third story, "Surrender," which might have been written first and could have dragged the others into existence after it, tells of Louise, the daughter/discontented mother: as it stands, this is a flashback, but it coheres with the stories of female frustration in *Winesburg*. Finally, in the last story ("Terror"; the first two have no individual names) the old man once more seeks a sign, and to coerce theophany this time vows to sacrifice a lamb. He takes young David, now

30. Ferres, p. 374.
31. Jarvis Thurston in Ferres, p. 341.

fifteen, with a lamb back to the same spot in the woods where the boy suffered his earlier fright and wound, muttering that he must put the blood of the lamb on the boy's forehead. David, naturally, is again seized by fear when he sees his grandfather approaching purposefully, and slings a stone at him from a slingshot! Jesse falls, and David runs away, for good this time. When Jesse revives, he tells everyone that a messenger from God took the boy: "'I was too greedy for glory,' he declared, and would have no more to say in the matter" (p. 102).

The story is funnier than most readers probably knew. The old man's fanatical project, according to the narrator, stems from the Biblical habit of mind in preindustrial America, before men were distracted by materialism and possessions and the glib new ideas of magazines and books. But Jesse is a comically creative mytho-poeist: he tries to enact the story of the founder of the Davidic dynasty, but it keeps turning into other stories, notably that of Abraham and Isaac. Finally it boomerangs on him when it becomes a combination of David and Goliath plus Oedipus and Laius. The rhetoric of the Cain and Passover stories, with that of Revelation, appears in the obsession about the blood of the lamb on the fore-head, while the stories of Enoch, Elijah, and others furnish the fantasy about the boy's being taken by a messenger of God. Other motifs swarm: the sought-for sign, the wound, the rock, many others. Clearly, the old man's Bible reading has produced a manic hodgepodge. But his confused thinking does reflect a backwoods version of the typological hermeneutic that the early Christians used to interpret and unify the two Testaments. For Paul, Adam was a type (in the old sense of *image*, as in "tintype" or "Daguerro-type") of Christ, Hagar of the Law, and so forth. The Old Testament prefigures the New, the New fulfills the Old. The Puritans were zealous typologists, and ingrained this habit into the American literary imagination—Melville's Ishmael, Ahab, and Leviathan are not coincidental. Anderson greatly admired Melville.

In "The Philosopher," Anderson has a character paranoiacally fearful of mob lynching exclaim that "in the end I will be crucified, uselessly crucified," and then go on to utter his grotesque "truth": "Everyone in the world is Christ and they are all crucified" (p. 57). (In the opening story, "The Book of the Grotesque," the old writ-er's figures are twisted into grotesques by embracing such "truths" as these.) Anderson's "Philosopher" anticipates the heyday of a type of criticism in which Christ figures were hunted throughout the length and breadth of American fiction. But though there is a tinge of mockery in his deployment of such folk typology, it also conceals a serious principle, the possibility of a kind of secular adaptation that interrelates the stories of *Winesburg* as the personages and events of the two Testaments are interrelated.

The clue lies in "Surrender," the third story of the "Godliness" tetralogy. This story, as noted, can stand by itself, although it now forms part of Jesse's saga. The evidence that it was written before the other parts (in their present form) links it to another story, called "Nobody Knows," on the basis of manuscript evidence apparently written just *after* "Surrender."[32] Both stories contain characters named Louise who write imploring notes to wished-for lovers. In "Nobody Knows," George Willard accepts a note, which he takes to be a sexual overture, from the lower-class Louise Trunnion, and acts on it. After this initiation into manhood he muses guiltily: "'She hasn't got anything on me. Nobody knows'" (p. 62). But "Surrender" puts this act into another context, for it tells the girls' side. The other Louise (Bentley), Jesse's daughter, leaves her father's farm and goes to live in Winesburg with a family named Hardy. She yearns for a loving relationship, and *in petto* nominates John Hardy, passive brother of two sisters who snub her. But she doesn't know how to approach him.

> She became obsessed with the thought that it wanted but a courageous act on her part to make all of her association with people something quite different, and that it was possible by such an act to pass into a new life as one opens a door and goes into a room. (p. 91)

Her thoughts are not sexual, but rather otherworldly. Then she accidentally spies on a courting scene between Mary Hardy and a young man, with the usual adolescent kissing and protesting, and this inspires her: she imagines "that to be held tightly and kissed was the whole secret of life." So she writes a note to John Hardy, saying "I want someone to love me and I want to love someone." This is her counterpart to Louise Trunnion's note to George Willard, which had read "I'm yours if you want me" (pp. 60, 94). The

32. William Phillips in Ferres, pp. 268 ff.

notes are not really sexual overtures, but desperate pleas for a kind of emancipation. Needless to say, both males reduce the notes to the most obvious meaning, and are accepted *faute de mieux*: "Louise Bentley took John Hardy to be her lover. That was not what she wanted but it was so the young man had interpreted her approach to him, and so anxious was she to achieve something else that she made no resistance" (pp. 95–96). With this clue we can read "Nobody Knows" as a story of George Willard's callow insensitivity and puerile ambition, which prevents him from seeing Louise Trunnion as anything but a sexual convenience. Like Don Juan, such juvenile lovers are really escape artists, and George Willard is glad to escape to other girls and ambitions. The forgotten and inarticulate Louise Trunnion has to have her story unfolded by her namesake Louise Bentley, just as Old Testament figures are unfolded by their counterparts in the revelation of the New.

Seeing how one story provides ways to look at another, and that linked stories can be interleaved in a typological way, we can generalize that each is incomplete by itself, and that there is apt to be an occulted element in each. Anderson tells us as much in the story "Loneliness," which again is his most obvious self-confession. The childlike artist Enoch Robinson, reacting to the prattle of New York "talking artists," cannot say what is hidden in his pictures, but can at least think it.

> "You don't get the point," he wanted to explain; "the picture doesn't consist of the things you see and say words about. There is something else, something you don't see at all, something you aren't intended to see. Look at this one over here, by the door here, where the light from the window falls on it. The dark spot by the road that you might not notice at all is, you see, the beginning of everything. There is a clump of elders there such as used to grow beside the road before our house back in Winesburg, Ohio, and in among the elders there is something hidden. It is a woman, that's what it is. She has been thrown from a horse and the horse has run away out of sight. . . . She is hurt and suffering but she makes no sound. Don't you see how it is? She lies quite still, white and still, and the beauty comes out from her and spreads over everything. It is in the sky back there and all around everywhere. I didn't try to paint the woman, of course. She is too beautiful to be painted. How dull to talk of composition and such things! Why do you not look at the sky and then run away as I used to do when I was a boy back there in Winesburg, Ohio?" (pp. 169–70)

This is Anderson telling us how to read his stories: we must look for the hidden suffering beauty as in this figure of the injured, inarticulate woman, this Susanna among the elders, as it were. (Anderson's taste for Biblical jokes was not limited to "Godliness.") There are many other suffering, inarticulate women in *Winesburg*; indeed they dominate the volume in a sense. And other relationships revealed here are also keys; for example, Enoch's remark about running away suggests that Anderson himself is to be seen in the figure of the fleeing boys, whether of the type of the coltish George Willard fleeing sexual entanglement or of the young David running away from his grandfather's Old Testament fantasies. In view of the latter, we must see that the essence of Anderson's work combines recovery of childhood memories with an adaptation of that same Biblical habit of mind that could, at times, seem so oppressive. As with the Professor in *The Secret Agent*, the religious heritage will out, in whatever displaced form.

The occulted woman in Enoch Robinson's painting appears throughout, as noted: Anderson did have a streak of hesitant, groping feminism, and he puts it into his characters. In "Surrender," Louise Bentley and John Hardy marry after the usual fears of pregnancy, and eventually young David is produced to satisfy old Jesse's dynastic cravings. But this is no happy ending. Louise becomes permanently embittered about the fate of women who are forced to seek in lovers the mysterious door to life for which they are searching, and at the end of the story she treats David indifferently. "'It is a man child and will get what it wants anyway,' she said sharply. 'Had it been a woman child there is nothing in the world I would not have done for it'" (p. 96). She almost, but not quite, gives a voice to all the suppressed, searching women in *Winesburg*, doomed to be misunderstood by practical husbands and dreamy young men (not only lovers but also pupils, as with the teacher Kate Swift and George Willard). These women all hunger for something for which "love" is a poor substitute, but they blindly seek it in men and regularly are forced into the game of ensnaring a husband. Whether or not they succeed, they remain frustrated, seeking, subject to wild impulses. They drive furiously through the streets, as does Louise Bentley, or even run naked through them, as does Alice Hindman in "Adventure"; or they walk in a storm with mind "ablaze," obsessed with the desire to pass something on to George Willard, as does Kate Swift in "The Teacher."

Following this train of thought, we can arrive at the notion that in *Winesburg*, as later in *The Waste Land*, all the women are one woman. (Had Anderson read Eliot's lines in "Preludes" [1914] about "some infinitely gentle/ Infinitely suffering thing"?) It could even be said that they all typologically incarnate the figure who appears in the story called "Mother." Secular typology can come to reinforce the child's vision in which all beings are seen through the schemata, as E. H. Gombrich would call them, of the parental figures.[33] "Mother" is now the third story in the volume, following to no apparent purpose the story "Paper Pills," about one Dr. Reefy. "Mother" seems to be about the relationship between Elizabeth Willard and her son George, but we know that the key element in any given story will not always be in focus. Only toward the end of the book, in "Death," do we learn of the importance of Dr. Reefy to Elizabeth. Near the end of her life he becomes her "one friend," communicant, confessor, and near-lover. Though she is gaunt and worn out, prematurely aged at forty-one from hard labor in her husband's hotel, she is seized by a strange energy as she confesses inchoate longings to the doctor, and this energy transforms her into a younger, beautiful person whom he begins to desire. She tells him that she had sought love from many men, but had finally decided to marry to resolve her quest. "'It wasn't Tom I wanted, it was marriage'" (p. 226). The crisis in her life came a few months after she found that marriage was not the answer, as the lovers had not been. She went for a drive:

> "I wanted to go at a terrible speed, to drive on and on forever. I wanted to get out of town, out of my clothes, out of my marriage, out of my body, out of everything. I almost killed the horse, making him run, and when he could not run any more I got out of the buggy and ran afoot into the darkness until I fell and hurt my side. I wanted to run away from everything but I wanted to run towards something too. Don't you see, dear, how it was?" (p. 227)

In answer he begins kissing her. At this point the reader should recall the earlier story in which Dr. Reefy appears, "Paper Pills,"

---

33. Cf. Waldo Frank in Ferres, p. 372: "The form of the mother, frustrate, lonely, at least desperate, pervades the variations that make the rest of the book."

in which an unnamed "tall dark girl" is married by the doctor after her failed quest, also involving other lovers, and an aborted pregnancy (and one of the lovers also substitutes kisses for words). It is no accident that "Paper Pills" immediately precedes "Mother," in which Elizabeth Willard's tall gaunt figure is emphasized; "Mother" even contains this sentence about her: "In her own mind the tall dark girl had been in those days much confused" (p. 46). The reader too may be "confused" about the two tall dark girls — or rather Anderson has "confused" them in a typological sense, with Elizabeth prefiguring the later unnamed wife (who is, however, described earlier).

As Dr. Reefy kisses Elizabeth Willard in "Death," the later story, he begins to mutter "You dear! You lovely dear! Oh you lovely dear!" echoing unaware the words of an earlier lover of hers before her marriage (p. 227). But this time the two are interrupted, the affair is never consummated, and a few months later the doctor is replaced by Death, whom she imagines as a lover reaching out to her. She dies before she can tell her son George of some money she has hidden away for him, money originally given to her by her father to make her independent, secreted by her in a wall after her marriage. This failed gift is part of a set of elements suggesting the point that her son is the last her human lovers, though he himself recognizes it only dimly: he is distracted by worldly thoughts while she is dying, particularly thoughts of the "red young lips" of another girl his own age, Helen White, who sends him a note and whom he hopes to court. But when he lifts the sheet from his mother's body, he (like Dr. Reefy earlier) sees her transformed into a "young and graceful" woman, "unspeakably lovely." And as he leaves the room, the final fusion of identities takes place. "'The dear, the dear, oh the lovely dear,' the boy, urged by some impulse outside himself, muttered aloud" (p. 232). Thus the son becomes the last term in a long series of lovers drawn to her, with Death as the only satisfying one: he succeeds in carrying her away. Death, Dr. Reefy, and all the premarital lovers become merged in the obscure knowledge, more valuable than the hidden money, that George Willard carries away with him: it obviously represents some kind of key to the past, and typological thinking, represented by the series of interchangeable lovers and by the links between stories, gives us a grasp of this key.

   This last twist, of the son as lover, raises once again the question
of influence or telepathic communion. If Anderson did not read
Sons and Lovers, how did he anticipate so closely the scene of the
mother's death, and the whole theme? In Lawrence, the mother
selects the sons, one after the other, as she rejects the husband:
relations in the Willard family are not so tempestuous, but the
similarity is undeniable. Indeed, when we put together all the stories in which she appears, it becomes clear that Elizabeth's quest
was for a son-lover all along.

> When that [sexual consummation] came she felt for a time released and
> happy. She did not blame the men who walked with her and later she
> did not blame Tom Willard. It was always the same, beginning with
> kisses and ending, after strange wild emotions, with peace and then
> sobbing repentance. When she sobbed she put her hand upon the face
> of the man and had always the same thought. Even though he were
> large and bearded she thought he had become suddenly a little boy.
> She wondered why he did not sob also. (p. 46)

The full significance of this, from "Mother," comes only at the end
of "Death" in which George is the last of the series. Once again
there is a synergetic combination of the typological perspective
with the quest for recovery of childhood. Malcolm Cowley once
made an observation about Anderson that is true, in the terms
meant, but also points to the effects of typological thinking: "Time
as a logical succession of events was Anderson's greatest difficulty
in writing novels or even long stories. He got his tenses confused
and carried his heroes ten years forward or back in a single paragraph. His instinct was to present everything together, as in a
dream."[34] So typology even helps account for the dreamlike quality
of the essential structure. And why not? The same objections could
be made to the typology of Paul or the Christian fathers: their
thought is, in the structuralist term for myth, a machine for the
abolition of time — and so, of course, is a dream. Anderson's clumsiness was not the only cause of his temporal inconsistencies; he
was using the child's sense of things as a typological instrument.
Finally, note how the passage above resembles some of Lawrence's
in its use of time: as at Morel's breakfast, a recurrent action is
given the quality of a unique event. So even that imperfect-tense

34. Ferres, p. 360.

effect has typological connections; the events of the Bible are both historically true, hence past, and yet forever present in the immediacy of the ongoing revelation for the believer. Typology, even in the folk forms in which Anderson would have known it, is in more than one way a template for the journey to the "land of lost content."

The passage also leads to consideration of yet another important Andersonian motif. The inner boyishness of the lovers comes forth at the touch of Elizabeth's hand: in *Winesburg*, as many critics have noticed, hands often speak more eloquently than lips, and what their gestures signify is more meaningful; in fact, they always imply the inadequacy of words. In "Death," recalling Elizabeth's quest for meaning, Anderson describes it thus:

> In her girlhood and young womanhood Elizabeth had tried to be a real adventurer in life. At eighteen life had so gripped her that she was no longer a virgin but, although she had a half dozen lovers before she married Tom Willard, she had never entered upon an adventure prompted by desire alone. Like all the women in the world, she wanted a real lover. Always there was something she sought blindly, passionately, some hidden wonder in life. The tall beautiful girl with the swinging stride who had walked under the trees with men was forever putting out her hand into the darkness and trying to get hold of some other hand. (p. 224)

In Anderson the questing spirit is always a woman, or — as in the case of George Willard — the female or maternal side of a man, and the gestural motif of the quest is the reaching hand. Indeed, hands are as typological as the characters themselves. Elizabeth's questing hand has its counterpart in almost every story, from that of the feminine Wing Biddlebaum ("Hands") onward.

The passage above continues: "In all the babble of words that fell from the lips of the men with whom she adventured she was trying to find what would be for her the true word." The true word can never be spoken, but the quest for it can be figured in the hands that reach out to touch lovers' faces or grasp their hands. When she hallucinates Death as a lover, Elizabeth thinks "that death like a living thing put out his hand to her. 'Be patient, lover,' she whispered" (p. 228). Because Death is typologically identified with her son, the last of her lovers, the reaching gesture also underlines the maternal aspect of the quest. Sons, who imply the deaths of their mothers, incarnate the quests in themselves, and ultimately the quest is for the door back into childhood, that is, back into the warm world of maternal care.

In following such maternal–sexual quests, the women in *Winesburg* are avatars of the mother: the two Louises, Kate Swift, the "tall dark girl" who married Dr. Reefy, and several others have this aspect. Even the unseen Nell Gunther in "The Untold Lie," who is reflected only in the dialogue between the two farmhands of the story (another occulted woman), should be classed as such a quester from what we can infer about her. And Belle Carpenter in "An Awakening" takes George Willard as a substitute lover in much the same way that Clara Dawes takes Paul Morel. All of these women are adventurous in Anderson's sense but also, by conventional standards, sexually suggestible or even roundheeled. They are not "nice girls." Their presence caused the book to be denounced as "a sewer" early on; Anderson claimed he got a letter from the wife of a banker acquaintance who said that after reading it she would never feel clean again.[35] But there is nothing erotic, much less sordid, about any of these stories. Many missed Anderson's repeated statements that for these questers love was a substitute.

Of the group of women who are not merely incidental to the stories, Kate Swift is perhaps the nearest to a fully realized, autonomous character in her several appearances. Yet, tellingly, her most memorable role is as occulted woman (object of a sexual fantasy, like Louise Trunnion) in "The Strength of God," in which she catches the eye of a minister as he writes sermons in his bell-tower study next to her house. She is seen first, scandalously, smoking a cigarette, then in various states of undress. The story seems to be about the minister's simpleminded prurience and his fight against it, but in a key sentence we are told that when he finally sees her naked on her bed, she is wildly agitated for no visible reason: "She wept and beat with her fists upon the pillow" (p. 155). This remains unexplained in the story; we have to read the next one, "The Teacher," to learn more about her agitation.

> The people of the town thought of her as a confirmed old maid. . . .
> In reality she was the most eagerly passionate soul among them, and more than once, in the five years since she had come back from her travels to settle in Winesburg and become a school teacher, had been

35. Ferres, pp. 17–18.

compelled to go out of the house and walk half through the night
fighting out some battle raging within. (p. 162)

In "The Teacher" Kate's quest is channeled into a half-sexual
urge to "blow on the spark" of talent within George Willard. She
shares Anderson's mistrust of glibness: "'If you are to become a
writer you'll have to stop fooling with words,'" she tells him. "'You
must not become a mere peddler of words. The thing to learn is to
know what people are thinking about, not what they say'" (p. 163).
Like a good Freudian the teacher knows that all utterances have
undergone encrypting and displacement; moreover, her advice curiously recapitulates what the boy's mother had wanted to say to
him all her life. In "Mother," George has developed a dreamy habit
of talking to himself, which gives Elizabeth a "peculiar pleasure."
To herself she thinks, "'He is not a dull clod, all words and smartness'" (p. 43). Though both women naturally fail to put into words
what they really want to tell him, a strange wisdom is implanted in
him nonetheless. He satisfies his mother's dreams (though she can
communicate them only by saying their very opposite) when he
declares "'I just want to go away and look at people and think'"
(p. 48). Similarly, he concludes that he has missed whatever Kate
Swift was trying to tell him, but it grows within him (p. 166).[36]

These interchanges have an obvious confessional aspect, and refer to Anderson's sense of his destiny to be a writer — one who
would go away to look at faces and think up fantasies to explain
them. The famous story that he grasped his destiny by simply walking away one day from his paint factory is of course too simple,
though he did have some form of nervous breakdown and did
escape from business into advertising and thence into writing, making himself the Gauguin of American fiction. It was for him a
removal from the world of facts to that of dreams, which meant a
return to childhood and the hometown of memory. As he put it in
a letter of 1921:

> I wish it would not sound to[o] silly to say I pour a dream over it
> [the town] consciously, intentionally, for a purpose. I want to write
> beautifully, create beautifully, not outside but in this thing in which I
> am born, in this place where . . . I have always lived, must always
> live.[37]

36. Compare the ending of this story with the ending of Joyce's "The Dead."
37. Sutton, p. 17.

This association of the town, the dream writing, and maternal-gestational images holds the key to his inspiration. *Winesburg* is dedicated "to the memory of my mother, Emma Smith Anderson, whose keen observations on the life about her first awoke in me the hunger to see beneath the surface of lives." In this instance, the dedication to the "memory" of the mother is more than a conventional gesture of piety; and since "beneath" here means projection of fantasies "behind every face" rather than any probing of aetiologies, it is clear that the mother's keen observations were of the type that spurred the boy's imaginative rather than his perceptive or analytical faculties.[38] From the first story on, George Willard is urged by one or another of the grotesques to forget "talk" and to cultivate "dreams." This project is given a maternal cast even before "Mother" (that telling title with its missing article!) In "The Book of the Grotesque" the old writer who dreams of the grotesques has something "inside him":

> He was like a pregnant woman, only that the thing inside him was not a baby but a youth. No, it wasn't a youth, it was a woman, young, and wearing a coat of mail like a knight. It is absurd, you see, to try to tell what was inside the old writer as he lay on his high bed and listened to the fluttering of his heart. The thing to get at is what the writer, or the young thing within the writer, was thinking about. (p. 24)

This passage, with its metamorphosing and androgynous figure "inside" the writer, calls out as displaced psycho-autobiography. And the last sentence is repeated with variations in Kate Swift's advice to George ("The thing to learn is to know what people are thinking about, not what they say"). So we are being urged to look for the deflections in the stories themselves — or to paraphrase Lawrence, never trust the artist or the tale either, look into them both for something within — as well as being given directions for understanding why the grotesques never are able to say what they mean.

But the key point is that Anderson's figure for "the buried life" is pregnancy, so that by his dream logic, the son-lover is impregnated by the mother figures.[39] The mother herself darkly recognizes

38. Anderson's mother was also tall and dark; see Sutton, p. 502.

39. On Anderson's use of pregnancy as a figure for artistic gestation, see Sutton, pp. 339, 458.

this. When she rejoices that he is "not a dull clod, all words and smartness," her inner rumination continues: "'Within him there is a secret something that is striving to grow. It is the thing I let be killed in myself.'" Her precious inarticulate gift is not advice, still less the money; it is a love that impregnates, and is nurtured in gestation by Kate Swift and the others. As Joyce hinted in his works that the feminine or maternal was the ultimate source of the artist's language and power, so Anderson pays his tribute by reversing the roles in the Lawrentian version of the Oedipal drama.

Anderson often asserted that his stories issued from visions, "dreams," "pure feeling," a dulling of the conscious and critical faculties and a subordination of them to fantasy.

> Again I begin the endless game of reconstructing my own life, jerking it out of the shell that dies, striving to breathe into it beauty and meaning [note that Paul Morel metaphor]. When I was a boy I lived in a town in Ohio and often I wandered away to lie upon my back, thinking, as I am doing now. I reconstruct and begin to color and illuminate incidents of my life there. Words said, shouts of children, the barking of dogs at night, occasional flashes of beauty in the eyes of women and old men, are remembered.[40]

The reconstruction and "coloring" of incidents that gave him the stories seemed to him a progenitive project, a series of birth-giving fantasies. So he identifies with the mother's lifeworld, although on other occasions he announced that his father's fabulistic propensities had engendered his own. But the male realm was for him predominantly a soulless domain of business, facts, and calculation, whereas the type of the artist was female. His marriage to a woman artist (Tennessee Mitchell, who had been Edgar Lee Masters' mistress) worked out no better than his others, but she did symbolize creativity for him, and those years (1916 to 1923) were his most fruitful period: four novels, a volume of poetry, many stories.

Poetry was another word that for Anderson had associations with the maternalistic, creative, visionary world of childhood recaptured. He often thought of himself as a poet in prose, and so did his best early critics. Rebecca West, reviewing *Winesburg* in 1922, admitted that it had deficiencies as fiction:

40. Sutton, pp. 17–18.

> But it is not fiction. It is poetry. It is unreasonable; it delights in places where those who are not poets could never find delight; it will not follow logic and find connections and trace "plots," but stands in front of things that are of no importance, infatuated with their quality, and hymns them with obstinate ecstasy; it seems persuaded that there is beauty in anything, in absolutely anything.[41]

West caught several important facets, including the dream logic, but her sense of the "obstinate" celebratory, unselective mode was most perceptive. Here Anderson owed much to Whitman, our pre-eminent loafer and dreamer, but also, again, to Joyce: Ezra Pound had diagnosed the inner Joyce as "the sensitive, the [poet]," and his sense of the necessary crossbreeding between poetry and prose has already been discussed in relation to Hardy. (Faulkner's opinion was that all novelists were failed poets.)[42] What Rebecca West identified as poetic in *Winesburg* was certainly Joycean, corresponding to Joyce's urge to find more and more meaning in things less and less important, to find Blake's infinity in a grain of sand.

In *Winesburg* "poetry" means finding significance in the trivial, but it also has strange connections with violence. At first this seems to contradict Anderson's own gentleness and his reverence for the maternal, but — by a Whitmanian logic of inclusiveness — violence must be celebrated as part of life; after all, Whitman hymned even the suicide "sprawl[ed] on the bloody floor of the bedroom."[43] We first notice this conjunction in the early pages of "Godliness," where Jesse's four older brothers are described on their Saturday afternoon forays into Winesburg.

> It was difficult for them to talk and so they for the most part kept silent. When they had bought meat, flour, sugar, and salt, they went into one of the Winesburg saloons and drank beer. Under the influence of drink the naturally strong lusts of their natures, kept suppressed by the heroic labor of breaking up new ground, were released. A kind of crude and animal-like poetic fervor took possession of them. On the road home they stood up on the wagon seats and shouted at the stars.

41. Ferres, p. 262; cf. Sutton, p. 341.
42. Pound, see Forrest Read, ed., *Pound/Joyce* (New Directions, 1970), p. 178; Faulkner, see James B. Meriwether and Michael Millgate, eds., *Lion in the Garden: Interviews with William Faulkner 1926–1962* (Random House, 1968), pp. 217, 238.
43. "Song of Myself," 8 (l. 152).

> Sometimes they fought long and bitterly and at other times they broke
> forth into songs. (p. 65)

One of them almost commits parricide in one such outburst of
"poetic fervor," from which violence and song are equally likely
results. The brothers are typical denizens of Andersoniana, inarticulate and driven; like their fellows they let their hands do most of
the talking for them. Their baffled urges foreshadow the end of
"Godliness," so that we see young David as a true kinsman of theirs
when he strikes at his grandfather with a slung stone. Perhaps the
linkage of violence and song owes something to the Biblical David's
eminence as both warrior and psalmist.

If we turn from this to an apparently puzzling passage in "The
Untold Lie," we see again a typological interillumination. In that
story, an older farmhand is stumped by a problem, of what advice
to give his fellow laborer who has "got Nell Gunther in trouble."
Should he confess, as he half-believes, that marriage is a trap?

> Along the path to his own house he trudged behind his wife, looking at
> the ground and thinking. He couldn't make out what was wrong. Every
> time he raised his eyes and saw the beauty of the country in the failing
> light he wanted to do something he had never done before, shout or
> scream or hit his wife with his fists or something equally unexpected
> and terrifying. Along the path he went scratching his head and trying
> to make it out. (p. 206)

His "poetic fervor" of response to the beauty of the countryside
becomes an impulse toward familial violence, as with Jesse's brothers, a declaration of a desire to return to an irresponsible boyhood.
(Note that Anderson like Lawrence sees archetypal power in domestic violence, but does not use it to condemn the father.) Of
course the "hand" is also frustrated by the mystery of what to say
about marriage. When he tries to speak his feelings to the younger
man, he loses his nerve, only to find that the problem has been
solved: the young rakehell has decided to reform, to "settle down
and have kids." The older man wisely concludes: "Whatever I told
him would have been a lie" (p. 209). Whether we say yea or nay,
we can never be inclusive enough. Moreover, though marriage is
no solution to the problem, the life-force will have its way; Anderson was heir to both Lawrence and the naturalists. (In *Sons and
Lovers* Mrs. Morel keeps getting pregnant despite her ever-deepen-
ing estrangement from her husband.)

What Anderson seems to be saying is that there is a weird beauty even in the moments of violence to which these inarticulate farmers and townsmen are prone. All readers of *Winesburg* will think of the story "Queer" in this connection. The most baffled and confused of all the Winesburgers is a young man named Elmer Cowley. His father is an ineffectual merchant whose person, store, and business practices have become a laughingstock; Elmer can't understand why and is determined not to be similarly labeled *queer* (not homosexual but laughably eccentric). He finds it impossible to "declare his determination not to be queer," although he tries to communicate his predicament to George Willard. Just before leaving town to run away from his problem, he demands that George listen to him once more, but when he starts to speak, he can only bring forth his father's hackneyed expression, picked up from a halfwit: "'I'll be washed and ironed and starched'" (p. 200). So, in frustrated fury, Elmer starts hitting George, and this gives him just enough release to cry as he jumps aboard the train, "'I guess I showed him. I ain't so queer. I guess I showed him I ain't so queer.'" The story can be glossed with a line from Williams: "The pure products of America go crazy."[44] And with *Billy Budd*—but that was published only after *Winesburg*, so do we have more telepathy? Presumably George Willard learns something from the furious assault, even in a sense something loving: it has its own strange beauty, and it relates to other episodes in which love and violence intermingle.

Winesburg can be seen as a celebration of the poetry of the inarticulate even when that rouses or turns to violence, when it is expressed with the fists: thus it becomes part of the theme of groping, searching hands, so familiar to all readers of the book.[45] We can now look back at the thematic story, "Hands," in which Wing Biddlebaum's homoerotic leanings as well as his belief in the necessity of "dreams" are communicated to George Willard through his poetic hands.

> The story of Wing Biddlebaum is a story of hands. Their restless nature, like unto the beating of the wings of an imprisoned bird, had given him

44. "Spring and All," XVIII; also known as "To Elsie."
45. Waldo Frank in Ferres, p. 371; David Anderson in Ferres, pp. 424–25.

his name. Some obscure poet of the town had thought of it. . . .
Sympathetically set forth [the story] would tap many strange, beautiful
qualities in obscure men. It is a job for a poet. (pp. 28–29)

So already in this, the first story set in the Winesburg locale, the
premise of "mute inglorious Miltons" in the village is latent; they
are all synecdochically represented by the narrator, but also by
Wing's own hands. Wing uses the hands only gently, but is driven
from his Pennsylvania home by lynchers, rope in hand, inflamed
by rumors of pederasty. Yet even this ugly, misconceived violence
has a tang of poetry to it, a gesture of violent passion by those
who have no other way to express themselves.

Part of the premise of *Winesburg*, as Rebecca West's sharp eye
discerned, is that hatred and ugliness and violence can have their
own beauty. This theme is brought forward most explicitly in "Respectability," the story of the town telegraph operator, Wash Williams. The opening compares him with a repellent monkey, "with
ugly, sagging, hairless skin below his eyes and a bright purple un-
derbody." Like the monkey, Wash is fascinating in his repulsiveness. "In the completeness of his ugliness he achieved a kind of
perverted beauty." Wash has deliberately cultivated an unkempt,
dirty appearance to go with his eunuchoid "immense girth" and
"feeble legs": "Everything about him was unclean. Even the whites
of his eyes looked soiled." Yet, revealingly, he "took care of his
hands," which were strangely "sensitive and shapely" (p. 121). They
represent the kernel of beauty that inheres even in the most grotesque creatures.

Wash's physical ugliness manifests a consuming inner hatred of
self and others, but this too has a "poetic fervor" to it. "Wash
Williams was a man of courage. A thing had happened to him
that made him hate life, and he hated it whole-heartedly, with the
abandon of a poet. First of all, he hated women" (p. 122). He tells
George Willard how he had been betrayed by a young wife—no
doubt another seeker—whom he drove away; she turned to other
men because Wash worshipped and pedestalized her, grovelled in
front of her, kissed her shoes, and trembled when the hem of her
garment touched his face (a Biblical touch). Worse still, the girl's
mother sought to reconcile them after the separation by pushing
the girl, naked, into a room where he waited aching "to forgive

and forget." Wash is, in the story, still so repulsed by this shameful device that he declares "all women are dead, my mother, your mother, that tall dark woman who works in the millinery store and with whom I saw you walking about yesterday—all of them, they are all dead" (p. 124). Anderson allows him to work himself up into a diseased denunciation of women as "rotten," "creeping, crawling, squirming things." Yet even in this Hitlerian hymn of nausea the narrator finds a "perverted beauty." "There was something almost beautiful in the voice of Wash Williams, the hideous, telling his story of hate. . . . [He] had become a poet. Hatred had raised him to that elevation." If the fool would persist in his folly he would become wise.

The sentence in which Wash asserts that all women are dead is worth rereading for its adumbration of typological linkages: "my mother, your mother, that tall dark woman." Wash's surreal litany of hatred runs them all together, culminating in the "tall dark" figure. Wash's series is a perverse variation of the child's proto-typological vision, as well as his awe at a world in which adults are more powers than personalities and in which violence is fascinating in spite of its fearfulness (cf. Stephen Dedalus at Christmas dinner, or Paul Morel, *passim*). Wash's violent hatred is an essentialization of the child's responses to felt betrayals, particularly by the mother.

This complicates the relation of the maternal to the violent, but it is already complicated in "Mother." Trying to prevent her son the dreamer, an Old Testament Joseph figure, from being misled by his father into a business career—the father is a would-be Babbitt *avant la lettre* who wants to make the boy "smart" and "awake"—she determines to stab her husband. She takes out a pair of sewing scissors and holds them like a dagger. "As a tigress whose cub had been threatened would she appear, coming out of the shadows, stealing noiselessly along and holding the long wicked scissors in her hand" (p. 47). Fortunately George forestalls her murderous plan by coming in to tell her of his decision to go away. But the gesture of maternal ferocity is as telling as that of maternal solicitude, of reaching out to touch son's and lovers' faces. From it we can deduce the meaning of the baffled violence in the acts of the women of Winesburg who are seekers and adventurers: all the beating of pillows, mad drives, naked runs. These are yet another poetry, that of frustration. Just as the male isolatoes of the town momentarily break free of their self-imposed bonds to tell George Willard their stories, so the women break out into parabolic acts that release their pent-up frenzies.

Besides illuminating the connections between the violent, the poetic, and the maternal, such motifs form part of a larger tableau: the inarticulateness of the people of *Winesburg*, the condition that enables their "poetry," leads to a vision of their being somewhat puppetlike; they are all moved by forces of which they have little or no understanding. Anderson displayed small overt interest in naturalistic determinism, yet recurrently he postulated biological and social forces that carry his characters along like leaves on a stream. His version of the era's fascination with atavism combines a vague sense of "animal" forces with an elegiac awareness of the passing of rural culture. Waldo Frank pointed out the importance of this latter perspective on his work:

> Sherwood Anderson liked to think of himself as a primitive or neo-primitive artist; as a naive unlettered storyteller. The truth is, that he belonged at the end of a cultural process. . . . That world was already drooping when it crossed the ocean; it had been, in England, a world of revealed religion and sacramental marriage, of the May dance and the sense of each man's life as mystery and mission. It lives in the past of *Winesburg*; it has become a beat and a refrain in the blood. In the actual experience of these men and women, it is a recidivism, a lapse away into organic echoes.[46]

By "recidivism" here, Frank means the preservation of forms of social life, based on religion, without the continuation of their original essence and meaning. "Sacramental marriage" illustrates his point, by 1900 a mere shell of its former self. So Anderson, by his account, was an elegiac artist, singing the passing of a world, and — in the age of naturalism — rendering accounts of human acts and motives with suggestions of biological explanations that fill out the emptiness of the forms.

At times Anderson does sound almost behavioristic. His characters are not rounded, in Forster's sense, because they derive from childhood apprehensions, so that they are forces rather than personalities; but also because they have no innerness that they can themselves comprehend. They don't even get ideas: ideas, and de-

46. Ferres, p. 374.

sires, get them, and dominate until they are exorcised. "Certain vague desires that had been invading her body" (p. 141) move Helen White in "The Thinker." Or, in the "Surrender" part of "Godliness": "The mind of the country girl became filled with the idea of drawing close to the young man" (p. 91). When Alice Hindman runs naked in the rain, it is because "mad desire . . . took possession of her"; one page earlier, "a passionate restlessness took possession of Alice" (pp. 118–19). Over and over the same trope, culminating in "Sophistication," in which "the sadness of sophistication has come to the boy." In this story George and Helen become "excited little animals," and Anderson allows himself one of his most unfortunate *sententiae*: "In youth there are always two forces fighting in people. The warm unthinking little animal struggles against the thing that reflects and remembers," and so on (p. 240). The use of "thing" here is characteristic.

Even the most verbal of the Winesburgers, Joe Welling, in "A Man of Ideas," is possessed by words, is the slave and not the master of them. "He was beset by ideas and in the throes of one of his ideas was uncontrollable. Words rolled and tumbled from his mouth" (p. 103). As a blind pig sometimes finds an acorn, Welling occasionally stumbles on an interesting insight, only to be carried away from it by a new rush of words. Heidegger's aphorism that language speaks itself through us is literally true for him: he cannot say what he wants to say, but only what words bid him. In "An Awakening," George Willard has a visitation with overtones that suggest that he too is at the mercy of obscure forces. "He had never before thought such thoughts as had just come into his head and he wondered where they had come from. For the moment it seemed to him that some voice outside of himself had been talking as he walked" (p. 183).

In furtherance of this trope Anderson does not simply use the passive construction: he abuses it. In "Loneliness," the story of Enoch Robinson the childlike artist, "two children were born to the woman he married" (p. 171). The wording underscores the nature of Enoch, absent in his own life, so self-absorbed that he is hardly aware of his wife, still less of impregnating her. The passive voice shows the Winesburgers at the mercy of forces that their moribund culture does not let them understand. (The title of one of Anderson's later works was *Puzzled America*.) And often the removal of agents from actions corresponds to the child's sense of the immediacy of what occurs around him: only with some training does he learn to think in our causative way. Here is an interesting passage from "Mother":

> In the evening when the son sat in the room with his mother, the silence made them both feel awkward. Darkness came on and the evening train came in at the station. In the street below feet tramped up and down upon a board sidewalk. In the station yard, after the evening train had gone, there was a heavy silence. Perhaps Skinner Leason, the express agent, moved a truck the length of the station platform. Over on Main Street sounded a man's voice, laughing. The door of the express office banged. (p. 42)

The disembodied noises are magnified by the silence between the two. But although their communion is inhibited and inarticulate, the narration preserves the child's instinctive wide-eyed responsiveness to the immediate stimuli around him. The oral lifeworld of the child is dynamic, dramatic, intensely personal, and mysterious. (Hence the overexcited confusion and culture shock of rural people in big cities, where the inhabitants learn to train themselves in sensory deprivation: in New York one must learn to ignore all eye contact and all noises, even screams.) The child's world, in contrast, resembles that of preliterate cultures, and *Winesburg* is full of parallels to this condition. The child perceives all beings, human and other, as parts of a fluid panorama of ultimately inscrutable powers. He does not learn until later to reduce beings to personalities, still later to abstractions. The isolatoes and seekers of *Winesburg* are reversions to this wonder-filled realm. Though they lack the solidity and credibility that more competent but less inspired fictionists could have devised for them, they have some of the mysterious compelling force of beings in cave or rock art. And though their language fails them, they have a poetry of inarticulateness such as a grown man himself feels in trying to recapture them. For him this gives them their strange beauty even when, by "normal" standards, they are twisted or truncated.

Anderson's judgment on Sinclair Lewis highlights his own reversion. "Wanting perhaps to see beauty descend upon our lives like a rainstorm, [he] has become blind to the minor beauties our lives hold."[47] Where Lewis saw mostly the numbing insularity and spiritual bankruptcy of the Midwestern town, Anderson takes the Whitmanian line. In the early decades of the century, critics often aligned the two as part of the "revolt against the village," but the remark above makes it clear that any social criticism in *Winesburg* is incidental to the inclusivist vision. Anderson cried out against constricting and trivializing forces, but even these cries were almost lost in his wonder. "One shudders at the thought of the meaninglessness of life while at the same instant, and if the people of the town are his people, one loves life so intensely that tears come into the eyes": a mawkish but revealing sentence. The difference between the two writers is that Anderson in the very act of writing was recovering his own childhood. The emotion of rediscovery, the wonder of finding again that which has been lost, is the joy that powers the work. Herbert Gold captured it in a memorable image: "He carried his childhood like a hurt warm bird held to his middle-aged breast as he walked out of his factory into the life of art."[48]

*   *   *   *   *   *   *   *

The idea that the best American writers of this century are deeply indebted to Anderson has been voiced repeatedly, yet the insights that come from seeing them as "sons of Sherwood" have been neglected recently. Malcolm Cowley put the standard claim for Anderson's paternity most succinctly:

> He soon became a writer's writer, the only story-teller of his generation who left his mark on the style and vision of the generation that followed. Hemingway, Faulkner, Wolfe . . . each of these owes an unmistakable debt to Anderson, and their names might stand for dozens of others. Hemingway was regarded as his disciple in 1920, when both men were living on the Near North Side of Chicago, Faulkner says that he had written very little, "poems and just amateur things," before meeting Anderson in 1925 and becoming, for a time, his inseparable companion. Looking at Anderson he thought to himself, "Being a writer must be a wonderful life." He set to work on his first novel,

47. Ferres, p. 402.
48. Ferres, p. 404.

Soldier's Pay, for which Anderson found a publisher after the two men had ceased to be friends. Thomas Wolfe proclaimed in 1936 that Anderson was "the only man in America who ever taught me anything"; but they quarreled a year later, and Wolfe shouted that Anderson had shot his bolt, that he was done as a writer. All his disciples left him sooner or later, so that his influence was chiefly on their early work, but still it was decisive. He opened doors for all of them and gave them faith in themselves.[49]

But the real gift was not so much the faith in themselves as in the hints of ways to regain the personal past. Access to childhood and adolescent feelings is demonstrably the key to Nick Adams, Quentin Compson, Eugene Gant, and other personae. Anderson unleashed a flood of subjectivism in American literature: if Hemingway and Faulkner and Wolfe and even Fitzgerald made their work out of their own youthful experiences (in a way that would have baffled and irritated, say, Henry James), much of the credit or blame must go to *Winesburg* and Anderson's other early stories in which the "island of the past" is re-created.

It is true, as Cowley's remark about Faulkner indicates, that he gave them a model to follow, an example of achievement and dedication that made them believe in the possibility of a writer's life. They all had dreams of literary glory, and were hero worshippers; Anderson proved to be a salutary hero, just what they needed. He was plainspoken yet devoted to craft, simple yet painstaking. And when he befriended them, he really did try to nurture their talents, rather than turn them into epigones. For this he was repaid, as Cowley notes, with rejection and ridicule. If such acts were inevitable declarations of independence, they still were petty. When his young friends repudiated or mocked him, Anderson did not reply in kind. He was hurt but not bitter, and he recognized that their talents transcended their personal failings. (The writers who followed him — at least the four just mentioned — all were more important than he, but there are only a few accounts of their helping still younger writers.) It may be that Anderson's generosity was due to his own sense that, as Wolfe said, he had shot his bolt, and would do as much for his own immortality by helping fresh talents as by cultivating his own: still he looks good, morally speaking,

49. Ferres, p. 357.

next to his former friends. (Yet they were all moralists, and probably distrusted him all the more because he seemed so nonjudgmental.) He was more subjective and self-absorbed than they, yet much less competitive and anxious about his supremacy: and generous almost to a fault, whatever the cause.

Anderson suffered a common fate in America, one that consists of early lionization and then unrealistic expectations from the public; typically, for writers, performance anxiety follows, leaving a mixed and regretful record. But why do we always ask that writers surpass themselves? Why should they be punished by having their early creditable works thrown up to them later? Why do we watch so closely for signs of decline? Are we like those ancient cultures in which the king's potency in the sacred intercourse is monitored for signs that the crops will fail? We seem to have an exaggerated psychic investment in the continuing productivity of writers, and we are quick with the term *has-been*: contrast our reluctant use of *master*. Apparently we are so eager to disown our image of ourselves as Philistines that we demand great crops of talent from our land. The result is that—to use Leslie Fiedler's borrowed aphorism—nothing fails like success, for American writers. So also with artists. One critic mordantly commented that the American avantgarde "will buy an artist until it kills him."[50] We shower attention on young unknowns, and later scorn them petulantly if they falter. Their usual recourse is to turn themselves into self-publicizing "media stars." But Anderson did no such thing; he lived out his decline with relative equanimity. Indeed, the lionization pattern took its worst toll not on him but on those who followed him and repaid him so badly for his good deeds, particularly Hemingway. Instead of his hoar head going down to the grave in peace, secure in friends and honors, Hemingway endured a sad, often desperate afterlife of celebrity. Among his many haunting guilty memories must have been his treatment of Anderson; moreover, he must have realized that the decay he so mercilessly forecast for Anderson, by satirizing his clumsinesses in *The Torrents of Spring*, had materialized in his own career.

Anderson himself concealed debts, as remarked earlier, and his

50. Thomas Hess, in Gregory Battcock, ed., *The New Art: A Critical Anthology* (Dutton, 1966), pp. 167–68.

disciples' backbiting must have covered over their own sense of indebtedness. They no doubt felt belated, for each of the young writers began, or first succeeded, with some form of the past-recaptured theme. Fitzgerald's debt is the least obvious, yet *This Side of Paradise*, although a breathy romance and not a real *Bildungsroman*, is his portrait of the artist as a young Prince(tonian). His later and more important work falls into dilemmas of self-dramatization that the Andersonian quest obviated. Thus Dick Diver's decline, in *Tender Is the Night*, is really Fitzgerald trying to explain to himself his own victimization by early success and his subsequent baffled, alcoholic anomie. In contrast, Andersonian motifs buoy the most lyrical moments of *Gatsby*, as when Nick grasps the relevance of geography, reasserts his Midwestern origins, and like Stephen Dedalus retravels the journeys home from school at Christmas:

> I remember the fur coats of the girls returning from Miss This-or-That's and the chatter of frozen breath and the hands waving overhead as we caught sight of old acquaintances, and the matchings of invitations: "Are you going to the Ordways'? the Herseys'? the Schultzes'?" and the long green tickets clasped tight in our gloved hands.

But in the sophisticated, meretricious East, those names have degenerated into the list of strangers who came to Gatsby's parties — the Cheadles and the Beckers and the Leeches — while the tickets have become merely "long green," the cash nexus of the world of bond salesmen and bootleggers. So the childhood world remained the locus of inner warmth, and transferred to the moralized and maternally eroticized landscape of unspoiled America, it became the vision of the last page of the book. Like Gatsby, we don't realize that our dream is already behind us, "somewhere back in that vast obscurity beyond the city, where the dark fields of the republic rolled on under the night."[51]

*   *   *   *   *   *   *   *

From Faulkner Anderson elicited admiration, imitation, and finally satiric rejection, but for the latter he made some amends by

51. *The Great Gatsby* (Scribner, 1953; originally published, 1925), pp. 176–77, 182.

offering a posthumous tribute. His memoir tells of what he learned from conversations with Anderson in New Orleans parks and bars; of their spontaneous collaboration to produce a Midamerican mythology about a "half-horse half-alligator [and now] half-shark" descendant of Andrew Jackson, left in the swamp after the Battle of New Orleans; and of Anderson's offer to recommend Faulkner's first novel for publication if he were excused from reading it. But the central advice that Faulkner remembered was the exhortation toward the local:

> "You have to have somewhere to start from. . . . It dont matter where it was, just so you remember it and aint ashamed of it. Because one place to start from is just as important as any other. You're a country boy; all you know is that little patch up there in Mississippi where you started from. But that's all right too."[52]

So it was Anderson who gave the hint that expanded the "little patch," the Compson square mile, into Yoknapatawpha County. Compare "one place to start from is just as important as any other" with Joyce's observation that Dublin for him was the particular that contained the universal. Faulkner's admiration for Joyce may have preceded Anderson's lesson, but it would hardly be just to depreciate the latter's catalytic role.[53]

The case of Faulkner raises a question, as to whether the Andersonian recapture of the personal past may not be an evasion of the task of confronting a larger, societal past.[54] Anderson claimed to

52. Ferres, pp. 491–92. Faulkner left few traces of specific debts to Anderson, but he did once describe *Absalom, Absalom* as a story "of a man who wanted a son through pride," which sounds like a memory of "Godliness." See David Minter, *William Faulkner: His Life and Work* (Johns Hopkins University Press, 1980), p. 145.

53. Faulkner sometimes denied having read *Ulysses* (to Henry Nash Smith, *Lion in the Garden*, p. 30). But at other times he admitted having read it "once" (*Lion*, pp. 197, 284). He knew it well enough to crib a poem for his mistress out of Stephen's gypsy ballad; see Minter, *William Faulkner*, p. 163; and *Ulysses* (Vintage Books, 1961; originally published, 1922), p. 47 (in the Gabler ed., 3.380). No doubt, given his rhetorical propensities, Falkner responded most sympathetically to Stephen's poetic monologue (cf. *Lion in the Garden*, p. 56: "My prose is really poetry"). Note also Faulkner's Joycean sense of the potentialities of colloquial language, and the fact that the art of both is that of accretion: a third of *Ulysses* was written on the proofs.

54. T. S. Eliot, among others, believed that the personal past was significant only as a window onto a cultural past. See Cairns Craig, *Yeats, Eliot, Pound and*

be telling the story of America, as Faulkner of the South, but both were thematically and philosophically imprisoned in their private sensibilities. Writers have no duties to their birthplaces, but again, if we compare as Trilling suggests the specificities of Lawrence's or Joyce's worlds with those of Winesburg or Jefferson, we can easily see the greater subjectivity of the Americans' work. No one has grappled more continuously with the "burden of Southern history" than Faulkner, no one has been more haunted by the dilemma of the meaning of the past; but his most Southern trait is his evasion of real history in favor of a quest for an imaginary world. Thus Anderson brought out only what was latent in him. The "history" of the South for its denizens is a combination of legend, theology, and kinship systems, like some archaic tribal epic. To know the South adds piquancy to Faulkner's work, but mainly because his South is as mythological as the average Southerner's — and both are also mythological in the sense that would have angered Mark Twain: demanding devotion to chivalric mystifications à la Scott, whose influence is deplored at great length in *Life on the Mississippi*. (Not by chance is the wrecked steamer in *Huck Finn* called the *Walter Scott*; it prefigures the highminded senselessness of the feuding Grangerfords and Shepherdsons.) Faulkner's South, like Hawthorne's New England, is an imaginary realm in which ancestral guilts may be worked through as impingements on the childlike sensitivities of the romancer's personae.

André Gide is often quoted to the effect that Faulkner's characters had no souls, meaning that they don't make moral choices but instead are driven, "doomed," possessed, programmed like robots.[55] To appreciate this observation, it helps to know that the region is populated by Scotch–Irish Calvinists, and this heritage forces individuals to suspect themselves constantly of falling into degeneracy. They don't have to commit actual sins; guilt is not in question, but eternal damnation is. If they feel certain urges, many

---

the Politics of Poetry (Croom Helm, 1982), esp. p. 132. On Faulkner's sense of the past in the present, see Hugh Kenner, *A Homemade World: The American Modernist Writers* (Knopf, 1975), p. 198: Faulkner told Malcolm Cowley that his ambition was to put everything into one sentence, "'not only the present but the whole past on which it depends and which keeps overtaking the present, second by second.'"

55. *Lion in the Garden*, p. 94; and Harold Bloom, ed., *William Faulkner: Modern Critical Views* (Chelsea, 1986), p. 5.

conclude they are predestined to hell and give themselves up to
"depravities"—sexual, alcoholic, whatever—and some (the literary
ones) even turn Catholic to get out from under Calvin's shadow.
There is a well-known linkage between this mentality and a high
incidence of fanaticism. Mississippi is not an easygoing, tolerant
place—or only so for good ole boys. And the fanatics are as self-
doomed as stiffnecked. Caddy Compson is no more a sensualist
than Quentin is; she simply assumes she is lost. Her daughter Quentin makes this explicit: "I'm bad and I'm going to hell, and I don't
care. I'd rather be in hell than anywhere where you [Jason] are."[56]

Faulkner's characters are often grotesques compounded from
childhood memories of the more vivid of these people, not realistic
in any helpful sense but rather, as in *Winesburg*, representing
forces more than personalities. Faulkner's subjectivism is not as
annihilating as Anderson's, but he is an artist of caricature, like
Dickens, and his playful collaboration with Anderson in spinning
tall tales of semihuman creatures is more diagnostic for his work
than any amount of regional sociology. Both of them had the
gift of access to the fantastic through the childhood imagination.
Faulkner's numinous animals— totemic bears, hellish horses, and
the like—are derived from a world of mythology that we allow to
children (pets, zoos, cartoons) but not to adults. And all his characters are seen through the wide eyes of the child, desperate to know
the adults' secrets. "My mother is a fish," indeed.[57]

A difference between them is that whereas Ohio is a dark dream
with luminous moments for Anderson, Faulkner presents Mississippi as something of a nightmare. The lurid Gothic-romance
elements dominate: obsessions, revenges, dark secrets (incest, adul-
tery, miscegenation), weird violence—not only murders and
suicides and rapes but bizarre castrations, real and fancied. Thus
Faulkner's real subject is not the South itself but the murky dark-
side of its self-image. Moreover, the artistic tone stems from a
Beardsleyan aesthetic that Faulkner took up in his adolescence,
combining grotesquerie and cold sensuality with strange folk elements, producing an effect that is at once phantasmagoric and

56. *The Sound and the Fury* (Vintage Books, 1961; originally published, 1929),
p. 207.
57. *As I Lay Dying* (Vintage Books, 1964; originally published, 1930), p. 279.

countrified.[58] In all of this we can see a child's fascinated horror at some of his birthplace's stories and scandals. Faulkner's characters, like their region, are burdened with their mythologized histories, hence like Quentin Compson they tend to be Supergatsbys: they want not simply to repeat the past with a new ending, but to repeal or deny time altogether, to create and worship an ideal unchanging world, safe from falling into real history. Quentin's suicidal project of renewing his sister's virginity is symptomatic. Faulkner's characters have always lived, not at Axel's castle, but at an antebellum version of Satis House.

*　*　*　*　*　*　*　*

What is true of Faulkner's South is also true, *mutatis mutandis*, for Wolfe's. Neither was a regional writer in the old sense; and both made the local readers very nervous by breaking the code of *omertà* that holds in the South as in Sicily, in the felt need to close ranks against outsiders. Wolfe's scandals were not as melodramatic as Faulkner's: he hinted at real-estate swindles and the like rather than Gothic horrors. Yet he too was more nearly ostracized than celebrated in the old home. Both writers were more place-centered in the Andersonian or Joycean sense than "Southern," as their fellow Southerners would have agreed. Wolfe was manifestly a chronicler of the forever lost country of the past, and of the poignancies of memory, not of any region: he treated New England and Brooklyn — which only the dead know — as he treated the South, in an unrelentingly elegiac way. Over and over he sounds his theme of the impossible but unrelinquishable quest to recapture the joys and sureties of childhood, with a special plaintive tone: "Remembering speechlessly we seek the great forgotten language, the lost lane-end into heaven, a stone, a leaf, an unfound door. . . . O lost, and by the wind grieved ghost, come back again."[59] The rhapsodic passages that punctuate his narratives are all suffused with the sense of loss, even the most exultant celebrations of richness in life and abundance in the earth. Indeed, Wolfe's well-known Gargantuan appetites, in life and in these passages, are simply attempts to as-

---

58. See Kenner, *Homemade World*, pp. 194–97.
59. *Look Homeward, Angel: A Story of the Buried Life* (Scribner, 1929), p. [2].

suage the hungers for the past that can never be satisfied. His litanies tell over familiar yet uncanny objects — real and yet visionary, like the unfound door: inexplicable talismans of memory, invested with unworldly portentousness — as if naming them over and over might open the caves and vaults of time. Wolfe sings dithyrambs to a vanished life and to vanished figures, parents or brothers, who stand for sudden joyful fulfillment that seems to lurk always just out of sight or grasp. Like Achilles reaching for the ghost of Patroclus, he knows he can never have him again, yet cannot cease trying.

At the age of twenty-four, when he gave up playwriting for prose, he chose as the theme of a sketch Goethe's line "Gib meine Jugend mir zuruck" (Give me my youth back again). Later he was to preface *Of Time and the River* with another Goethe poem, "Kennst du das land," which ends "O Vater, lass uns ziehn!" (O Father, let us go — [to the blessed land]). These mottoes, with those from Wordsworth's *Ode* that he thought of prefacing to *Look Homeward, Angel*, sum up his vision.[60] The narratives pile up quest on quest, multiplying the hungers of life many times over, making them all flow into a furious, maddening search for completion that can never be satisfied but that leads to temporarily exhilarating states of exhaustion. They are full of catalogs, topheavy enumerations that owe more to the "Cyclops" chapter of *Ulysses* than to Homer's catalog of ships, but without Joyce's comic effects. Wolfe is painfully serious; he has a compulsion to consume, and to make lists, like Don Giovanni, of his experiences. He writes paeans to food, baseball in autumn, and real or imaginary women, that could well go on forever. But the note of loss is constant underneath the sometimes manic joy, as in the following passage in which the 1912 World Series is seen simultaneously on the field and as a box score in a store window in Asheville:

> And suddenly, even as the busy figures swarm and move there in the window before the waiting crowd, the bitter thrilling game is over! In waning light, in faint shadows, far, far, away in a great city of the North, the 40,000 small empetalled faces bend forward, breathless, waiting — single and strange and beautiful as all life, all living, and

60. Richard S. Kennedy, *The Window of Memory: The Literary Career of Thomas Wolfe* (University of North Carolina Press, 1962), pp. 103, 145.

man's destiny. There's a man on base, the last flash of the great right arm, the crack of the bat, the streaking white of a clean-hit ball, the wild, sudden, solid roar, a pair of flashing legs have crossed the rubber, and the game is over!

And instantly, there at the city's heart, in the great stadium, and all across America, in ten thousand streets, ten thousand little towns, the crowd is breaking, flowing, lost forever! That single, silent, most intolerable loveliness is gone forever. . . . Now it is done, the crowd is broken, lost, exploded, and 10,000,000 men are moving singly down 10,000 streets—toward what? Some by the light of Hesperus which, men say, can bring all things that live on earth to their own home again—flock to the fold, the father to his child, the lover to the love he has forsaken—and the proud of heart, the lost, the lonely of the earth, the exile and the wanderer—to what?[61]

The crowd, embodying the Heraclitean law that all things flow, dissolves itself and brings to young Eugene the message of loss and mortality: the passage ends with the boy's realization that his brother, posting the score in the window, is doomed: "The boy knows in that one instant Ben will die." As he says in a neighboring passage: "But this was the reason why these things could never be forgotten—because we are so lost, so naked and so lonely in America."[62] The image of the abandoned, anxious child, almost as if taken from the last stanzas of Coleridge's "Dejection," suggests itself irresistibly.

Wolfe appears to have suffered from prolonged separation anxiety, and from what grief therapists call "searching behavior." It is a well-known symptom of those who have suffered loss but cannot let go psychically, who retain unadmitted fantasies that the loved one will somehow reappear. All of us are familiar with this syndrome in dreams, but acute sufferers apparently carry dreams over into waking life. The unresolved mourning drives them into questing patterns that they don't understand and can't account for: they find themselves seeking out crowds, so as to walk as if looking for a familiar face; but they can't admit to themselves whose face it is. They only know that they keep finding themselves doing such things.[63]

61. *Of Time and the River: A Legend of Man's Hunger in His Youth* (Scribner, 1935), pp. 206–7.

62. Ibid., p. 155.

63. See Colin M. Parkes, *Bereavement: Studies of Grief in Adult Life* (International Universities Press, 1972), pp. 39–56. Cf. Ezra Pound's poem "Coda":

Wolfe obviously had a chronic case. As a young man he walked city streets, rode trains, journeyed everywhere driven by what he calls, in Eugene Gant, "fury"; but it was plainly a form of grief. The most memorable parts of his novels deal with the endlessly drawn-out, compulsively reexperienced deaths of his brother and father, as achingly protracted in their own way as is the music of unconsummated desire in *Tristan und Isolde*. His *mot juste* is having Eugene Gant reply, when asked whether his father is still living, "No! He's still dying."[64] In the writing of these epics of loss — and all epics are about loss, in fact — Wolfe relived all the searching behavior of his own young manhood. His notorious inability to edit, or trim, or even stop writing except from exhaustion, came from the same compulsiveness that drove all his being. No wonder Wolfe revered Anderson: George Willard's train ride out of Winesburg turned into Eugene Gant's endless journeys, always fleeing from but also toward home. Stylistically the two writers were a world apart, with Anderson always seeking spareness and simplicity, Wolfe piling up adjectives and attributes in a trance of oracular copiousness. Yet repetition was a key to the strategy of both, to gain access to the memory of home through incantations or magic formulas that name the dream fragments that will open those "unfound doors." Anderson's quest was only somewhat less intense than Wolfe's. His urge to "tell the stories" of the faces that he met was, surely, another form of searching behavior. Out of his labor Wolfe drew the painful lesson that you can't go home again, but neither he nor Anderson could stop trying, or really wanted to.

* * * * * * * *

Flat, monosyllabic repetitiveness had already marked the style of Gertrude Stein even before that of Anderson. Their most apt pupil took repetition in a very different direction from that of Wolfe, but in a sense made it the key to his work. As Philip Young long

---

O my songs,
Why do you look so eagerly and curiously into
 people's faces,
Will you find your lost dead among them?

64. *Of Time and the River*, p. 197.

ago demonstrated, Freud's "repetition-compulsion" precisely diagnoses the behavior of many Hemingway protagonists.[65] They obsessively relive their traumas, and Hemingway relives them in each act of writing; the oeuvre is *Sons and Lovers* over again, with differences. The whole corpus reads like a gigantic expansion of *Beyond the Pleasure Principle*, which began as an investigation into "shell-shock," the reliving of overwhelmingly painful, life-threatening war wounds. Whether Hemingway actually suffered a form of shell-shock from his own wound is not a wholly relevant question; he had plenty of opportunity to observe the symptoms, and he found he could write stories that embodied them. Evidence exists, cited by Young, that Hemingway knew very well the night horrors of the traumatized, and indeed that he kept seeking out violent and dangerous situations in his life, in order to fulfill the irrational dictates of the drive to master the wound somehow. To infer this from Hemingway's recurring injuries is very tempting, although many macho types develop accident-proneness simply from a childish need to keep proving their courage. It also might be argued that any psychic wound stemmed not from the war but from a domineering mother and a passive father.[66] But the work is the evidence that Hemingway, either by autobiographical transposition or imaginative recreation or both, made repetition-compulsion a standard part of twentieth-century psychic imagery as well as of its stylistic armory. Once more it is a version of Anderson's quest for the past—not in this case for the warmth of childhood, but for something more dark and sunken, perhaps Thanatos itself.

The clearest examples come from some of the Nick Adams stories. No one can now read "Big Two-Hearted River" as a fishing story, but must interleave it with "A Way You'll Never Be," in which Nick's shell-shock is openly introduced. "Big Two-Hearted River"—the title suggesting both freaks and duplicity in Nature, either or both appropriate to the theme of the wound as a betrayal by powers above—by this light becomes an example of Hemingway's "theory of omission," according to which one can leave out

---

65. *Ernest Hemingway: A Reconsideration* (Harcourt Brace, 1966), pp. 16–17, 165–70.

66. Hemingway himself diagnosed this pattern in his parents: see Carlos Baker, *Ernest Hemingway: A Life Story* (Scribner, 1969), pp. 348, 465. Cf. Young, p. 136.

much seemingly vital exposition if there is some form of implication to convey to the readers that they must fill in the gaps.[67] This
device is related to Symbolist evasiveness (to convey "the horror of
the forest" without "the intrinsic, dense wood of the trees") and to
Flaubertian economy, discipline, and hatred of the obvious and
superfluous.[68] Both came to Hemingway through Ezra Pound and
Ford Madox Ford, as part of the Francophile "prose tradition,"
but Hemingway's adaptations are original and striking; they account for the forcefulness of his short stories, the one form in
which he outshone all his coevals.[69]

But the novels, especially the earliest and best, are equally dependent on the wound and its eternal return. On these broader can-
vases we can most clearly see that the verbal echolalia that marks
Hemingway's signature-style has its thematic counterpart in the
repetition that reverberates through and structures the books. In
The Sun Also Rises, characterization is typically achieved by recurrence of pet phrases and motifs (especially because Hemingway
ruthlessly employed his "theory of omission" in the original opening chapters of exposition, acting on a hint from Fitzgerald),[70] and
these verbal formulas are given extra emphasis by reproducing the
inane repetitiveness of conversation. A revealing example is Brett's
constant recourse to the word *rot* in all its forms; Jake hears the
word in his mind as he rolls on his bed in insomniac suffering:

> What a lot of bilge I could think up at night. What rot, I could hear
> Brett say it. What rot! When you were with English you got into the
> habit of using English expressions in your thinking. The English spoken
> language—the upper classes, anyway—must have fewer words than the
> Eskimo. . . . The English talked with inflected phrases. One phrase to
> mean everything. I liked them, though. I liked the way they talked.[71]

67. See Baker, pp. 109, 125, 170–71; also Hemingway interviewed by George
Plimpton in *Writers at Work: The Paris Review Interviews, Second Series* (Viking,
1963), pp. 235–36.
68. See Arthur Symons, *The Symbolist Movement in Literature* (Dutton, 1958;
reprint of 1919 ed.; originally published, 1903), p. 71.
69. Astonishingly little has been written on Hemingway's debt to Pound: the
best discussion, though diffuse and oblivious of Flaubert, is in Linda Wagner's
Hemingway and Faulkner: Inventors/Masters (Scarecrow, 1975), Chap. 2: "Hemingway as Imagist."
70. Baker, p. 170.
71. *The Sun Also Rises* (Scribner, 1954; originally published, 1926), p. 149.
Subsequent page references are to this edition.

Ezra Pound liked them, too, at first; the "laconic speech of the Imagists" must have owed something to the effect that the habitual understatement of the British educated classes would have made on impressionable young Americans like Pound and H. D.[72]

Hemingway's native informant on English speech was "Chink" Dorman-Smith, whose stiffly restrained comments on the late war were enshrined in the interchapters of *In Our Time*: "It was simply priceless. . . . It was absolutely topping," and so on.[73] Compare the first story, "On the Quai at Smyrna":

> The Greeks were nice chaps too. When they evacuated they had all their baggage animals they couldn't take with them so they just broke their forelegs and dumped them into the shallow water. All the mules with their forelegs broken pushed over into the shallow water. It was all a pleasant business. My word yes a most pleasant business.[74]

Hemingway made ironic laconism a salient feature of his art, as Pound had done earlier in another mode. Brett became the perfect vehicle: she could be made to use "a lot of rot," "a rotten shame," and their congeners so often that the whole book was suffused with the odor of decay, moral but insistently physical too as in the whore's rotted teeth. Jake's obsession with Brett is foreshadowed even before she is introduced into the story as it now stands, in his anticipation of her favorite word. Cohn, he tells us, "had married on the rebound from the rotten time he had in college," and "I have a rotten habit of picturing the bedroom scenes of my friends" (pp. 8, 13).

The theme of rottenness and decay and concomitant disgust pervades to the last pages of the book, in which Jake's gorge rises again and again as he futilely serves as ineffectual peacekeeper among his companions and all-too-effective pimp for Brett. Mike calls Robert Cohn a "steer," a gelded, patient beast who "tries to make friends" with the bulls to keep them from fratricidal self-

---

72. See my *Ezra Pound: The Image and the Real* (Louisiana State University Press, 1969), pp. 31–32; and Donald Davie, *Thomas Hardy and British Poetry* (Oxford University Press, 1972), p. 46.

73. Baker, 53–54.

74. *In Our Time: Stories by Ernest Hemingway* (Scribner, 1958; originally published, 1925), pp. 11–12. "On the Quai at Smyrna" was put first only in the 1930 second edition, but obviously reflects Hemingway's fascination with the speech of another British officer Hemingway met while a correspondent in the Greco-Turkish war. See Baker, p. 98.

destruction, but obviously Jake is the real steer: early on he tells us "I try and play it along and just not make trouble for people" (p. 31). Jake's emasculating wound not only pushes him into the steer role, but also gives him the waking nightmares of the shell-shocked. When he remarks on his "rotten habit" of picturing his friends' bedroom scenes, he prefigures his own night visitations:

> My head started to work. The old grievance. Well, it was a rotten way to be wounded. . . . Probably I never would have had any trouble if I hadn't run into Brett when they shipped me to England. I suppose she only wanted what she couldn't have. . . . I lay awake thinking and my mind started jumping around. Then I couldn't keep away from it, and I started to think about Brett and all the rest of it went away. I was thinking about Brett and my mind stopped jumping around and started to go in sort of smooth waves. Then all of a sudden I started to cry. Then after a while it was better. (p. 31)

In the next chapter one of his casual acquaintances asks, "What do you do nights, Jake?" (p. 36). It is the cruelest moment in a cruel book.

Jake does have bedroom scenes with Brett, but like those without her they consist of sterile regrets and recriminations, conducted in the monosyllabic repetitive style that envelops the two of them and, like a fog, allows the real issues to be visible only intermittently. The futile repetitions of the dialogue typify the pointless, barren quality of the dependence between them and of its self-parodying reenactment of true love affairs. When Brett and Jake and the Count go dancing in Montmartre, her facade of cheerfulness begins to crumble as they dance (Jake is "a rotten dancer," Brett says). "'Oh, darling,'" Brett said, "'I'm so miserable,'" and Jake thinks "I had that feeling of going through something that has all happened before" (p. 64). Indeed, she had made exactly the same complaint four chapters earlier, when she entered another dance hall with a crowd of homosexuals and found Jake. But Jake's sense of déjà vu stems not only from her words; he realizes that the two of them are condemned to a restless weary dance of togetherness without consummation, like Dante's Paolo and Francesca. He must continue to lend her out to other men — Mike, Cohn, Romero — and take her back again: "That was it. Send a girl off with one man. Introduce her to another to go off with him. Now go and bring her back. And sign the wire with love. That was it all right" (p. 239).

No possible end to this cycle can be foreseen. To gratify Brett's compulsive desires Jake sacrifices not only his concept of manhood but his cherished *aficion*, as he alienates his old friend Montoya, the hotel owner and *genius loci* of the bullfights, by introducing Romero into Brett's Circean clutches. All Jake gets out of it is a beating from Cohn, some heavy anesthetic drinking, and frustrating reunions with Brett. In short the whole cycle consists of putting himself through trauma, over and over. He and Brett both see themselves as paying: "I thought I had paid for everything. Not like the woman pays and pays and pays," the latter referring to Brett's "Don't we pay for all the things we do, though? . . . When I think of the hell I've put chaps through. I'm paying for it all now" (pp. 26, 148). Jake tries to believe, with the Count, that paying is simply "exchange of values," that "you gave up something and got something else," but in his despair senses that life for him will always be repetitive, endless "paying" for having suffered the wound in the first place. Surely many shell-shocked victims must have felt just that way.

As Young comments, "This is structure as meaning, organization as content. . . . [The book is] Hemingway's *Waste Land*, and Jake is Hemingway's Fisher King," calling attention to Jake's much-loved fishing.[75] To Eliot's evocation of sterility and lovelessness and self-humiliation, Hemingway adds the force of the Freudian concept, the dark suspicion that life is obscurely ruled by an instinct prior to and inexplicable by the pleasure principle. Young dramatizes the concept further: "Then [Freud] took another step, and went on to account for the destructive drives in the human personality by tracing them back to this death instinct: in order not to destroy ourselves, we destroy other things."[76] The smashup of people and things in the novel emblematizes the destructive potential of the repetition-compulsion.

Destruction and decay, always just out of sight as part of the war background if not present in the foreground, are invoked in the mantra "rot." Hence the characters often resemble those sufferers known as obsessive-compulsives, who are driven to wash themselves, their hands, their surroundings, in futile repetition, like

75. P. 87.
76. P. 166.

Lady Macbeth. In the novel this mania for cleansing becomes a series of temporary and ineffectual erasures of various insults, injuries, offenses, or other taints: constantly one character or another is "wiping out" something by some obsessive ritualistic action. Indeed this is the whole point of the bullfighting: repeated brushes with death, skillfully performed, cleanse the souls of all observers, at least temporarily. Jake explains superior technique:

> Romero never made any contortions, always it was straight and pure and natural in line. The others twisted themselves like corkscrews, their elbows raised, and leaned against the flanks of the bull after his horns had passed, to give a faked look of danger. Afterwards, all that was faked turned bad and gave an unpleasant feeling. (pp. 167–68)

Bad bullfighting produces more "rot," but good provides catharsis for all wounds: "The fight with Cohn had not touched [Romero's] spirit but his face had been smashed and his body hurt. He was wiping all that out now. Each thing that he did with this bull wiped that out a little cleaner" (p. 219). That the catharsis entails the torture and death of the animal only tightens the link to primitive sacrificial ritual.

With the same metaphor, Brett takes some joy in the affair after relinquishing Romero: "I'm all right again. He's wiped out that damned Cohn" (p. 243). She adopts a hair-of-the-dog strategy for sexual taints, wiping out hangovers by starting another affair. All her affairs are compulsive substitutions for her love for Jake, though they torture him, just as her earlier affairs were to "wipe out" the death of her "true love" in the war. The pattern of her alcoholic's strategy underlines the thematization of alcohol as a cathartic. Jake, disgusted by the crowd of "fairies" accompanying Brett, wants to "swing on one, any one, anything to shatter that superior, simpering composure. Instead, I walked down the street and had a beer at the bar at the next Bal. The beer was not good and I had a worse cognac to take the taste out of my mouth" (p. 20). All these acts provide palliative remedies for the various "rots" but must be incessantly repeated in one or another form.

The very dialogue of the book is subjected to repeated erasure, wiping out. Brett, who believes that "talking's all bilge," silences herself by truncating her sentences, talking in a begrudging telegraphic style (pp. 55–58). Jake agrees with her premise. Of any valuable experience, he says, "You'll lose it if you talk about it" (p. 245). He makes a point of telling us that there is no Spanish word for *bullfight* (p. 173). The black drummer in Montmartre is eloquent although his words are reduced to pure ellipsis:

> The drummer shouted: "You can't two time—"
> "It's all gone."
> "What's the matter?"
> "I don't know. I just feel terribly."
> " . . . " the drummer chanted. Then turned to his sticks.
> "Want to go?"
> I had the feeling as in a nightmare of it all being something repeated, something I had been through and that now I must go through again.
> " . . . " the drummer sang softly.
> "Let's go," said Brett. "You don't mind."
> " . . . " the drummer shouted and grinned at Brett. (p. 64)

His message elaborating "you can't two time" is so painful that it is clear without words. Jake's admiration for the monosyllabic reserve of the British is part of this motif, though it ties in with native-American, Andersonian mistrust of words and homage to inarticulateness. But Hemingway makes it take the form of compulsive censoring, silencing, "wiping out" of untrustworthy words, as if some linguistic purging could quiet the demons unleashed by the wound.

Concerning that which cannot be spoken of, we must be silent. What is interdicted above all in the novel is the wound itself. In the supposedly pastoral interlude in Spain, Jake and Bill joke about writers, expatriation, degeneration, and "fake European standards."

> "It sounds like a swell life," I said. "When do I work?"
> "You don't work. One group claims women support you. Another group claims you're impotent."
> "No," I said. "I just had an accident."
> "Never mention that," Bill said. "That's the sort of thing that can't be spoken of. That's what you ought to work up into a mystery. Like Henry's bicycle."
> He had been going splendidly, but he stopped. I was afraid he thought he had hurt me with that crack about being impotent. I wanted to start him again.
> "It wasn't a bicycle," I said. "He was riding horseback."

"I heard it was a tricycle."

"Well," I said. "A plane is sort of like a tricycle. The joystick works the same way." (pp. 115–16)

The reference is obviously to Henry James, who also suffered from an obscure hurt rumored to be emasculating.[77] Jake and James both have "joystick" trouble; the unmentionable wounds make their status as writers ambiguous, like their sexuality. There is even a hint that writing is a debased or perverse form of sexual activity, suitable for those who lack man-roots and must therefore expatriate themselves.

The novel is laden with sexual ambiguity: Brett calls herself a "chap," wears a man's hat, innovates the boyish hairstyle and figure ("curves like the hull of a racing yacht" are not mammary protuberances), and treats herself to a sex life traditionally reserved for males. Although occluded in the novel itself, these motifs can be further traced in Hemingway's life and unpublished writing; the posthumous work put together and published as *The Garden of Eden* shows clearly his fascination with gender mutations and permutations.[78] Like many men he was fascinated by lesbianism; he oscillated between maternal and boyish types in his choices of wives, and especially in turning from the older, well-rounded Hadley Richardson to the slighter Pauline Pfeiffer (who looks like a male in some photos, had a lesbian sister and tried it herself in later life), he gave a hint of interests that later included pederastic fantasies.[79] Hence *The Garden of Eden* is the most psychobiographical of his works. But what it reveals of his musing on reversed sex roles is only part of the story; the other motif that emerges from occlusion in those pages is that of childhood betrayed by paternal forces. Hemingway, like Sylvia Plath, never forgave his father for dying. He felt betrayed not only by the

77. See Kenneth S. Lynn, *Hemingway* (Simon & Schuster, 1987), pp. 231, 327–28. This is a remarkable work, not least because it contains no entry for "Freud" in the index.

78. *The Garden of Eden* (Scribner, 1986). See Lynn's index, s.v. "Hemingway . . . gender identity as obsession of."

79. See Jeffrey Meyer, *Hemingway: A Biography* (Harper & Row, 1985), pp. 436–37; cf. Lynn, *Hemingway*, p. 533. See also Lynn, pp. 100–1, on the rumored lesbianism of Hemingway's mother; p. 142, on a lesbian incident in Hadley's early life; and pp. 318–25, on Hemingway's lesbian acquaintances in Paris.

suicide itself, but also by its implied surrender to the mother. The early story "The Doctor and the Doctor's Wife" tells all one needs to know about Hemingway's belief in the castrating mother; her manipulation of social and religious pressures is a form of unmanning. (And the evidence indicates that this was an accurate view of Grace Hemingway.)[80] In *The Garden of Eden*, the father betrays the child's world of immortal chthonic powers by killing the elephant, bringing in a cruel revelation of mortality that mixes the elephant's with his own; the beneficent god is unveiled as only a venal, vulnerable man.[81] Here Hemingway recapitulates the Freudian logic of the Romantic revolt against theodicy: and this loss of faith in patriarchal goodness and power ties in with erosion of sexual identity and thus with the sexual explorations of each other by the young man and his wife—one passage even hints that she penetrates him with a dildo.[82] No wonder Hemingway never published any of this work. It has long been suspected that his macho posturing screened some homosexual inclinations, but this manuscript reveals that he must have grasped this, and that he was more honest with himself than might have been predicted. This honesty seems to have restored his waning stylistic powers, and thus the novel, even in its synthetic form, is more interesting than such works as *Across the River and into the Trees* and *Islands in the Stream*. But its suppression was not only a matter of privacy; it was the logical terminus of the censorings and occlusions that typify *The Sun Also Rises*. The "theory of omission" had been suggested by the Flaubertian lessons he learned from Pound and Ford but came to be laden with the force of the repetition-compulsion.

The reliving of the wound is atavism with a vengeance, the return of the past in a way both unavoidable and unbearable. But besides all the psychic motivation that pushed Hemingway to use fiction as

80. Baker, p. 474, paraphrases letters from Hemingway that include a report of his mother boasting that she had made her husband "live to regret" an early transgression against her.

81. The story runs through the latter part of the book, but see esp. pp. 180–82, 197–202.

82. The wife, having cut her hair to look like her husband's, says, "'But now I'm a boy too and I can do anything and anything and anything'" (p. 15). Then comes the mysterious lovemaking with her on top, when he feels "the weight and the strangeness inside," and she says, "'Now you can't tell who is who can you?'" (p. 17).

a form of repetition, as Lawrence did, there were aesthetic motivations as well. Chief among these was the link to Anderson: it must be seen that the unending wound is a dark and twisted version of Anderson's quest for the past. Hemingway learned of the quest as the key to authorship from his erstwhile mentor, and originally intended to employ it in a straightforward way. He was going to write a "wonderful" novel about Oak Park but held back to keep from hurting living people, if we can believe that.[83] But the upper Michigan peninsula, his boyhood summer home, was even more psychically potent than his hometown, and in the Nick Adams stories it is the locus of various forms of initiation, several of which foreshadow the failure of fatherhood in *The Garden of Eden*. Michigan is as important in Nick's background as the wound itself; they are compounded together into psychic shocks that make Anderson's idyllic visions seem grotesquely sentimental, yet recapitulate his patterns of construction and style.[84] Hemingway observed of his father that sentimental people are cruel; he might as well have been commenting on himself, and especially on his attempts to controvert Andersonian themes — and this includes the implication that his repudiation of Anderson covered over not only his sense of indebtedness, but also his exorcism of his detestably "soft" father.[85]

Stylistically, the debt to Anderson is present throughout Hemingway's work. The nastiness of *The Torrents of Spring* was probably multiplied several powers by his irritation at its inescapability, and by his prophetic sense that he too would one day be reduced to stylistic mannerisms. The constant praise of integrity and purity in his work is not only a sign of his bad conscience about his ruthless treatment of people, especially benefactors, but also his sense that his own art was irreducibly a matter of gestures and techniques. Lacking a college education, he was both too old-fashioned and too self-conscious about this disadvantage to accept style as pure artistic value, which increased his ambivalence about his stylistic mentors and resulted in the character assassinations he practiced

83. Fenton, *Apprenticeship*, p. 1.

84. Hemingway felt that a writer's duty to the place he knew best was "either to destroy it or perpetuate it," an interesting choice: Meyer, p. 144.

85. See the patently autobiographical "Fathers and Sons" in *The Complete Short Stories of Ernest Hemingway* (Scribner, 1987), p. 370.

throughout his life. Having repaid Anderson for his kindness with
Torrents, he finished off Stein and Ford in *A Moveable Feast* —
brilliant writing in a totally meretricious and self-serving cause. At
least with Stein he had the excuse that she had called him a coward.
The gift from Ford and Pound of the Flaubertian "prose tradition"
was priceless for his work, yet all he remembers of Ford is snobbish
pretentiousness, lying self-aggrandizement, and halitosis — a portrait contradicted by Pound himself, Williams, Robert Lowell, and
others. (Did Hemingway let Pound off because of the treason indictment? Even a compulsive ingrate must have some hesitations
about kicking people when they're down.) Petty malice, anti-
Semitism, and other factors were at work in Hemingway's treatment of Harold Loeb and like victims, but obviously his most
disfiguring psychic wound came from his feelings about indebtedness.[86]

And so *A Farewell to Arms*, though written after the break
between them, is not really less Andersonian than *The Sun Also
Rises*: which shows the tar-baby futility of trying to exorcise
wounds. Certainly the presence of the past is equally vital; *A Farewell* elaborates at vast length a motif that first surfaced as drunken
byplay in *Sun*, about buying some stuffed dogs:

> Brett smiled at [Bill] again.
> "You've a nice friend, Jake."
> "He's all right," I said. "He's a taxidermist."
> "That was in another country," Bill said. "And besides all the animals
> were dead." (p. 75)

---

86. On Hemingway picking quarrels with "erstwhile benefactors" and other
forms of compulsive hostility, see Baker, pp. 81–82, 86, 133, 135, 159–63, 170, and
passim. Meyer quotes a letter (p. 152) to Fenton from Hemingway about picking
quarrels to get rid of obligations that casts light on the story "The Doctor and the
Doctor's Wife" but even more on Hemingway himself. Meyer also quotes (p. 171)
Donald Ogden Stewart, the original of Bill Gorton in *Sun*: "The minute he began to
love you, or the minute he began to have some sort of obligation to you of love or
friendship or something, then is when he had to kill you."
  The debt to Anderson would have rankled most since it involved near-plagiarism.
See Young, p. 177, on the incredibility of Hemingway's denial that his story "My
Old Man" owed anything to Anderson's well-known "I Want to Know Why." In
view of the boldness of Hemingway's appropriations, it is not farfetched to see even
his "theory of omission" (the "iceberg under water") as derived from Anderson's
employment of occulted elements. Cf. his description of how *The Old Man and the*

This is a parody of some lines from Marlowe's *Jew of Malta*, used
by T. S. Eliot as an epigraph for "Portrait of a Lady":

> Thou hast committed —
> Fornication: but that was in another country,
> And besides, the wench is dead.[87]

Shortly after *Sun* Hemingway had written a bitter short story, "In
Another Country," about loss and wounds, with the news of the
death of a young wife coming to a soldier in a hospital. The germ
of the novel of "transalpine fornication," as Hemingway called it,
is thus evident.[88] The Marlovian phrase must have been keyed to
the idea of a harmless "sin" returning from a buried past to accuse
and kill: a variation on the "paying" motif in *Sun*, where the wound
takes its own endless retribution. Catherine, only slightly varying
Brett's pattern, takes her new lover to reincarnate the dead one and
to give him the sex she foolishly withheld in life, whereas Frederic
survives his wound without overt consequences, yet is marked by it
as much as Jake, in his new awareness of mortality. "Another
country" in this context is Italy as against Switzerland, but more
profoundly signifies the realm of the past, from which we are revisited by the deadly consequences of what we did not even know was
a sin. It is another kind of nightmare, of pursuit by nameless and
faceless agents; what seems to be refuge proves no barrier against
pain and fear and death. This time the wound literally recurs, in
the form of a lethal, fruitless Caesarean "operation." Ultimately it
is the war that pursues and kills; the ambiguity of "sides" in the
war intensifies the fear, as the very cause for which one was fighting turns out to be as hostile as the supposed enemy. Frederic had
gone to the war in what seemed to be a noble gesture, but his
lighthearted entry envelops him in a net of forces he cannot escape.
His illusions crumble, his camaraderie erodes, and what is left of
his admiration for warriors washes away in the river of escape, but
he finds no refuge in his attempt to declare a separate peace. He is

---

Sea was constructed by leaving things out (Plimpton, *Writers at Work*, p. 236) with
my discussion, in this book, of Anderson's "Loneliness" and related stories.

87. Hemingway tried to disguise his fascination with Eliot by writing a dismissive
comparison of him with Conrad, a typical gesture. See Lynn, pp. 246–48.

88. Baker, p. 199.

pursued by a past as implacable as the Furies, and like them it knows nothing of his original good intentions.

The story "In Another Country" had begun with a sentence much admired by Fitzgerald: "In the fall the war was always there, but we did not go to it any more."[89] It seems obvious that this grew into the famous opening paragraph:

> In the late summer of that year we lived in a house in a village that looked across the river and the plain to the mountains. In the bed of the river there were pebbles and boulders, dry and white in the sun, and the water was clear and swiftly moving and blue in the channels. Troops went by the house and down the road and the dust they raised powdered the leaves of the trees. The trunks of the trees too were dusty and the leaves fell early that year and we saw the troops marching along the road and the dust rising and leaves, stirred by the breeze, falling and the soldiers marching and afterward the road bare and white except for the leaves.[90]

Many critics have analyzed this passage, from many different points of view; few have commented on how its apparently domestic and pastoral quality degenerates at the close. The beginning is too lyrical for Frederic Henry, and really belongs to a more child-like, Andersonian point of view. But the ending vision has a nightmarish emptiness, turning the scene into a dream fragment with an inexplicable malevolent quality, like the "long yellow house" that haunts the shell-shocked dreams of Nick Adams in "A Way You'll Never Be." Perhaps only after Hiroshima can it be easily seen that the few human traces in the paragraph are made by the dust of transient, impersonal "troops." The troops march off to be pulverized, the ominous dust raised by them settles on the leaves that begin to fall, and the road is left uncannily bare and white. Even the deceptive clarity — white of the boulders, blue of the water — takes on an alienating, lifeless quality in the light of the dehumanized closing. The war is all the more threatening for being hidden within such peaceful images.

In the following paragraphs cars and armies, guns and Kings are paraded before us, and we are told that with autumn came the

---

89. Baker, p. 190.

90. *A Farewell to Arms* (Scribner, 1957; originally published, 1929), p. 3. Subsequent page references are to this edition.

rain, "and with the rain came the cholera. But it was checked and in the end only seven thousand died of it in the army" (p. 4). Ironic laconism has rarely produced a better sentence. In the rain (which Catherine later fears because she presciently sees herself dead in it) the troops put on capes that cover the cartridge boxes on their belts, and look "as though they were six months gone with child" (p. 4, cf. p. 131). Besides foreshadowing death in birth, this image makes us look back to Anderson. No doubt Hemingway had suppressed any memory of the pregnant old man in "The Book of the Grotesque," or of the figurative impregnation of George Willard by his mother. But his disturbing image of the soldiers suggests some linkage; in any case, it gives new twists to the intertwining of love and death, sexuality and aggression. To exploit them, Hemingway enforces a running parallel between the course of the war and of the love affair. Catherine gives Frederic his first "wound" when he tries to kiss her:

> We looked at each other in the dark. I thought she was very beautiful and I took her hand. She let me take it and I held it and put my arm around under her arm.
>   "No," she said. I kept my arm where it was.
>   "Why not?"
>   "No."
>   "Yes," I said. "Please." I leaned forward in the dark to kiss her and there was a sharp stinging flash. She had slapped my face hard. Her hand had hit my nose and eyes, and tears came into my eyes from the reflex. (p. 26)

Note the structural similarity as Frederic becomes aware of his body after the Austrian mortar-shell explosion, which also comes in "a flash, as when a blast-furnace door is swung open":

> I sat up straight and as I did so something inside my head moved like the weights on a doll's eyes and it hit me inside in back of my eyeballs. My legs felt warm and wet and my shoes were wet and warm inside. I knew that I was hit and leaned over and put my hand on my knee. My knee wasn't there. (p. 58)

In both traumas, Frederic remains the medical corpsman, clinically tallying the effects.

Catherine accepts Frederic as a purposeful hallucination, in that he reincarnates her dead lover, "blown all to bits." Fittingly, their love is consummated in a hospital bed, where she provides illusory refuge: he "loves" for her to take her hair down, "and we would both be inside of it, and it was the feeling of inside a tent or behind a falls" (p. 118).[91] Later, Catherine in Switzerland thinks of how little she knows about her approaching delivery, and Frederic gives the love–war theme an Andersonian turn:

> "I'll find out what is necessary."
> "You ought to know. You were a nurse."
> "But so few of the soldiers had babies in the hospitals."
> "I did."
> She hit me with the pillow and spilled the whiskey and soda. (p. 318)

They have been chased into Switzerland by the nightmare image of the battle police, who would have shot Frederic simply as an example and now compel him to be no different from the deserters that he himself had to shoot in the great confusion of the retreat. The anonymous, rigid police, often rumored in the conversations of the common soldiers, have "that beautiful detachment and devotion to stern justice of men dealing in death without being in any danger of it" (p. 232); indeed they are not mortal, but avenging underworld figures. They combine Freud's notion of the superego with a modern version of the Furies (later borrowed by Cocteau). They cannot reach into Switzerland, but the inescapable war, which they embody, simply takes another form, and Catherine's attempt to give life turns into a lethal trauma, in which the ambiguities of

91. Catherine's hair, when she wants to cut it to look like Frederic's (p. 310), also manifests Hemingway's obsession with gender mutation; see Lynn, p. 388, which brings in the unfinished short story "The Last Good Country," in which the fleeing lovers are Nick Adams and his little sister. This nexus, with *The Garden of Eden* and a passage in "Soldier's Home," comprises Hemingway's attempt to work out an incestuous Lolita-complex with overtones of pederasty and narcissism, and other trimmings. The pattern is all the more interesting in comparison with Faulkner's equal obsession with the "little sister"–narcissism–death motif: see Minter, esp. pp. 62, 100–1, 124–25, 163; and the classic study by John Irwin, *Doubling and Incest/ Repetition and Revenge: A Speculative Reading of Faulkner* (Johns Hopkins University Press, 1975).

Mark Spilka gives the Hemingway pattern a much more healthy-minded reading: see "Original Sin in 'The Last Good Country': or, The Return of Catherine Barkley" in Lawrence B. Gamache and Ian S. MacNiven, eds., *The Modernists: Studies in a Literary Phenomenon* (Associated University Presses, 1987), pp. 210–33 (also in a forthcoming book).

operation and wound, doctor and enemy, operating room and trench, are mercilessly explored. Her labor is protracted until she can be helped only by gas (it is worth remembering that in the world of the trenches those who were gassed were after all delivered from their pains).

> Poor, poor dear Cat. And this was the price you paid for sleeping together. This was the end of the trap. This was what people got for loving each other. Thank God for gas, anyway. (p. 330) . . .
> I thought Catherine was dead. She looked dead. Her face was gray, the part of it that I could see. Down below, under the light, the doctor was sewing up the great long, forcep-spread, thick-edged, wound. Another doctor in a mask gave the anaesthetic. Two nurses in masks handed things. It looked like a drawing of the Inquisition. (p. 336)

No wonder the image of torturers occurs to him. The invasive scalpels are the instruments of the unseen war itself, incarnating fear, pain, mutilation, and death.

Fertility and fatality, the great apparent opposites, lead to the same end, in this vision of a nightmare universe. Some victims die on the spot, some walk away zombielike to haunted afterlives. Frederic, "croyant" only at night, is doomed to *una nox perpetua* (p. 270).[92] Feminist critics have alleged that Catherine has to die to exorcise Hemingway's fear of women; indeed this fear is a vital component of his spiritual universe, but Catherine's death is demanded by the implacable logic of the repetition-compulsion itself.[93] Her agony provides Frederic with his most vivid and undeniable shell-shock nightmare, and brings to a climax the twisting together of love and war that the book has foreshadowed in so many ways, from the whores at the front and Rinaldi's syphilis to all the ones cited above.

Hemingway is able even to make the weather of the novel manifest the treacherous ambiguity of this motif. The rain is always an omen of gratuitous, undeserved death, as in the wry notation about cholera, but snow at first seems to have beneficent properties of respite and refuge (reminiscent of *The Waste Land*): "Looking out at the snow falling slowly and heavily, we knew [the war] was all

92. Catullus, V, 6.
93. For example, Judith Fetterley, *The Resisting Reader: A Feminist Approach to American Fiction* (Indiana University Press, 1978), pp. 46 ff.

over for that year" (p. 6). The images of the hard-packed snow of the Abruzzi reinforce this association and forecast the flight to Switzerland—these lovers too parody Mary and Joseph, though their escape is attended with crucifixion rather than birth imagery. A snowy country, "where nothing makes any difference," seems a natural sanctuary: compare the deceptive fiesta in *Sun* (originally titled *Fiesta*) where "it seemed as though nothing could have any consequences. It seemed out of place to think of consequences during the fiesta."[94] Those fleeing the war—that is, repetition-compulsion—must always seek such states, but they are tricked as usual. Frederic grasps this when he reads, in Switzerland, "that they were still fighting in the mountains because the snow would not come" (p. 301). The laggard snow is like the baby, "young Catherine, that loafer," whose delay is similarly fatal and similarly deceptive. The snow finally comes as deadly rain, and the child comes as a stillborn boy.

The ethos of the book is that of a lifelike dream in which faceless men and blank Nature conspire to hunt down soldiers and lovers indifferently. One finds oneself accused and judged like a Kafka character, never knowing what the crime was. Frederic's famous rumination on the ants in the campfire looks back to the image from *Lear*—"As flies to wanton boys are we to th' gods;/ They kill us for their sport"—but mixes it with that answering precept from the same play: "The gods are just, and of our pleasant vices/ Make instruments to plague us."[95] We can't even know whether our suffering is guilty or not. It's arbitrary, like a game of baseball, but "the first time they caught you off base they killed you": so much for our pleasant vices. The bucolic baseball image, so Midamerican, yet reveals once more that the story is a nightmare version of Anderson's dream visions. Anderson constantly sought to get back the past, Hemingway to exorcise it, but it loomed relentless over them both, beyond their control, dwarfing their efforts. "So we beat on, boats against the current, borne back ceaselessly into the past."[96]

---

94. *The Sun Also Rises*, p. 154; see Baker, p. 166, on the "fiesta concept of life."
95. *Lear* IV,i, 36–37, and V, ii, 171–72. Cf. these ants with the grasshoppers in "Big Two-Hearted River."
96. This, of course, is the last sentence of *Gatsby*.

5

Ezra Pound:
The Archaeology of the Immanent

well in contrast to the *god*-damned crooning
put me down for temporis acti

80/499

The decisive moment in the history of Modernism's self-definitions came just before the First World War, when the Vorticists, led by Wyndham Lewis and Ezra Pound, rejected an alliance with the Futurists, led by Filippo Marinetti. Marinetti had come to England to propagandize for his noisily nihilistic demands that the entire past of Western culture be scrapped, museums destroyed, and so forth; he sought to broaden the base of his movement, though its natural locus was Italy, where (as he complained) the whole country was a museum. The Vorticists had initially welcomed Futurism's strident self-advertising as a way to wake up the somnolent British public, but began to gag when they saw the covert sentimentalism of Marinetti's nostalgia for the future. In the Vorticist journal *BLAST* Futurism was condemned as "accelerated impressionism" and "automobilism." Marinetti was written off for having merely updated nineteenth-century worship of the machine, and Pound condemned his nihilistic demands, for example that Venice be torn down, as childishness:

> The vorticist has not this curious tic for destroying past glories. . . .
> We do not desire to evade comparison with the past. We prefer that
> the comparison be made by some intelligent person whose idea of "the
> tradition" is not limited by the conventional taste of four or five centu-
> ries and one continent.[1]

In those sentences are contained not only the seeds of Pound's personal aesthetic but more obviously the nucleus of the doctrine of "tradition," worked out at greater length by Pound and T. S. Eliot during the war years. It was most coherently expressed in Eliot's 1919 essay "Tradition and the Individual Talent," the nearest Modernist equivalent to the Communist Manifesto. The burden of that essay, as is widely known, was that new art is not really a break with the past but a synergetic incorporation of it; old and new combine to reshape and revitalize each other, and the only meaningful art is produced by those who have a true "historical sense," which requires "a perception, not only of the pastness of the past, but of its presence."[2]

Before we examine more closely the significance of Eliot's essay, however, we should note that this evolution in literary history is crucial mostly because of the personal energy and determination of Ezra Pound. Insofar as Anglo-Hibernio-American Modernism was a movement, it was largely Pound's creation; it is not too much to say that he was the only one of the figures we now call Modernists for whom the movement as such had any importance. Even those who refuse to honor Pound's achievement as a poet can hardly deny the importance of his presence. If his lasting poetry were judged to consist only of the usual anthology pieces, it would still be accurate to call this period "the Pound era" simply because of his dynamic role — to use Eliot's metaphor — as a literary catalyst. In fact there is no figure quite like him anywhere in literary history. Though he was actually a rather shy person, according to many of his intimates, the intensity of his aesthetic convictions led him to make friends, allies, and projects of almost the whole roster of contemporary artists and writers. He became in effect the best

1. "Vorticism," written in 1914, in Pound, *Gaudier-Brzeska: A Memoir* (New Directions, 1960; originally published, 1916), p. 90. Cf. *BLAST*, June 20, 1914, p. [8]: "The futurist is a sensational and sentimental mixture of the aesthete of 1890 and the realist of 1870."

2. *Egoist* (1919), in *Selected Essays of T. S. Eliot* (Harcourt Brace, 1932), p. 4. Pound had said again in 1914 that the "futurists are evidently ignorant of tradition. . . . We do not desire to cut ourselves off from the past. We do not desire to cut ourselves off from great art of any period" ("Wyndham Lewis," *Egoist*, January 15, 1914, p. 234). The similar phrasing to that quoted above suggests that the term *tradition* first became powerfully invested for Pound, and then probably Eliot, in the course of the dismissal of Futurism.

literary friend, successively, of William Carlos Williams, Ford
Madox Ford, William Butler Yeats, T. S. Eliot, Wyndham Lewis,
and James Joyce; later he befriended Ernest Hemingway, e.e.
cummings, and others. Though no feminist, he sponsored and
catalyzed the work of the two preeminent women poets of the era,
H. D. and Marianne Moore; he did his best to publicize all new
talents in poetry even when he did not like them personally, as with
Robert Frost and D. H. Lawrence. It would be shorter work to
list those who were unaffected by his tireless efforts, for example
Wallace Stevens, than those who benefited in one way or another.
And though he was remarkably catholic in his tastes — from Hardy
to Cocteau — and never forced even devoted protégés to conform
to his own ideology, he did give Modernism its essential character
simply by his example and leadership. As early as 1916, someone
as remote from his interests and milieu as Carl Sandburg could
testify that anyone who wanted to think about modern literature
had to take account of Pound's work and activities, since he "had
done most of living men to incite new impulses in poetry."[3] If some
Pound briefly championed have faded in retrospect, such as Edgar
Lee Masters, still his links to the giants of the age overshadow
these. And to say so much is to say nothing of his relationships
with artists like Henri Gaudier-Brzeska, Francis Picabia, and Con-
stantin Brancusi.

Recounting the diversities of Pound's roles in Modernism makes
one wonder where he got the time and energy for them and for his
own work too. He brashly thrust himself upon Yeats's attention in
1909, concealing his diffidence with bravado, and started taking
charge at Yeats's weekly salons. Within a short time Yeats began
to employ him as reader-companion during winter stays in Sussex,
and set him the task of going over his work to hunt out "abstractions." Eventually they became almost in-laws; Pound married
Dorothy Shakespear, daughter of Yeats's onetime lover, and was
best man at Yeats's wedding to Dorothy's good friend and step-
cousin. In 1914 Pound discovered Eliot, then an unpublished grad-
uate student, and started him on his career by forcing "Prufrock"
on an ambivalent Harriet Monroe, whose nascent *Poetry* magazine

3. "The Work of Ezra Pound," *Poetry*, February 1916, p. 249.

Pound had lately commandeered. He performed much the same feat for Joyce, though by mail since Joyce was in Zurich and the two did not meet until after the war: he instantly grasped the genius in Joyce's work, and by getting it into print ended Joyce's years of obscurity and frustration. At Pound's instigation Yeats, through Edmund Gosse, sent the penurious Joyce a grant from the Royal Literary Fund, which must be the most ironic event in literary history. Meanwhile Pound was more or less running the *Egoist* and then the *Little Review*, as well as *Poetry*, turning them into vehicles for Modernism and especially for the chapters of Joyce's *Portrait* and *Ulysses*; he was crusading for other writers too, having started Imagism partly to get H. D.'s work published; he abandoned Imagism to Amy Lowell and started Vorticism with Lewis; and he shepherded other careers and projects besides, constantly pushing Ford and the "prose tradition in verse." All this time he was keeping up a lively and sometimes acrimonious correspondence with his college chum Williams, cajoling him into awareness of all the new developments in spite of Williams' nativism. There is no comparable figure even in a movement like Romanticism, in which the major figures were better acquainted with one another.[4]

Indeed, most of the participants in Modernism disliked or ignored the others, and that makes Pound's activities in holding them together appear even more amazing. Eliot sniffed at Yeats as a mere "minor survivor of the '90s";[5] Williams thought Eliot was a literary disaster, who had sent us all back to the classroom and to rootless cosmopolitanism; Joyce was first isolated, then self-absorbed after his isolation ended; Yeats, with his attention fixed on Ireland, hardly noticed the younger men; Hemingway slandered Ford; and Lewis expressed contempt for everybody. But except for Amy Lowell, Lawrence, and a few others, all those who had any part in modern literature and art liked Pound and testified to his generosity and helpfulness. Even when his manic politics led him from Fascism to a treason indictment and then to an insane asy-

---

4. The best collection of biographical facts — though remarkably obtuse about the work — is Humphrey Carpenter's *A Serious Character: The Life of Ezra Pound* (Faber, 1988).

5. "Ezra Pound" (1946), quoted from Walter Sutton, ed., *Ezra Pound: A Collection of Critical Essays* (Prentice-Hall, 1963), p. 17.

lum, most stood by him because of what he had once done, and several were instrumental in having him eventually released.

Pound's role in reshaping the work and ideas of his friends is well documented. Yeats credited him with "getting toward the clear and natural," helping eliminate "rhetoric" and "modern abstractions," and thus pointing the way toward the hardening of tone and technique in the post-1914 poetry.[6] Eliot dedicated *The Waste Land* to him as *il miglior fabbro*, and also called him "cher maître," in recognition of his midwifery of the poem.[7] His influence on Williams was less direct, but it is hard to believe that Imagism had no effect on Williams' shorter poems, or *The Cantos* on *Paterson*. Even some of Pound's economic ideas—such as Social Credit— turn up in Williams' long poem. Hemingway claimed to have learned much from him; although it has been little noticed, the influence of ideas from Imagism and the "prose tradition" on *In Our Time* and *The Sun Also Rises* is clear. On all of his friends Pound exerted an effect that caused them to be more aware of other developments and precedents, even on Joyce who had no desire to be part of any movement. (The rest had no real desire either but were at least alert to developments in other arts.) Thus, what validity there is to the name and concept of "Modernism," as a conscious literary effort, is largely due to Pound's personal force.

Such sharp observers as Eliot and Lewis noticed a paradox in Pound's leadership, in that his own work before 1912 had an "old-fashioned" quality, which is probably why he hit it off so well with Yeats; Lewis smirked that Pound's "fire-eating propagandistic utterances [in Vorticist days] were not accompanied by any very experimental efforts in his particular medium. . . . [His work's] novelty lay largely in the distance it went back, not forward." Lewis diagnosed Pound's major flaw as antiquarianism: "He has never loved anything living as he has loved the dead."[8] It is true that

6. See A. Norman Jeffares, *W. B. Yeats: Man and Poet* (Routledge & Kegan Paul, 1949), p. 167; and the unsigned "Poetry's Banquet," *Poetry*, April 1914, p. 27.

7. See *The Letters of Ezra Pound 1907–1941*, ed. D. D. Paige (Harcourt Brace, 1950), p. 170.

8. Eliot interviewed by Donald Hall, in *Writers at Work: The Paris Review Interviews, Second Series* (Viking, 1963), p. 95. Note also the phrases "touchingly

when Pound went to London in 1908, to try to sit at Yeats's feet, he had in mind an ideal for poetry that combined the dreamy, obscure Symbolism of Yeats's early work with the imitative medievalism that he drew from his own research into Provençal and early Italian literature. But his antiquarian urge was turned into other channels by Ford, who ridiculed the "derivative" emotions and mannerisms in his poems and convinced him, finally, that all poetic affectations were an abomination, that poetic language must be aggressively contemporary and speakable, and that "Paolo and Francesca loved and suffered precisely as love and suffer the inhabitants of the flat above him."[9] As Hugh Kenner puts it: "And Pound left [Ford in 1911] to become a modern poet: the figure we have known ever since: the revolutionary."[10] But he did not simply abandon his love for the past: the significance of his repudiation of Futurism is that he saw not the pastness of the past, but its presence. This is why his work's revolutionary quality is a revelation of artistic atavism, a manifestation of the ongoing power and immanence of "the tradition." The *Cantos* involve the past in an uncompromisingly direct way that dispenses with the derivativeness of his early work, and eschews the "romance of time-travel."[11] They share this achievement with such works as *Ulysses* and *Finnegans Wake*, as well as with *The Waste Land* and *Four Quartets*, so that Modernism was activated by the force of the past erupting into the present.

Even in the most revolutionary of his entrepreneurial works, Pound insisted on aligning their experimental qualities with ancient practices. For instance, in introducing H. D.'s poems to Harriet Monroe, Pound emphasized the classical connection:

> I've had luck again, and am sending you some *modern* stuff by an American, I say modern, for it is in the laconic speech of the Imagistes, even if the subject is classic. . . . Objective—no slither; direct—no excessive use of adjectives, no metaphors that won't permit examination. It's straight talk, straight as the Greek![12]

incompetent" and "romantic . . . cloak-and-dagger kind of stuff." Lewis, *Time and Western Man* (Harcourt, 1928), pp. 39, 71.

9. Ford Madox Hueffer, *The Critical Attitude* (Duckworth, 1911), p. 187.
10. *The Pound Era* (University of California Press, 1971), p. 81.
11. *Pound Era*, pp. 24–25 ff.
12. *Letters*, p. 11.

(Pound didn't bother to inform Monroe that he had just created "Imagisme" himself, or that H. D. was an old girlfriend.) Vorticism, two years later, was much more consciously avant-garde than Imagism, but in one aspect it was an attempt to create an English parallel to Cubism, and Pound's judgment on Picasso is illuminating: "The strength of Picasso is largely in his having chewed through and chewed up a great mass of classicism; which, for example, the lesser cubists, and the flabby cubists have not." No wonder Pound declared that "there is no effective revolution in art save that which comes from men who have cast off bonds which they show themselves able to bear."[13]

So Modernism, bearing Pound's stamp, brought revolutionary fervor to the effort to recapture "tradition." But this was not the worship of Milton and the Romantics with which the term was then identified. Pound's urge to go back beyond such narrow, conventional conceptions, and his belief that "all ages are contemporaneous," led directly to Eliot's famous essay with its insistence on a collective, glacial "mind of Europe. . . . which abandons nothing *en route*, which does not superannuate either Shakespeare, or Homer, or the rock drawing of the Magdalenian draughtsmen."[14] (Pound would have insisted on going beyond Europe too, but here that term stands as a rebuke to British insularity.) About a year before writing his essay Eliot, in his *Egoist* columns, had diagnosed current poetry as "deficient in tradition," and thus gripped by mortmain:

> England puts her Great Writers away securely in a Safe Deposit Vault, and curls to sleep like Fafner. There they go rotten; for if our predecessors cannot teach us to write better than themselves, they will surely teach us to write worse; because we have never learned to criticize Keats, Shelley, and Wordsworth (poets of assured though modest merit), Keats, Shelley, and Wordsworth punish us from their graves with the annual scourge of the Georgian Anthology.[15]

The Georgian poets have now disappeared into the dustbin of his-

13. *Letters*, p. 113; and "America: Chances and Remedies," *New Age*, May 29, 1913, pp. 115–16.

14. See Pound's *Spirit of Romance* (New Directions, n.d.; originally published, 1910), p. 8; and Eliot's "Tradition and the Individual Talent," *Selected Essays*, p. 6.

15. "Observations," T. S. Apteryx, *Egoist*, May, 1918, p. 69.

tory, just as Eliot foresaw, because they failed to guard against a stillborn derivation from the past.

In the "Tradition" essay, many of the most notorious pronouncements are similarly topical; they continue the waspish attacks on current notions of poetic composition, especially on the vulgarized dregs of Romantic "genius" theory (great minds expressing great thoughts, etc.):

> What happens is a continual surrender of [the poet] as he is at the moment to something which is more valuable [i.e., the tradition.] The progress of the artist is a continual self-sacrifice, a continual extinction of personality. . . .
>
> If you compare several representative passages of the greatest poetry you see . . . how completely any semi-ethical criterion of "sublimity" misses the mark. For it is not the "greatness," the intensity, of the emotions, the components, but the intensity of the artistic process, the pressure, so to speak, under which the fusion takes place, that counts. . . . And emotions which [the poet] has never experienced will serve his turn as well as those familiar to him. Consequently, we must believe that "emotion recollected in tranquillity" is an inexact formula. For it is neither emotion, nor recollection, nor, without distortion of meaning, tranquillity. . . . Poetry is not a turning loose of emotion, but an escape from emotion; it is not the expression of personality, but an escape from personality. But, of course, only those who have personality and emotions know what it means to want to escape from those things.[16]

For Eliot the key word was *surrender*: the artist surrenders his unruly personality to "something" greater than himself, outside him. This obviously prefigures his Christian conversion, some years later. Eliot's Donnean sense of the intertwining of religious and sexual surrender led to the lines from *The Waste Land*:

> The awful daring of a moment's surrender
> Which an age of prudence can never retract
> By this, and this only, we have existed . . .

These should make us think of Donne inviting God to ravish him, and they frame all the painful sexual failures and degradations in the poem with a sense of redemptive possibility. Eliot's ability to project himself into victims, particularly violated women — see especially "The Death of Saint Narcissus" and the chorus of women

16. *Selected Essays*, pp. 6–7, 8, 10–11.

in *Murder in the Cathedral*—gave him the power to dramatize the paradox of such figures, "Torn and most whole."[17]

But in the essay, the provocations directed at the Georgians and other tradition-starved contemporaries have no poignant notes. The main thrust is against the vulgar conception of originality: "Not only the best, but the most individual parts of [a poet's] work may be those in which the dead poets, his ancestors, assert their immortality most vigorously." Surely Eliot was thinking of Pound when he wrote this; a few years later he commented: "Now Pound is often most 'original' in the right sense, when he is most 'archaeological' in the ordinary sense." In 1919, he described the principle of the *Cantos* as "a final fusion of all [Pound's] masks, a final concentration of the entire past upon the present." His judgment was that Pound's success was the triumph of totalized atavism: "As the present is no more than the present existence, the present significance, of the entire past, Mr. Pound proceeds by acquiring the entire past."[18] Even with the hyperbole, the analysis points to the key to Pound's project, and to the depth of concord between the two of them.

Eliot's postulation of a tradition that "has a simultaneous existence and composes a simultaneous order" is essentially typological, in that the new work somehow transforms the older works, although they are already self-sufficient before "the supervention of novelty." Thus the Old Testament was complete and yet supplemented, both added to and fulfilled, by the New. Thus, long before Harold Bloom, Yeats influences Milton (Eliot wrote that "Pound has influenced the Chinese and the Provencals and the Italians and the Saxons").[19] Eliot also adds to the typological language an apothegm that recapitulates the position of the "ancients" in the seventeenth-century "querelle" with the "moderns," an ironic and strangely unnoticed point. "Some one said: 'The dead writers are remote from us because we *know* so much more than they did.'

17. *Waste Land*, 11. 404–6; *Ash Wednesday*, II; *Poems Written in Early Youth* (Farrar & Straus, 1970), p. 28.

18. *Selected Essays*, p. 4; "Introduction: 1928," in *Ezra Pound: Selected Poems* (Faber, 1959), p. 11; 1919 *Athenaeum* review of Pound's *Quia Pauper Amavi*, quoted in Ronald Bush, *The Genesis of Ezra Pound's Cantos* (Princeton University Press, 1976), p. 211.

19. "Introduction: 1928" (see preceding note), p. 15.

Precisely, and they are that which we know."[20] This is simply a variant of the old trope that we moderns can see far because we are standing on the shoulders of giants, the ancients themselves. Eliot's essay completes the Modernist repudiation not only of nostalgia for the future, but also of the nineteenth-century fear of atavism: the giants have awakened at last, and they turn out to have capacious shoulders. Gone is the image of mortmain, the deathgrip of the past; here the tenacious hold of the dead brings strength to the living. The last words of the essay, fitting for Eliot's typological theme, figure renewal through resurrection: the poet must live in "what is not merely the present, but the present moment of the past"—the same phrasing, from the same year, as in his judgment of the *Cantos*—and must be "conscious, not of what is dead, but of what is already living." The very vitality of the present comes from the past nourishing it; the present can grow because the past has come to life again in it.

In the light of this figuration, we can read Eliot's words about Joyce's "mythical method" in *Ulysses*, giving shape and control to the "immense panorama of futility and anarchy" that is the present, as something more than reactionary exasperation.[21] Eliot's own work from that point on was infused and invigorated by a substratum of mythological and chthonic motifs, obviously in *The Waste Land* but more fruitfully in *Sweeney Agonistes*, subtitled "Fragments of an Aristophanic Melodrama." His sense of mythic vitality was more classically oriented than Pound's, more attuned to that of the Cambridge anthropologists: thus the process bore fruit for him typically in the use of Greek tragedies as matrices for his own plays. The motif of a sacrificial self-surrender underlies all his dramatic work, combining the Greek and Christian vectors; even Sweeney is potentially a "tragic hero" in this sense. Eliot's power to put himself in the place of the victim fits naturally into such work, which drew on the idea that the Greek tragedies were themselves atavistic revivifications of an original ritual involving the self-sacrifice of Dionysus. The concept of the substitute victim, whose suffering or death is redeemed by the renewed life he gives to others, not only suffused Eliot's later work but retrospectively

---

20. *Selected Essays*, p. 6.
21. "Ulysses, Order, and Myth," *Dial* 75 (1923): 483.

transformed and gave new meaning to his earlier poems, as old and new revivify each other in his "tradition."[22]

For Pound, the motif of resurrection had already appeared in his creation of masks or personae, a poetic process he envisioned as that of raising the dead. In his substitute for an M.A. thesis, *The Spirit of Romance*, he praised the poetic heroes who more or less bracketed his sense of the tradition in 1910: "Ovid, before Browning, raises the dead and dissects their mental processes; he walks with the people of myth." Later Pound spoke of his *Propertius* as bringing "a dead man to life,"[23] but an even better exhibit is Canto I, in which the blood for the ghosts is an analogue for translation, giving the dead power to speak: not only in the sense of putting a text into another language, but also in the sense of handing on a live cultural tradition, as in the great Western myth derived from the *Aeneid*, that the *imperium* of culture was carried from Troy to Rome and finally embodied in Europe. (This, of course, is why Barbarossa's medieval Germany was called the Holy Roman Empire, though all three terms were misnomers, and why "Czar" and "Kaiser" are titles translating *Caesar*; even the republicans of revolutionary France and America thought Rome was immanent in their regimes. Current debaters about "Western Civilization" courses ought to recognize the mythical basis of the concept.) Known formerly as the *translatio imperii*, its cultural counterpart was the *translatio studii*, with alternative itineraries involving Athens or Jerusalem. These concepts comprise a resurrectional and typological idea of "tradition," a word whose basic meaning is very similar to that of "translation."[24]

22. See "Euripides and Professor Murray" (1920), *Selected Essays*, p. 49: "Few books are more fascinating than those of Miss Harrison, Mr. Cornford, or Mr. Cooke [*sic*], when they burrow in the origins of Greek myths and rites." For Murray's most important contribution to Eliot's practices, see his "Excursus on the Ritual Forms Preserved in Greek Tragedy," in Jane Harrison's *Themis: A Study of the Social Origins of Greek Religion* (New American Library, 1962; originally published, 1912), pp. 341–63.

23. *Spirit of Romance*, p. 16; *Letters*, p. 149.

24. See Ernst Robert Curtius, *European Literature and the Latin Middle Ages*, trans. Willard Trask (Harper & Row, 1963), pp. 29 et seq.; also see Walter Burkert, *Structure and History in Greek Mythology and Ritual* (University of California Press, 1979), p. 25, on the role of the Greeks in idealizing all their enemies as "Trojan" and thus creating the Romans' spurious genealogy.

Pound, who used Propertius' "Troica Roma resurges" as an epigraph in 1911, meant Canto I to illustrate the live force of the Odyssey being transmitted to the Renaissance through the Latin "crib" of Andreas Divus.[25] It also speaks less obviously of Pound's own journey to London, a city "covered with close-webbed mist." For the callow young poet, bounced from his teaching job, the trip in 1908 was a voyage to the land of the illustrious dead, from whom he hoped to draw inspiration and poetic sustenance. As he wrote in 1913: "Besides knowing living artists I have come in touch with the tradition of the dead. . . . [In] this sort of Apostolic Succession . . . people whose minds have been enriched by contact with men of genius retain the effects of it."[26] Through Ford and Yeats and their friends, especially the older ones, he received a "laying on of hands" that, he believed, transmitted the spark of tradition, not only from them but also from those they had known in youth. He sought out all the great survivors, but was too shy to approach Swinburne, who died in 1909; hence the lines in Canto 82 (quoted in Chapter 1): "Swinburne my only miss/and I didn't know he'd been to see Landor." This was written in 1945, and his mind was still vivid with the "Apostolic Succession"; the immediately preceding Canto ends with his memory of visiting Wilfrid Scawen Blunt in 1914, with Yeats and others, "to have gathered from the air a live tradition," and is followed by the regret that leads to the thought of Swinburne: "Here error is all in the not done,/all in the diffidence that faltered . . . " For Pound in Pisa, imprisoned by the American army, the names of Blunt, Swinburne, and Landor form an ideogram of both poetry and politics: they were all in different ways at odds with their countrymen, and suffered for it. Blunt, a vehement anti-Imperialist, had toasted Pound and Richard Aldington, on another visit, with "Damnation to the British government!"[27]

"The tradition" had acquired its political overtones in 1919, when Pound fell under the spell of C. H. Douglas and his analysis of industrialism's built-in deflationary tendencies. Douglas's concept of the "cultural heritage," that element of production he thought

25. The poem was "Rome."
26. "How I Began," *T.P.'s Weekly*, June 6, 1913, p. 707; see note 48 to ch. 1.
27. Carpenter, *A Serious Character*, pp. 228–29.

slighted in the wrangling about capital and labor, sounded to Pound like another name for *tradition*. But to see the force of this alignment on Pound, and why he pursued it to the political dead end that left him in an asylum, we must emphasize the mystical component rather than the economic: he was *jusqu'au-boutiste* because the whole matter was essentially a religious belief. The spark handed on by the "Apostolic Succession" was not for him a mere figure of speech; the numinous, he would have said, is sometimes most easily seen in its transmission.

Critics have not known what to make of Pound's mystical tendency; of those who mention it, only a few comment usefully. For most it seems something to apologize for, like his anti-Semitism. But it must be interpreted if we would comprehend his role in modern literature. For him, it combined the recondite with the matter-of-fact. He could write casually in a letter: "The minute you proclaim that the mysteries exist *at all* you've got to recognize that 95% of yr. contemporaries will not and can not understand *one* word of what you are driving at. And you can *not* explain."[28] The ultimate secrets are esoteric, reserved for the initiates, but he talks about them without hieratic mystification; to state it briefly, this is because the divine is immanent in the commonplace, not in some far-off realm of the transcendent. We can see this by tracing what can be known of his beliefs.

In evidence from Pound's early years we find hints of many kinds of psychic explorations. The adolescent courtship of Hilda Doolittle—before she was H. D. the poet, she was the daughter of a Penn professor of astronomy, and both Pound and Williams called on her—seems to have consisted of the use of exploratory sex play to produce visionary states. They taught each other, by means Pound later ascribed to Troubadour love cults, how to attain experiences of *ek-stasis*, standing outside oneself. In a transport of unconsummated ecstasy, with the right kind of stimuli and autosuggestion, one could experience what Pound always thought of as the divine principle, metamorphosis, and become "a tree amid the wood": see "The Tree" from *Hilda's Book*, which Pound de-

28. *Letters*, pp. 328–29. Leon Surette, in *A Light from Eleusis* (Oxford University Press, 1979) offers much useful information on the background of Pound's beliefs.

creed should stand at the beginning of all his *Personae* collections. This erotic mysticism bore fruit in many poems and several essays.[29] Hints of it are also seen in the recently published letters to his future wife, Dorothy Shakespear. In the London years we also hear of readings in occult traditions, conversations with authorities such as Evelyn Underhill, and even acts like horoscope casting.[30] Many of these activities seem linked to the developing friendship with Yeats; Pound heard much about Yeats's own zealous psychic researches into magical symbols and other esoterica, undertaken on the principle that "one should believe whatever had been believed in all countries and periods, and only reject any part of it after much evidence, instead of starting all over afresh and only believing what one could prove."[31]

Yeats had been the major figure in the "Apostolic Succession" linking back to poets of earlier ages, and was the source for Pound's knowledge of such figures as Lionel Johnson, whose appearance in *Mauberley* ties together once more the esoteric and the political. Johnson stands for a chain of poets going back to "Swinburne/ And Rossetti still abused," not for political views as such but because of their mystical, antimaterialist interests: in Johnson's case, the mysteries of the Church. These figures are alienated, ignored, or persecuted by a mercantile, Philistine public goaded by hirelings of the press (Oscar Wilde is the hidden symbol in the poem), and go off into evasions, retreats, defeats of various kinds. Since Pound portrays culture as a struggle between the artist and the banker—not only here but spectacularly in the *Cantos*—we must see that Yeats's long-smoldering resentment against the English with their shopkeeper mentality, and against those Irish politicians who deal with or are "hotfaced bargainers," was a prime source for Pound's attitudes.[32] But unlike Yeats, Pound sees no

29. See Kevin Oderman, *Ezra Pound and the Erotic Medium* (Duke University Press, 1986); and H. D. [Hilda Doolittle], *End to Torment: A Memoir of Ezra Pound*, ed. Norman Holmes Pearson and Michael King (New Directions, 1979).

30. *Letters*, p. 21; and Omar Pound and A. Walton Litz, eds., *Ezra Pound and Dorothy Shakespear: Their Letters 1909–1914* (New Directions, 1984), pp. 3–11, 32, 113.

31. *The Autobiography of William Butler Yeats* (Doubleday, 1958; originally published, 1936), p. 52.

32. *Autobiography*, p. 311.

gap between the political or economic realm and that of the spirit. On the contrary, they interact on the same plane, and each ignores the other to its cost.

However, Yeats powerfully reinforced Pound's conviction that the numinous could be found in inherited traditions. He had written not only of the value of accepting all traditional beliefs, but of something he called the Great Memory (later, in "The Second Coming," the *Spiritus Mundi*), which our minds could fitfully join.[33] Pound never overtly subscribed to the Great Memory, and indeed sometimes demonstrated impatience with Yeats's mystical habits, but belief in transmissible, cumulative mental energy became ever stronger in his work. A wonderful irony is that although Pound surely played some part in the modernizing of Yeats's verse after 1914, he preferred the early poems on which he had grown up and which had formed his spiritual ideals, the volumes such as *The Wind Among the Reeds* in which he had first seen so many enchanted codes and messages. Pound never saw Yeats as a Modernist, but took him at his own evaluation as "the last Romantic." In contrast to the aggressively contemporary Ford, he was "a great dim figure with its associations set in the past," a late-roaming mammoth: "Mr. Yeats is a romanticist, symbolist, occultist, for better or worse, now and for always. That does not matter. What does matter is that he is the only one left who has sufficient intensity of temperament to turn these modes into art."[34]

The effect of all these influences and investigations was that Pound eventually made himself into a pagan fundamentalist, not in believing in myths as scriptures but in believing that the gods are as real as ever, and immanent in the world around us. He "accepted [the] greek deities," he said in *Guide to Kulchur*, apparently mean-

33. See "Magic" (1901) in *Essays and Introductions* (Macmillan, 1961), p. 28; and my "Pound and Yeats: The Question of Symbolism," *ELH*, 32, June 1965, esp. p. 228.

34. For Yeats, see his poem "Coole Park and Ballylee" (1932); Pound, *Letters*, p. 21; and "Mr. Yeats' New Book," *Poetry*, December 1916, p. 151. By 1920 Pound thought Yeats "faded" (*Letters*, p. 158) but they remained friends—Yeats even moved to Rapallo for a while—although Pound continued to prefer his early work (letter to William Carlos Williams of September 9, 1957, in the Beinecke Collection at Yale University).

ing that pagan numens are for him crystallizations of eternal processes in nature that humans can apprehend with reverence and
training.[35] The gods are incarnate insights, and may appear in sudden revelations among perfectly ordinary circumstances. Thus one
must work to become an "halluciné," like Gaudier-Brzeska or
Ford, who, according to Pound, was capable of seeing "the Venus
immortal crossing the tram tracks."[36] Yeats seeing Helen in Maud
Gonne, and Joyce seeing Odysseus in Bloom, are symptomatic of
related trends in Modernism, but Pound's version is remarkable
for insisting on the equal reality of the divine and the mundane,
the mystery and the city (Joyce is not as literal about the mystery
as Pound). The cave of Eleusis can run underneath those tram
tracks, and does so "In a Station of the Metró." Pound recreated
in himself the state of mind of those sophisticated ancients and
tribesmen we call primitives, in our patronizing way, for whom the
phenomenal world is a series of personal encounters:

> Primitive man simply does not know an inanimate world. For this very
> reason he does not "personify" inanimate phenomena nor does he fill
> an empty world with the ghosts of the dead, as "animism" would have
> us believe.
>
> The world appears to primitive man neither inanimate nor empty but
> redundant with life; and life has individuality, in man and beast and
> plant, and in every phenomenon which confronts man — the thunder-
> clap, the sudden shadow, the eerie and unknown clearing in the wood,
> the stone which suddenly hurts him when he stumbles while on a hunt-
> ing trip. Any phenomenon may at any time face him, not as "It," but
> as "Thou." . . .
>
> . . . When the river does not rise, it has *refused* to rise.[37]

All this is similar to Pound's belief that "a god is an eternal state of
mind" — which, like Blake's dictum that all gods reside in the human breast, should not be confused with subjectivism. Gods are
manifestations of the permanent world to which humans have occasional, flickering access.

35. *Guide to Kulchur* (New Directions, [1938]), p. 301.

36. From Pound's obituary notice of Ford, *Selected Prose 1909–1965*, ed. William Cookson (New Directions, 1975), p. 461.

37. H. Frankfort and H. A. Frankfort, "Myth and Reality" (1946), in their *The
Intellectual Adventure of Ancient Man* (University of Chicago Press, 1977), pp. 5–
6, 15.

When is a god manifest?
When states of mind take form.
When does a man become a god?
When he enters one of these states of mind.
. . . .
What are the kinds of knowledge?
There are immediate knowledge and hearsay.
Is hearsay of any value?
Of some.
What is the greatest hearsay?
The greatest hearsay is the tradition of the gods.
Of what use is this tradition?
It tells us to be ready to look.[38]

Immediate knowledge is direct psychic experience, but we can see the numinous in events all around us if we revere the "tradition of the gods." From this follows Pound's definition of myth: a person attuned to the tradition encounters "delightful psychic experience," but finds it "necessary to screen himself from persecution," and therefore puts it into coded form because others could not understand what was meant by "'I turned into a tree.'"[39] As we have seen, Pound began cultivating such experiences no later than adolescence, and metamorphosis—entering the state of being of some other entity, sometimes of a god—was the form in which such transports occurred; moreover, metamorphosis was linked with resurrection, raising the dead, into whose being one could also enter by "delightful psychic experience." This explains Pound's otherwise puzzling assertion that Ovid's *Metamorphoses* was "a sacred book"; it and the writings of Confucius were "the only safe guides in religion."[40] Ovid is conventionally dismissed as a purveyor of entertaining fables, with no real religious belief or even spiritual impulse. Pound dissents completely, and in the final form of the *Cantos*, the Ovidian Metamorphosis of Canto II balances the Homeric Nekuia, the journey to the underworld, of Canto I. For Pound, these two *topoi* apparently divide the tradition between

38. *Selected Prose*, p. 47.
39. *Spirit of Romance*, p. 92; and *Literary Essays of Ezra Pound*, ed. T. S. Eliot (New Directions, 1954), p. 431.
40. *Letters*, p. 183; cf. *Guide to Kulchur*, p. 299, and *Literary Essays*, p. 179.

them. Writing to his father, he described Canto II as "the 'magic moment' or moment of metamorphosis, bust thru from quotidian into 'divine or permanent world.' Gods, etc."[41] Especially the term "bust thru" and the laconic "gods, etc." exemplify once again Pound's determination not to swathe these cherished and intensely serious beliefs in mystifications of language: as the divine world and the quotidian interpenetrate, so must the mysteries and the most down-to-earth way of speaking of them.

Pound's practice accords with the principles of ancient and primitive people. Typically the divine and natural worlds are the same for them, and Western tradition, which prefers absolute gulfs between the sacred and the profane, has a hard time understanding this.[42] But Pound understood it by intuition, just as he instantly saw the genius in the early work of Eliot and Joyce. (In fact "Mr. Nixon," in *Mauberley*, is correct: "No one knows, at sight, a masterpiece"—for, as E. H. Gombrich has shown, without proper schemata we cannot really "see" the new work of art.[43] But Pound transgresses this rule, and others.) He was thus able to recapture the mind-set of polytheism, to see the polymorphous potential in the tradition of metamorphoses. This kind of thinking was playful enough at the beginning, but he really did become a zealot of this religion. D. S. Carne-Ross, one of the few critics to comment usefully on Pound's beliefs, asserts that the test can be read in the Pisan Cantos:

> What these cantos show is that Pound won through [over despair] because he felt himself sustained by the powers he had always believed in. He himself went down into the unending labyrinth of the souterrain, a dark night of the soul that left no room for "poetry," for make-believe. And he came up, to look on the eternal elements and a nature once again brilliant with divinity. The army gave him a patch of ground to lie on and he found Demeter there and celebrated the marriage of Heaven and Earth. It must be the most astounding breach of military discipline since Coleridge joined the 15th Dragoons.[44]

41. *Letters*, p. 210.
42. See my *Sacred Discontent: The Bible and Western Tradition* (Louisiana State University Press, 1976), chap. 2.
43. *Art and Illusion* (Princeton University Press, 1960), *passim*.
44. "The Music of a Lost Dynasty: Pound in the Classroom," *Instaurations* (University of California Press, 1979), pp. 212–13.

Thus, when Pound sees the infant wasp as a chthonic messenger (Canto 83), it is not a picturesque allegory or a reprise of Wordsworth wishing to hear old Triton blow his wreathéd horn. Pound had no nostalgia for the good old days of myth; he believed their way of seeing the world is available to us now.

Polytheism, entailing respect for many forms of truth, became one of Pound's strongest commitments, and consequently he hated monotheistic religions for their coercive tendencies — blaming "some unpleasing Semite or Parsee or Syrian" for degrading spiritual insights into loyalty oaths. Obviously this was a powerful reinforcement, if not the source, of his anti-Semitism, but he tended to attack Christianity more directly.[45] He believed that some seeds of pagan wisdom had been carried along in Church traditions, but had been largely rooted out; and so the Church declined into bureaucracy and disputatious theology, until "it no longer believed or even knew what [its own doctrine] meant."[46] Only those who can now uncover the truths of the Albigensians, or of philosophers like Erigena, Grosseteste, or Richard of St. Victor can again see what was latent in the traditions. Modern Christianity in its contemptible torpor turned to enforcing orthodoxy and an obsession with belief: "Belief is a cramp, a paralysis, an atrophy of the mind in certain positions."[47]

Pound's undivided way of seeing the cosmos, with the realms of sacred and profane interpenetrating, accounts for another puzzling aspect of his views: the combination of mysticism with an unabashed empiricism. Agassiz (see the anecdote of Agassiz and the fish at the beginning of the *ABC of Reading*) was one of his heroes, just as was Ovid. As this story shows, the only useless knowledge for Pound was abstract, cataloged "book learning": Ernest Fenollosa's *Essay on the Chinese Written Character* reinforced this conviction at great length. What unified the esoteric and the empirical was Pound's concept of "direct" or "immediate knowledge." One could have immediate knowledge of the gods, as he said in "Re-

45. *Literary Essays*, p. 431; cf. *Selected Prose*, p. 52: "Inasmuch as the Jew has conducted no holy war for nearly two millennia, he is preferable to the Christian and the Mohammedan." This opinion of 1919 changed shortly afterwards, when he was persuaded that Jews financed wars.
46. *Selected Prose*, p. 57.
47. Ibid., p. 49.

ligio," and equally one could have nonconceptual, nonproposi-
tional knowledge of, say, painting. In 1911 he wrote: "A few days
in a good gallery are more illuminating than years would be if
spent in reading a description of these pictures."[48] In 1937, writing
Guide to Kulchur, he was still using the example: a gallery-goer
acquires a "form–colour" discrimination,

> a certain real knowledge which would enable me to tell a Goya from
> a Velasquez, a Velasquez from an Ambrogio Praedis. . . . There are
> passages of the poets which approximate the form–colour acquisition.
> And herein is clue to Confucius' reiterated commendation of such of
> his students as studied the Odes.[49]

Knowledge, even mystical knowledge of the gods, is in the particulars of the world, the *hekasta* (the "eaches") from which the *Kath-
'olou* (the general) must be drawn. The *Cantos* imply a tradition,
similar to that of the Confucian Odes, that "tells us where to look."
So also "Art does not avoid universals, it strikes at them all the
harder in that it strikes through particulars."[50]

In Pound's epistemology, "direct" knowledge is related to another kind, which provides yet another set of exempla for the belief
in traditions of transmissible mental energy. According to Pound,
this kind was emphasized by the anthropologist Frobenius:

> The value of Leo Frobenius to civilization is . . . [that] he has in espe-
> cial seen and marked out a kind of knowing, the difference between
> knowledge that has to be acquired by particular effort and knowing
> that is in people, "in the air." He has accented the value of such record.
> His archaeology is not retrospective, it is immediate.
>
> Example: the peasants opposed a railway cutting. A king had driven
> into the ground at that place. The engineers dug and unearthed the
> bronze car of Dis, two thousand years buried. . . . "Where we found
> these rock drawings, there was always water within six feet of the
> surface." That kind of research goes not only into past and forgotten
> life, but points to tomorrow's water supply.[51]

Once again the combination of esoteric and empirical is characteristic. Frobenius is surely a presiding genius for the *Cantos*, which

---

48. *Selected Prose*, p. 23.
49. *Guide to Kulchur*, p. 28.
50. *Literary Essays*, p. 420; cf. Canto 74/441.
51. *Guide to Kulchur*, p. 57.

also aspire to an archaeology of the immediate, one that will reveal the fault lines caused by the rot of *usura* but also the continual upspringings of "the tradition," the spiritual equivalent of living water.

The concept of such traditions or cumulative transfers of mental force is indispensable background for Pound's vision of a succession of literary works that pointed toward his own and other Modernist texts. In 1928 he outlined a version and rationale for this succession in a defense of William Carlos Williams against charges of formlessness:

> Very well, he does not "conclude"; his work has been "often formless," "incoherent," opaque, obscure, obfuscated, confused, truncated, etc.
>
> I am not going to say: "form" is a non-literary component shoved on to literature by Aristotle or by some non-litteratus who told Aristotle about it. Major form is not a non-literary component. But it can do us no harm to stop an hour or so and consider the number of very important chunks of world-literature in which form, major form, is remarkable mainly for absence.[52]

Pound lists the Iliad ("a corking plot . . . but it is not told us in the poem"), Aeschylus' *Prometheus*, the works of Montaigne and Rabelais, Lope de Vega, and finally Flaubert (*"Bouvard and Pecuchet* wasn't even finished by its author") as exemplars. From this Pound went on to imply that form was not always necessary in literature, and could be restrictive and devitalizing: "The best pages of Williams — at least for the present reviewer — are those where he has made the least effort to fit anything into either story, book, or (in *The American Grain*) into an essay." This statement inevitably looks forward to a most revealing remark Donald Hall recalls Pound making about the form of the *Cantos*, that it had to be one that "wouldn't exclude something merely because it didn't fit."[53] Evidently formlessness — or kinds of form that somehow incorporated excess, overflow, transgression, and the like — had positive values in light of the tradition. Though grudgingly conceding the merit of "the 'accomplished,'" Pound seemed to be defending the *Cantos* as well as Williams's work in speaking of "the other satisfactory effect, that of a man hurling himself at an indomitable

52. *Literary Essays*, p. 394.
53. *Writers at Work* (see note 8), p. 38.

chaos, and yanking or hauling as much of it as possible into some sort of order (or beauty), aware of it both as chaos and as potential."[54] If so, he implied the existence of great precedents for such projects.

Pound's interest in formlessness seems to come from his sense that Procrustean homogenizing of different materials denatures them and impedes their effective relationship to one another. A clue to his cast of mind here can be found in his paraphrase of the principle of entropy in his advocacy of Henry James:

> Peace comes of communication. No man of our time has so laboured to create means of communication as did the late Henry James. The whole of great art is a struggle for communication. All things that oppose this are evil, whether they be silly scoffing or obstructive tariffs.
>
> And this communication is not a levelling, it is not an elimination of differences. It is a recognition of differences, of the right of differences to exist, of interest in finding things different.[55]

As Peter Makin observes: "Difference is what Pound wants; it creates 'discharge' between 'charged surfaces,' one of his governing images in physics, sexual relations, and the aesthetics of art."[56] When form is imposed, there is a risk of planing down the potential for discharge. So mistrustful of making things fit was Pound that he willingly ran the risk of widespread rejection of his lifework rather than compromise on the point. He would do nothing to force his materials into predetermined shapes, or relationships with one another. If they could not find their own places, too bad.

Like other great poetic and artistic pioneers, Pound was not risk-averse. As Wordsworth risked ridicule and disdain for his convictions, so did Pound; both of them could have secured much wider readership by taking more conventional paths. Pound's stub-

---

54. *Literary Essays*, p. 396. Note that Pound's sense of the tradition is more occult, or Eleusinian, than that of Eliot, or for that matter, anyone else. Hence his interest in Troubadours and the like. The ideas of "trobar clus" and "gai saber" recur often, in fact, in the drafts for the early Cantos. This point has not only poetic but also political implications. See especially Cairns Craig, *Yeats, Eliot, Pound, and the Politics of Poetry* (Croom Helm, 1982) about the differences among Pound and the others: Yeats and Eliot revered a more aristocratic, less secret tradition, though all of them had their mystic touches.

55. *Literary Essays*, p. 298.

56. *Pound's Cantos* (Allen & Unwin, 1985), p. 69.

bornness was based on his sense of the modern, that is, on the belief that the new wave in literature must be experimental and novel, but even more on his sense of a tradition. If a current ran from the Greeks to Williams that could be seen as undermining ideas of form, he too was part of it. He credited Williams with "Mediterranean equipment," alluding to his Spanish heritage but also to his descent from the predecessors named above. This concept must lie behind the great tradition, described in "How to Read" and other such essays, that included all Pound's favorite authors: Homer, Sappho, Catullus, Propertius, Ovid, Dante, Chaucer and so on up to Joyce — *Ulysses* was quintessentially "Mediterranean," and Pound saw it as directly continuing *Bouvard et Pécuchet*.[57] With the obvious exception of Dante, the authors in Pound's lists tend to be either cavalier toward form themselves, or preserved for us in fragmentary but revealing texts: their *virtú* or power survives the erosion of form.

Given what Pound says in the *Dichten = condensare* section of *ABC of Reading*, we can deduce that concentration and compression, always for him the highest values of literary technique (because "great literature is simply language charged with meaning to the utmost possible degree"), were the ultimate motives behind the transcendence of canons of form.

> Pisistratus found the Homeric texts in disorder, we don't quite know what he did about it. The Bible is a compendium, people trimmed it to make it solid. It has gone on for ages, because it wasn't allowed to overrun all the available parchment. . . . Ovid's Metamorphoses are a compendium, not an epic like Homer's; Chaucer's Canterbury Tales are a compendium of all the good yarns Chaucer knew. The Tales have lasted through centuries while the long-winded medieval narratives went into museums.[58]

It seems clear that here Pound privileges a tradition that has as its touchstone a combination of particularist concentration and farraginous inclusiveness, in which the works have an apparently randomized form: the very devices of the *Cantos*, as of *Ulysses*, which calls itself "this chaffering allincluding most farraginous

---

57. *Literary Essays*, pp. 27 ff., also pp. 403 and 416.

58. *Literary Essays*, p. 23; and *ABC of Reading* (New Directions, 1960; originally published, 1934), p. 92.

chronicle."[59] The bloodlines of Modernism, then, descend through these "Mediterranean" compendia. Since the *Cantos* are neither an epic nor a Menippean satire, though partaking in both, perhaps we ought to call them a compendium, or even an anthology, in the sense of Chaucer's *Tales* or the Bible.[60]

Pound was never comfortable with "the fitting," in any sense. In Vorticist days he adopted a deliberate, programmatic vulgarity, taunting and insulting the public; this stance became very ugly when it turned anti-Semitic. But it had its more fortunate counterpart in the concept of the work as a play of uncontainable forces, resulting in farraginous collections of concentrated "gists and piths."[61] While more self-contained works go into museums, the exuberant, transgressive, apparently randomized works become part of great traditions. The whole idea reveals Pound's relish for dynamic change and polymorphous diversity: very likely he wanted the form of his major work to be metamorphic, which is why it is so hard to say just what "a Canto" is. Once again the most modern aspects of his work are derived from the most ancient.

Pound's convictions about these things were so powerful that he distrusted all appearances of unity in ancient texts, as his remarks on Pisistratus and on the absence of "plot" in the Iliad suggest. (Of course there is a plot in the Iliad, but it is synecdochic to the larger story of the Trojan War and is not self-contained in the formal sense.) In a letter he went much further:

> I suspect neither Dante nor Homer *had* the kind of boring 'unity' of surface that we take to be characteristic of Pope, Racine, Corneille.
>
> The Nekuia shouts aloud that it is *older* than the rest, all that island, Cretan, etc., hinter-time, that is *not* Praxiteles, not Athens of Pericles, but Odysseus.[62]

These sentences are vital for the *Cantos*, and for Modernism. As a gloss on Canto I they are most illuminating (especially if we add a

59. *Ulysses* (Vintage Books, 1961; originally published, 1922), p. 423; Gabler ed., 14.1412.

60. See the running debate in *Paideuma* between Max Nänny and Michael André Bernstein: vol. 11, Winter 1982, pp. 395–405; vol. 12, Fall–Winter 1983, pp. 269–74; and vol. 13, Fall 1984, pp. 263–68.

61. *ABC of Reading*, p. 92.

62. *Letters*, p. 274. For Pound, Dante's apparent unity may have been a "screen" for mystical contents.

passage written in 1912: "I have, moreover, sought in Anglo-Saxon a certain element which has transmuted the various qualities of poetry which have drifted up from the South").[63] They also show that for Pound Homer is not the beginning, but that his Nekuia already contains the archaic within it, buried but waking: it "shouts aloud." The eruption of atavism is already there in his work.

More generally, this passage illustrates the great shift in taste and understanding that occurred as a result of the "primitivism" of Picasso and others, from (as Charles Olson put it) the classical-representational to the primitive–abstract, from the polished humanism of Praxitelean sculpture to the earlier, Egyptian-stylized hieratic statuary and thence to comparable shifts in art from other provenances.[64] For Pound, the immediate source here was Gaudier-Brzeska, who attacked the classical Greeks for embodying in their art what Pound called "the caressable," forms in which the viewer delighted to fantasize an idealized version of him or herself: what they wanted instead was "sculpture with [the god] inside."[65] The point, for Pound, Picasso, and the rest, was not that there was something noble about this preclassical savagery or that it fell in with the pastoral ideals of otium and content; rather it represented the sudden liberating appearance of a heritage that had been carried unseen within the present, as in Yeats's favorite figure of "mummy wheat." Not primitivism in the old sense, this impulse was not only artifactual instead of allegorical, but also lacked the antiquarian "romance of time-travel," and jaded escapist complaints against the decadence of the present. It celebrated the atavistic energies of a reawakening, a resurrection of that which is immanent but invisible to the timid or ignorant—to paraphrase Eliot's essay, or Picasso's pictures.[66]

So the tradition all along was atavistic as well as cumulative,

63. *Selected Prose*, p. 24.

64. Charles Olson, *Selected Writings*, ed. Robert Creeley (New Directions, n.d.), p. 28.

65. Pound, *Gaudier-Brzeska: A Memoir* (New Directions, 1960; originally published, 1916), p. 97; and *Literary Essays*, pp. 152–53.

66. Reed Way Dasenbrock, *The Literary Vorticism of Ezra Pound and Wyndham Lewis* (Johns Hopkins University Press, 1985), esp. pp. 78–102, discusses the issue of primitivism and use of the past very helpfully, but with some emphases that differ from mine. He says that the apparent primitivism of Vorticism was more a "kind of modernism or presentism" (p. 82).

each work drawing strength from the energizing past. Pound had been nurturing anticipatory forms of these ideas throughout his Modernist activities, and even before them. In the enthusiasms of his antiquarian phase—for Yeats and Browning for instance—we see the importance of mysticism and "the Apostolic Succession" for the one, and of "raising the dead" in the dramatic monologues for the other; the importance to him of Hardy's sense of the past has already been discussed at length; these qualities of theirs combined with the others that attracted him, such as the acceptance of "difficulty" and awkwardness by Hardy and Browning, and their feeling for the materiality and potentiality of language. But when Pound began to shape what was later to be called Modernism, further crystallizations took place. An epitome of his sense of things shows up in his usage of the term *vortex*, in *BLAST* (1914):

> The vortex is the point of maximum energy. . . . All experience rushes into this vortex. All the energized past, all the past that is living and worthy to live. All MOMENTUM, which is the past bearing upon us, RACE, RACE-MEMORY, instinct charging the PLACID, NON-ENERGIZED FUTURE.
>
> The DESIGN of the future [is?] in the grip of the human vortex. All the past that is vital, all the past that is capable of living into the future, is pregnant in the vortex, NOW.[67]

This was Pound's way of answering Lewis's contention that the Vorticists were concerned only with the present, not with the past, while continuing the repudiation of Futurism in which he agreed with Lewis. But it also shows the way in which the idea of transmissible mental energy could metamorphose into various forms, how it could reach back to the primitive as well as the classical, and how it could emerge in Eliot's "tradition."

As an efficient cause of the structure of the *Cantos*, the premise of the farraginous tradition was that fragments and truncated quotations could transmit the force of *nous* better than the usual forms of sustained discourse or narrative. In 1910, Pound had written that "Art is a fluid moving above or over the minds of men." As his thoughts matured he took the mushy idealism out of such

---

67. *BLAST*, June 20, 1914, p. 153. Note that thus by 1914 we hear no more about the dead hand of the past: Pound's early fear of mortmain (as in "Commission") had turned into delight in atavism, as with Joyce (see the Introduction to this book).

formulations by specifying power that could be transmitted in jagged flashes, fragmentary revelations, "luminous details."[68] If within the apparently random and superficial stories of Chaucer or Ovid there could be preserved irregular arrays of detail embodying "Mediterranean" wisdom, then he could construct a work using these templates (along with those of Homer and Dante, the more obvious exemplars) to continue the tradition.

Pound was dedicated to an essentially fragmentary poetics for the reasons implied above, not — as in the standard classroom explanation — because he believed that a culturally fragmented age demanded such a thing. Indeed, for him the fragment as such had a kind of Scriptural aura, as Hugh Kenner has argued: especially his growing awareness over the years of the potentialities of Sappho's "manuscraps" opened for him such a poesis:

> As Agamemnon from being his "wisdom" had become his "relics" [when Schliemann's archaeology turned Homer from myth into verifiable artifacts] so poets ceased to be their Castalian gush [and became] their utterly idiosyncratic way of joining six words, the only words some mangled scrap affords. Yet we know how to feel sure whose words they are. Fragments compelled a new kind of detailed attention from minds already prepared by Poe and *Symbolisme* to find virtue in brevity, or by Pater to find it in the fleeting glimpse. . . . There was virtue in scraps, mysterium in fragments, magical power in the tatter of a poem, sacred words biting on congruent actualities of sight and feeling and breath.[69]

The scattered words and phrases manifested their *virtú* all the better for being fortuitously highlighted: freed from the sometimes domesticating and misleading entanglements of ordinary syntax, they stood naked, open to intense inspection. Pound reversed the Swinburnian habit of "restoring" Sappho's fragments with fanciful fillings-out, just as he eschewed Browning's habit of writing slices of historical novels from sources found in used-book stalls. The nineteenth century had been an age of "nostalgia for an imagined fullness," to be achieved by fantasized time-travel: the restored cathedral, disfigured by what Proust's Swann thought of as the petrified excretions of Viollet-le-Duc, and so on. Sappho was made

---

68. *Spirit of Romance*, p. 7; *Selected Prose*, pp. 22–23.
69. *Pound Era*, p. 51.

"caressable" by Swinburne, Emily Dickinson was swaddled in layers of regularization.[70] Pound moved for stark and suggestive isolation, positing an aesthetic of arrested attention. We are to do with the scraps what the student does with the sunfish in the Agassiz anecdote: look, really look at them. "At the end of three weeks the fish was in advanced state of decomposition, but the student knew something about it."[71] Decomposition can even facilitate knowledge: it can serve as a kind of dissection and display.

Pound's new appreciation of the heuristic possibilities of fragmentation and dissociation consorted with another impulse he was nurturing, along with Joyce and Eliot, to break away from the use of "voice" as a unifying device. Dickens' and Twain's prose and Browning's poetry, so suitable for platform performance, bring to perfection the convention of the tale-teller (note Conrad's ambivalence on this). But the *Cantos, Ulysses*, and *The Waste Land* are in different ways assaults on this fiction, which derives from post-neoclassical projections of Aristotle's "unities" and from the nineteenth-century engrossment in "character." Pound wanted to jettison unity in favor of farrago, and bridled at quasi-dramatic interest in character, despite his love for Browning. He had an instinctive aversion to the theater, as noted in Chapter 1: "The reason I loathe all stage stuff is that it is split. . . . to think of effect or how it wd. be on stage distracts from reality of fact presented. . . . Means the author not obsessed with reality of his subject." Mauberley, he specified, was not a character but a "mere surface."[72] The unidentified, sometimes echoic voices of *Mauberley*'s various sections prefigure the techniques of Modernist polyphony, most audible in many lines of *The Waste Land*. Against the figure of "character" as a three-dimensional depth, Pound (like the anti-illusionists in art) opposed the surface, the fragmentary phrase, the jagged phalanx of detail: no luxuriating in fullness of character or incident.

There is a more obscure and debatable background to the Modernist move against voice and character, stemming from the post-Cartesian dilemmas of the Romantic poets. Ever since the philoso-

---

70. *Pound Era*, pp. 59 ff; Marcel Proust, *Swann's Way* (vol. 1 of *Remembrance of Things Past*), trans. C. K. Scott Moncrieff (Modern Library, 1928), p. 421.

71. *ABC of Reading*, p. 18.

72. *Letters*, pp. 306, 180.

pher divided the internal from the external world, *res cogitans* from *res extensa* ("What is mind? No matter. What is matter? Never mind"), fear has lurked at the hearts of men that whatever they have to say may be valid only for themselves, since there is no sure way to prove that other minds can be reached. Fear of solipsism appears throughout our age, even in Marxist attacks on individualism, and has its ancestry in the affirmative assertions of the Romantics as well as in their despairs. Coleridge's labors to establish the mutual presupposition of subject and object, like Wordsworth's to articulate the "real language of men," have a dark underside in their dejections and despondencies, fearful premonitions of "mighty poets in their misery dead" (i.e. unread).[73]

This fear reappears with ironic emphasis in Eliot's work, derived from F. H. Bradley who voiced the extremity of the dilemma: a celebrated footnote transports Bradley into the Waste Land where he sings, as if out of a well: "My external sensations are no less private to myself than are my thoughts or my feelings," and concludes that souls are "opaque" to other souls. Hence the poem itself says, "Thinking of the key, each confirms a prison." Prufrock had feared that "one" would say to his Lazarus revelation, "That is not what I meant at all;/ That is not it, at all."[74] The wraiths in Eliot's early poems — they too are not characters — reach out futilely from the prison of self, and thus these poems, once past impercipient editors, found a huge audience (any adolescent knows those feelings). Eliot is thus not an heir of the Romantics, but a thematizer of their problems.

Breaking up the unity of character and voice appeared to be a way to strike a blow against the demons of solipsism, as did "the tradition." Meanwhile, from Homeric scholarship and studies of epic, destructive vectors converged on the concept of authorial voice. The belief that Homer was no isolated phenomenon, perhaps not a single person, followed from awareness of Greek epic cycles and editorial redactions; his poems, subjected to disintegrationist probings, came to be seen as layered like an archaeological site. That they could thus be composite artifacts, cumulative if not col-

73. See my essay, "Pound's Poetics of Loss," in Ian F. A. Bell, ed., *Ezra Pound: Tactics for Reading* (Vision/Barnes & Noble, 1982), pp. 103–20.

74. *Waste Land*, l. 415 and note to line 412; "The Love Song of J. Alfred Prufrock," penultimate section.

lective, opened many eyes, and Pound's comment on the Nekuia that "shouts aloud that it is older than the rest" shows how it seized his imagination, though he retained his belief in a personal Homer. In the *ABC of Reading*, his praise of Homer's accurate geography and anatomy resurrects the old view that Homer summed up all the knowledge of his culture, as Dante did that of the Middle Ages, and the belief in cumulative traditions gave this all the more credibility, as did the postulation that coded phalanxes of detail embedded in the narrative comprised the truly vital portion of the work.[75]

Eric Havelock states the mnemonic rationale for such hypotheses:

> The narratives enabled useful experience to be remembered in the form of vivid events arranged in paratactic sequence, while the compendious plot served as an over-all reference frame; the narrative is from this point of view to be regarded not as an end in itself but as a vehicle for transmitting the material of the tribal encyclopedia, which is presented not as such, but as dispersed into a thousand narrative contexts. Here then in the compendious epic of Homer is contained all philosophy and all history and all science.[76]

With this view in mind, one could retain a personal Homer, or discard him. By the late nineteenth century Nietzsche had decided that Greek tragedy had been the product of forces not only transauthorial but transcultural, so his analysis concerns itself hardly at all with the well-known authors, except for occasional slaps at the etiolated individualist Euripides. Individuation appears as a counterforce to the original spirit that created tragedy, in which all auditors awake to a deeply repressed sense of mortality, loss, and suffering. Nietzsche's violent rebuke to the complacent post-Romantic assumption of authors as self-begetting sources (*Oedipus* as an expression of the musings of Sophocles) still reverberates. Although writings are still produced by individuals, we no longer see this as Q.E.D.: authorship is not autonomy. Thanks to structuralism, we know that there are many motives and constraints (not just obvious "social forces") of which an author cannot be conscious. The simplest illustration is that, in any message in En-

75. See pp. 43–44.
76. *Preface to Plato* (Grosset & Dunlap, 1967), pp. 291–92.

glish of sufficient length to be randomized, the letter *e* will occur most frequently. The recently proclaimed "death of the author" among poststructuralists and advocates of "cultural poetics" points up self-contradictions and anomalies in our concepts of ourselves, our self-control, and our discourses. Disintegrationist theories make an interesting background for such assertions.[77]

Pound's evolution toward the contention that the *Cantos* were "not a work of fiction/ Nor yet of one man" (99/708) followed a predictable course. In 1909 he was defining an epic as the "speech of a nation through the mouth of one man," which is simply the nationalistic form of Romantic "genius" theory, and which he got from the unlikely duo of Yeats and Whitman.[78] In the drafts of the Ur-Cantos, he played variations on Browning, indeed haranguing him as a Muse-interlocutor. Most of this was canceled, and the remnants that appear in the present text are among the least satisfactory parts of the poem (see, e.g., the opening of Canto III). In the course of writing *Mauberley* and *Propertius*, supervising the appearance of *Ulysses*, and criticizing the drafts of *The Waste Land*, Pound clarified his sense of the "compendious epic," the farraginous tradition, juxtaposition of ensembles to replace narrative, and the possibilities of unspecified voices.

Eliot and Joyce had worked out differing theories of "impersonality," which were announced in the "Tradition" essay and in Stephen Dedalus' aesthetic theory in *Portrait*. Naturally these theories reflect ironic lights on the work of their proponents—who are these persons promulgating such impersonality?—which ironies are further ironized within the works, as when Stephen in the next book proposes a completely biographical explanation of Shakespeare's plays, or when a footnote to *The Waste Land* assures us that all the voices ultimately "meet in Tiresias," which seems to be Eliot's concession to the very convention he was outmoding, but which is better read as itself part of the poem, like the Bradley footnote.[79] *Ulysses*, with its different styles for each chapter, and *The Waste*

77. Friedrich Nietzsche, *The Birth of Tragedy*; cf. Michel Foucault, "What Is an Author?" in Josué Harari, ed., *Textual Strategies: Perspectives in Post-Structuralist Criticism* (Cornell University Press, 1979), pp. 141–60.

78. Quoted by Michael André Bernstein, *The Tale of the Tribe: Ezra Pound and the Modern Verse Epic* (Princeton University Press, 1980), p. 18.

79. Note to *Waste Land*, l.218.

Land with its succession of disembodied voices, undercut the reader's efforts to find a controlling speaker or narrator, express or implied. No such "voice" can be found, but rather the works seem to be reading themselves and commenting on themselves as they go along. *Ulysses* is particularly self-reflexive, and Joyce seems to have anticipated the present currency of the phrase "mind of the text." But the footnotes of Eliot's poem can also be so read, and there are many passages in both works in which the only specifiable source for what is said is the work itself, as no narrator or "arranger" is a satisfactory conception.[80] It is as if *Ulysses* wrote *Ulysses*. Joyce mischievously adapted the premise of the godlike creator everywhere present and nowhere visible, and his work's supertypological structure (every part latent in every other part) reflects the idea that God was the "real" author of the Bible, superseding the human authors who were mere amanuenses. So his book transcends him; *Ulysses* is obviously a parody of a sacred book, specifically of the Bible in a medieval reading with multiple levels, and so forth.

Pound's solution was naturally a little different; he worked out a poetics in which things, so to speak, could say themselves. Such thoughts were instigated by Fenollosa's meditation on the Chinese characters that stand out as icons in the *Cantos*. "In reading Chinese we do not seem to be juggling mental counters, but to be watching *things* work out their own fate."[81] Fenollosa theorized that we could see from Chinese a basic truth of language, that it was even more homologous with nature than Romantic theorists like Shelley or Emerson had dared to believe. "The sentence form was forced upon primitive men by nature itself. It was not we who made it; it was a reflection of the temporal order in causation. All truth has to be expressed in sentences because all truth is the *transference of power*." For Pound, these sentences were self-enacting "transferences"; their power validated the concepts in-

80. See Hugh Kenner, *Joyce's Voices* (University of California Press, 1978), *passim*; and his *Ulysses* (Allen & Unwin, 1980), pp. 64–65. Kenner accepts David Hayman's "arranger," but why multiply entities?

81. Ernest Fenollosa, *Essay on the Chinese Written Character*, often reprinted : all quotations from Fenollosa are from this essay. On "events narrating themselves," see Emile Benveniste, *Problems in General Linguistics*, trans. Mary Elizabeth Meek (University of Miami Press, 1971), p. 208.

volved in his ideas of tradition. Moreover, they reinforced his speculations on modern forms of energy: electricity, the radio, the
stored energy in gasoline or dynamite, were all "transferences of
power," and Allen Upward had predisposed him to think of electricity as "only the most coarse and obvious of the ethereal . . .
influences forever at work weaving the woof of Life upon the warp
of Matter."[82] Therefore Fenollosa's vision — one that seemed to include modern technological forces in continuum with natural process, cultural evolution, and timeless wisdom — offered him a powerful validation of his syntheses of esoteric and empiric, spirit and
matter, myth and politics, archaic and modern, *du côté de chez*
Yeats with that *chez* Ford.

Fenollosa had mocked the notion of language as a subjective
human production:

> The subject is that about which I am going to talk; the predicate is that
> which I am going to say about it. The sentence according to this defini-
> tion is not an attribute of nature but an accident of man as a conversa-
> tional animal.
>
> If it were really so, then there could be no possible test of the truth
> of a sentence. Falsehood would be as specious as verity.

Pound no doubt found this argument overwhelming, the more so
because it defiantly begs the question of the Cartesian separation.
So he followed Fenollosa into an even more visionary, heuristic
hypothesis: that all parts of speech had grown out of verbs, even
prepositions and conjunctions. The verb was the most primitive
and revealing linguistic form because it embodied process, and "a
true noun, an isolated thing, does not exist in nature." (Pound was
predisposed to see the cosmos as process by, among other things,
his reverence for metamorphosis.) Nouns and other parts "are naturally verbs. The farmer is one who tills the ground, and the rice is
a plant which grows in a special way." From this train of thought,
Fenollosa derived the conclusion that subject and predicate are
simply aspects of a unitary self-articulating process: "The true formula for thought is: the cherry tree is all that it does. Its correlated
verbs compose it." Not what we say of it, but what it does.

Poets, because of their uneasy sensitivity to Cartesian dilemmas

82. Upward, *The Divine Mystery* (Ross-Erikson, 1976; originally published,
1913), p. 2.

(not necessarily by that name), see such thoughts as liberating. Charles Olson was following Fenollosa, and Pound, when he wrote his enormously influential "Projective Verse," of which this is the kernel:

> Objectism is the getting rid of the lyrical interference of the individual as ego, of the "subject" and his soul, that peculiar presumption by which western man has interposed himself between what he is as a creature of nature (with certain instructions to carry out) and those other creations of nature which we may, with no derogation, call objects.[83]

This also borrows from Mallarmé, the point being that poets over several generations have dreamed of a united front against subjectivism. Pound took up the quarrel by actually constructing a poetic of objective predication, of letting things say themselves.

As Carne-Ross has observed, Pound's repudiation of subjectivism gave his poetic the character of a Copernican revolution in favor of a disconcerting literalism: "Poetry [before Pound] has had to point away from the first, literal level to deeper levels of meaning. . . . The thing, however concretely rendered, always 'stands for' something else supposedly more important. But Pound is not polysemous; his first level doesn't point beyond itself." This leads to poetic as well as pagan fundamentalism:

> We feel something is missing [in Pound's poetry]; the whole reverberating dimension of inwardness is missing. There is no murmurous echo chamber where deeps supposedly answer to deeps. Not merely does the thing, in Pound's best verse, not point beyond itself: scandalously, *it doesn't point to us.* The green tip that pushes through the earth does not stand for or symbolize man's power of spiritual renewal. . . . Pound's whole effort is *not* to be polysemous but to give back to the literal level its full significance, its old significance, I would say. That green thrust is itself the divine event, the fruit of the marriage at Eleusis. Persephone is in that thrusting tip.[84]

No matter how deluded we think Pound's visionary sense of immanence, or how logocentric we judge Fenollosa's linguistics to be, we must admit that this literalism accords with the thrust in modern art against subjectivism, mere symbolism (the dregs of allegory),

83. *Selected Writings*, p. 24.
84. *Instaurations*, pp. 213–14.

and representationalism in its older forms. Pound was part of a wave of anti-illusionist, anti-perspectival flatness and fragmentation, among painters as well as writers like Stein and Anderson. And there can be no doubt that the effort to break the old forms was revivifying.

Moreover, few can regret the challenge to "the great principle of inwardness or internalization" that Carne-Ross sees in Pound's poetic. As if recapitulating Olson, Carne-Ross says that this challenge "gives back to the visible world — a world 'out there' which is not of our construction nor dependent on our collaboration — an importance it hasn't had for centuries."[85] Many, including Olson, found Pound ultimately too egoistic to carry through successfully on this rebuke to human pretensions, but insofar as "the religious attitude" is part of Modernism, there ought to be less discussion of Eliot's more churchy pronouncements and of T. E. Hulme, and more of Pound's pagan fundamentalism. Here as elsewhere, of course, pagan and Christian beliefs cohere. Fenollosa was following Biblical tradition, echoing Psalm 100, with his assertion that "it was not we who made [the sentence form]."

Pound's earliest endorsements of Fenollosa's essay concentrate on that "true formula for thought": "'All nouns come from verbs.' To primitive man, a thing only IS what it *does*. That is Fenollosa, but I think the theory is a very good one for poets to go by."[86] And from this point on, his own poetry showed a taste for verbal force and predicational function, with little reliance on copulas, which Fenollosa disparaged ("Rarely will you find an 'is' in [Shakespeare's] sentences"). Like his construction of a polymorphous, form-breaking, exuberant "tradition," his poems reveal his predilection for change, dynamism, activity. Along these lines, Fenollosa had pointed out that the components of an ideogram act as verbs, or predicates, for one another. He gave as an example the *ming* ideogram, "sun" plus "moon": "It serves as verb, noun, adjective. Thus you write literally, 'the sun and moon of the cup' for 'the cup's brightness.' Placed as a verb, you write 'the cup sun-and-moons,' actually 'cup sun-and-moon,' or in a weakened thought, 'is like sun,' i.e., shines." So, in the "east" ideogram (sun in tree

85. *Instaurations*, p. 214.
86. *Letters*, p. 82.

branches) tree and sun are not analogous, but together form a predication through the implication of a relationship: "Relations are more real and more important than the things which they relate." The constituents act as predications for one another.

One can see Fenollosa's propositions active in all of Pound's work after 1914, in various ways, and they surely helped him decide to transform the Ur-Cantos, jettisoning their "speaker" and his method. Cantos I and II now are especially rich in examples of verbal force underlying other words and phrases. The first lines don't even have a noun-subject; moreover, the initial *And* "works like a verb, transmitting force. The emphatic *forth* works verbwise also, and *godly* pervades the sea with animate forces."[87] In Canto II, Ovidian metamorphosis and Dionysian epiphany are linked to Protean shape-shifting (possibly suggested by the third chapter of *Ulysses*). Nouns and adjectives turn into verbs: "The blue-gray glass of the wave tents them"; "the gulls broad out their wings." The *Cantos* throughout show that Pound conceived predication as a force arising from concise presentation of imaginatively conceived particulars: this, and not analogy or metaphor, is the basis of the "ideogrammic method." ("Ornamental" or showy metaphor had always annoyed Pound, and as early as 1910 he had sought a "language beyond metaphor.")[88] Such ideogrammism tied in with "direct knowledge," another term for what Fenollosa was urging, and with such Imagist practices as the abandonment of "comment" (read "subjective predication"). The strictures of Flaubert comprising the "prose tradition," via Ford, had anticipated Fenollosa's points:

> [Clear presentation] is what may be called the "prose tradition" of poetry, and by this I mean that it is a practice of speech common to good prose and good verse alike. . . . It means constatation of fact. It presents. It does not comment. It is irrefutable because it does not present a personal predilection for any particular fraction of the truth.[89]

87. *Pound Era*, p. 351.
88. *Spirit of Romance*, p. 33. The mistrust of metaphor is a key to much in Pound: see my *Ezra Pound: The Image and the Real* (Louisiana State University Press, 1969), pp. 47–48 and 64, and "Wisdom Past Metaphor: Another View of Pound, Fenollosa, and Objective Verse," *Paideuma* 5 (Spring–Summer 1976): 15–29. See also Pound's *Selected Prose*, p. 51, where he argues that defective religious insight relies on analogy.
89. "The Approach to Paris," *New Age*, October 2, 1913, p. 662.

[Whereas subjective predication is endlessly arguable, as Fenollosa had pointed out. Compare also the more warmhearted but similar critique of the grotesques' "truths" in the opening pages of Anderson's *Winesburg*.]

Elsewhere Pound had identified "presentation or constatation" with the "mot juste," and somewhat earlier had written: "The artist seeks out the luminous detail and presents it. He does not comment. His work remains the permanent basis of psychology and metaphysics."[90] Such credos prepared the way for his instant enthusiastic agreement with Fenollosa. Though Pound did not apply the term *ideogrammic* to the *Cantos* until relatively late, the force of Fenollosan ideas can be seen as soon as the poem emerged from its Ur-Cantos husk and metamorphosed into an exemplar of the farraginous tradition. The key was abandonment of the subjective, rambling harangue for the technique of letting things say themselves.

Objective predication—by whatever term Pound would have thought of it—enabled him to believe that he had defeated the most insidious of human pretensions, the creation of the Cartesian gulf between mind and world, language and nature. This gave him the confidence with which he disposed of "voice" in the *Cantos*. If after Heisenberg we take it for granted that mind and matter interact in acts of perception, we can see how Fenollosa enabled Pound to preserve his instinctive sense of the interpenetration of these realms, and of their equal validity. (Objective predication did not mean pretending that things say themselves without a catalytic poet or that a poem writes itself.) Renewed confidence—and what is poetry but supreme verbal confidence?—enabled him to venerate the tradition of transmissible mental energy, *nous*, but also to reaffirm triumphantly and religiously its involvement in "reality."

In the poem, the results can be seen most directly in the handling of autobiographical material: it is notoriously there but is not subjective comment in the sense of presenting "what I'm going to say about it." Details of Pound's life are "factual atoms" (from which "all knowledge is built up") like other details in the poem: together, all these form predications through their relationship.[91] All the past

90. *Selected Prose*, p. 23.
91. *Guide to Kulchur*, p. 98.

must become present for the catalytic poet; it must "carve" itself in the poet's mind to be recovered, often as a divinity. "Wherever the quality of the affection — Aphrodite — is strong enough to carve a trace in the mind, the past is preserved and its content, its images rise up again and are renewed like the moon — Artemis — who renews herself each month." Thus Carne-Ross paraphrases Canto 76.[92]

A further effect of Pound's belief in objective predication was to reinforce his already-stated intention to deploy chunks of documents, fragments of poems, and the like as displays that could speak for themselves. Philip Furia, whose name ironically occurs in Canto 22, has published an analysis of the poem as a collage of passages from the farrago of history.

> The *Cantos* can be read as a counter conspiracy against . . . historical blackout, an attempt to recover and recirculate lost documents: ecclesiastical edicts, commission reports, municipal records, diary entries, judicial writs, parliamentary statutes, contracts, mandates, treaties, log books, legislative codes, and regulations governing that most pervasive document of all, money. . . . In the *Cantos* the heroes are the archivists — men like Kung, Coke, and an army of scholars, editors and translators who preserve and "make new" the important documents of the past in palimpsests that mirror the *Cantos* themselves.[93]

Palimpsest is a key word. Canto I tells us that the Nekuia is an atavistic resurgence, Homer's reinscription of a more ancient text; at the same time, it is Divus' unpretentious, literalistic translation: we see it as a "transference of power." A similar role is played by Pound's own paraphrase of a French Jesuit's version of Chinese chronicles. Such projects were implicit in Pound's veneration for documents, from *razos* to Constitutions, that like paintings required "direct knowledge." As early as 1911, he recommended looking for the "luminous details" in statesmen's diaries and papers (showing his weakness for "strong men" in history):

> If one wished an intimate acquaintance with the politics of England or Germany at certain periods, would one be wiser to read a book of generalities and then read at random through the archives, or to read

92. *Instaurations*, p. 206.

93. *Pound's Cantos Declassified* (Pennsylvania State University Press, 1984), pp. 2–3.

through, let us say, first the State papers of Bismarck or Gladstone? Having become really conversant with the activities of either of these men, would not almost any document of the period fall, if we read it, into some sort of orderly arrangement? Would we not grasp its relation to the main stream of events?[94]

The progression from this to the poem itself is not hard to trace. Documentation was another force making the poem irreducibly polyphonic: Allen Tate called the *Cantos* a "many voiced monologue," but that description really fits *Mauberley* better, where Pound speaks in momentarily assumed accents, showing himself behind the masks so much that Mauberley is not even a persona, much less a character (hence the phrase "a mere surface").[95] The obtrusive "quotations newly energized" make the *Cantos* different, not a monologue, even a many-voiced one.[96]

Pound conceived his polyphony literally, on the analogy of that new transmitter of verbal force, the radio: explaining Cantos 18 and 19 to his father, he wrote: "Simplest parallel I can give is radio where you tell who is talking by the noise they make."[97] In 1940 he asserted that he had prophesied radio's effects, although cursing it for having become a distraction: "I anticipated the damn thing in first third of Cantos."[98] Presumably he meant that the *Cantos* were like twirls of the dial through history, fragments of significant language interspersed with squawking. (There is a multiedged irony here, given the trouble that Pound got into by making use of Rome Radio for his hysterical attacks on Allied leaders.) The radio parallel could lie behind *The Waste Land* too, and Joyce used both radio and television for "voices" in *Finnegans Wake* (only the phonograph, of course, in *Ulysses*). Pound's claim that his poem was "not the work of one man" echoes Joyce's sense that all users of language were contributing to his polyglossia: "Really it is not I who am writing this crazy book [the *Wake*]. It is you, and you, and you, and that man over there, and that girl at the next table."[99]

94. *Selected Prose*, pp. 42–43.

95. Tate, quoted in Bush, *The Genesis of Ezra Pound's Cantos*, p. 6n.

96. *Pound Era*, p. 126.

97. Quoted in Max Nänny, "The Oral Roots of Ezra Pound's Methods of Quotation and Abbreviation," *Paideuma* 8 (Winter 1979): 382.

98. *Letters*, p. 343. Whether he meant that he had prophesied its vulgarizing effects or its potential for transmitting luminous details of speech is not clear.

99. Quoted in *The Pound Era*, p. 126.

Polyphony entails discontinuity, but discontinuity like decomposition (as in the erasure of manuscraps by time) isolates particulars for intense scrutiny, arresting the flow of homogenizing discourse that can submerge the particulars, and so promotes concentration. Yet discontinuity also opens the door to a certain arbitrariness, even an episodic quality in the poem. The hidden continuities in the *Cantos*, like those of the symbolic correspondences in *Ulysses*, are interesting in themselves, and certainly Pound's procedures have only superficial resemblances to Dadaist or truly random jumbles. However, in a sense Yeats was right, the suits could all be laid out in a different order.[100] Given Pound's choice of dynamic over formal values, it follows that a Canto is more of a process, a way of doing (or displaying) something, than a static receptacle. Hence Pound was able to write to C. K. Ogden: "You watch ole Ez do a basic Canto" [he meant in Basic English].[101] The project accords with his epistemological beliefs, but presupposes that the content of the Canto would be more or less arbitrary. Is this a fatal flaw? The painters had been hammering on the idea that a work of art's value is not in its subject, and Pound had quoted an unnamed Russian on himself: "You wish to give people new eyes, not to make them see some new particular thing."[102] The principle of visionary metamorphosis was behind those "new eyes," but also the precedents of other arts. Like a Cubist painting, a Canto is something of a demonstration, and testing, of possibilities.

Modernism entails a demandingly episodic structure. Like those of Joyce's work, the devotees of Pound can open the *Cantos* anywhere and skip around at will. Indeed, these works can't be read any other way, for their devices have defeated much of the kind of processing we call "reading," meaning ingestion of certain lines of continuity. The first law of Modernism is that the works are easier to study—even to write books about—than to read casually, for one simply cannot go from the first to the last pages with the habitual ease of a novel-reader. Reading them is more like reading a picture (a phrase that is something more than a metaphor, as Gombrich has taught us); we must inspect and jump around, and

---

100. *A Vision* (Macmillan [New York], 1961: originally published, 1938), p. 4.
101. *Letters*, p. 266.
102. *Gaudier-Brzeska*, p. 85.

do it again and again. Like pictures, these works have no *telos*, no predetermined climax to which they lead up by conventional rhetorical structures (George T. Wright once observed that Pound's poems are often like jokes with the punch lines missing).[103] Jung's sneer that *Ulysses* could be read as well backwards as forwards was simply fitting praise for the work of an author who was fascinated by chiastic and palindromic structures.

Hugh Kenner calls *Ulysses* "as discontinuous a book as its author can manage."[104] We can in fact read it consecutively, but it's better when we don't; to do so is against the grain. At some points, notably the lists in the "Cyclops" chapter, we simply can't: the eye and the interior vocalization become exhausted. To savor such comic grotesqueries, we must come at them indirectly, as if sideways. (And they lead to the hilarious but exhausting pages of *Finnegans Wake*, where each sentence must be read as a work in itself.) Even where we think we can read consecutively, we will miss much if we don't pause over every phrase. They have been calculated in a way that none ever were before: part of Joyce's secret is simply the time and attention he spent. The very first sentence is a key to the techniques of *Ulysses*, not only in what it says but also in what it doesn't. "Stately, plump Buck Mulligan came from" — what? Not "a social class that allowed him to look down on graduates of the National University"; that would be a possible *Dubliners* sentence, but Modernism entailed eschewing such "comment" and the implied speaker that goes with it, with all his baggage of unity, continuity, climax, and the rest. Instead, Buck comes "from the stairhead," with his mock-eucharistic shaving paraphernalia, which leads on to the book's demonstration that the sacramental is in the commonplace even where that appears as mockery, just as the Yeatsian–Theosophical play with "metempsychosis" enables Bloom to be Odysseus. The omissions, like the constellations of detail, speak volumes, but only if we go back over them many times. And they speak them without an implied consciousness, as if events narrated themselves. The only unifying "zone of consciousness" is that of the book itself. Thus the book

103. *The Poet in the Poem: The Personae of Eliot, Yeats, and Pound* (University of California Press, 1960), pp. 125–26.

104. *Flaubert, Joyce and Beckett: The Stoic Comedians* (Beacon Press, 1962), p. 59; cf. p. 41.

is, as it were, three-dimensional instead of two: rather than the eye's linear progression across a flat surface, we need a vision that will take in the submerged hidden mass of the iceberg, the unspoken implications that bulk beneath. All books have such a dimension, but the mark of a Modernist work is that the writers are aware of this as never before, and work in this dimension as much as on the surface flow. The Modernist work is not so much written as constructed, and the out-of-sight level is calculated with what Pound called "hyperscientific precision" throughout years of preparation (see Joyce's mounds of note sheets).[105] Buried scaffoldings, symbolic correspondences, and other hidden integrities are synonymous with Modernism; the surface is synecdochic to a degree never consciously intended before.

Ulysses is open-ended in the amount of detail Joyce could pour into it, "never finished, but only abandoned."[106] The *Cantos* are still more open-ended. Because of his concept of objective predication, Pound's lines exist in a conceptual space that is different from that of other Modernist works, one in which he himself appears as "ego scriptor cantilenae" amid the other things of the poem.[107] But equally for his work we must apply Joseph Frank's saying that it cannot be read, only reread. (In Joyce's case this has to do with the fact that a third of the book was written on the proofs; so to speak, it was never written, only rewritten.)[108] To read the poem from first page to last is to ignore, in the first place, that it was compiled (not composed) over more than forty years—he did not, after the one false start, go back years later for extensive revisions of earlier Cantos—and what goes along with that fact, namely the importance of Pound's beliefs that economics and politics interpenetrate with glimpses of a world full of the immanent divine. An epic is a poem including history, said Pound, and history without economics is just bunk.[109] It is equally bunk without mystery, but also vice versa. If we read the *Cantos* without glossing international politics

105. *Spirit of Romance*, p. 87. On Joyce, see the next note.

106. A. Walton Litz, *The Art of James Joyce* (Oxford University Press, 1961), p. 7 (quoting Paul Valery).

107. For example, 24/112.

108. Frank, quoted in Litz, *The Art of James Joyce*, p. 56. For proof-writing, see Hans Walter Gabler, "Afterword," in *Ulysses* (Vintage Books, 1986), p. 649.

109. *Letters*, p. 247; and *Literary Essays*, p. 86.

and correlating them with the years of composition as we go (an edition with dates of publication would be helpful), we'll miss as much as if we disdain his mystical fundamentalism.

* * * * * * * *

This brings us to the point of the immediate, as opposed to the formal and material, causes of the *Cantos*. They would not be true to their author's inmost beliefs if they were not topical, and in fact it is obvious that they were galvanized not only by other Modernist works but also by the aftermath of the Great War, specifically of the recriminations and accusations that arose from the frenzied attempts to understand it. Pound's attitudes toward the war are of the utmost importance, both for his politics and for his poetics — which, as all recent critics agree and as he always insisted, are far more continuous than previously acknowledged.

In 1914 Pound and the other Vorticists were, if anything, pleased at the outbreak of war; they claimed to have foreseen it. "While all other periodicals were whispering PEACE . . . 'BLAST' alone dared to present the actual discords of modern 'civilization,' DIS-CORDS now only too apparent in the open conflict between teutonic atavism and unsatisfactory Democracy."[110] In consonance with Vorticist hostilities, Pound maintained an evenhanded irony about the war during its first months:

> Blunt has brought out a two volume collected edition. Also they say he has barred his front door and put up a sign "BELLIGERENTS WILL PLEASE GO ROUND TO THE KITCHEN." . . . Ricketts has made the one mot of the war, the last flare of the 90's: "What depresses me most is the horrible fact that they can't all of them be beaten." It looks only clever and superficial, but one can not tell how true it is. This war is possibly a conflict between two forces almost equally detestable. Atavism and the loathsome spirit of mediocrity cloaked in graft. . . . One wonders if the war is only a stop gap. Only a symptom of the real disease.[111]

110. *BLAST*, July 1915, pp. 85–86. The irony of the use of the term *atavism* for Germany (here and in the next quotation) has its grimly humorous side, in view of Pound's siding with the Axis, and the argument I develop later that Fascism and Naziism were parodic versions of the forces that produced Modernist revivals of atavism.
111. *Letters*, pp. 46–47.

Within the year, however, the enormity of the slaughter precluded all irony. Tracing Pound's attitudes through his journalism, one sees that he felt the predicament of the noncombatant alien living in a country being bled of its youth. His writing grew more and more strident, not with hatred of Germany, or with British official propaganda, but with a conviction that only American intervention could end the murderous stalemate. Perhaps he had this thrown up to him often. His exasperation at President Wilson's neutralism expressed itself in taunts to the American public: for example, for not understanding "the last public act" of Henry James, who took British citizenship just before he died in 1916.[112] From stridency Pound went on to hysteria, just as he was to do on the radio in the next war. He seems to have felt as exposed as a soldier in no-man's-land.

When it ended, Pound's relief was darkened by a growing conviction, widespread in the postwar disillusion, that wars were sinister blood purges, irrational cataclysms into which lemminglike populations were lured by munitions makers and profiteers. This would have been a nearly irresistible idea in 1918, when no one could authoritatively assign a cause to the war or even say what had been won and lost — except a generation of young men. For what did those millions die? How did the English, and Germans and French and Russians, explain to their children that the Serbian assassin of an Austrian archduke had dragged Europe into a maelstrom that decimated all its towns and villages? The "causes" proposed were so out of proportion to the results that logical thought itself seemed discredited; the eruption of Dadaism was as inevitable as that of Bolshevism (both from Zurich, from whence one could sit back and contemplate the madness or write *Ulysses*.) Because there was no obvious reason, seekers had to go beyond reason. Freud began the explorations that resulted in *Beyond the Pleasure Principle* to explain the repetition-compulsions of shell-shocked victims, but he might as well have been examining the self-destructive urges of civilized nations (which he did later).

The answers that Pound grasped at came from neither psychiatrists nor statesmen, but from an amateur economist who proposed that war was a crude self-correcting device for the inequities and

112. *Literary Essays*, p. 295.

chronic depressive forces of industrial capitalism. C. H. Douglas theorized that the system produced more goods than purchasing power, because the price of the goods always contained bank charges and the like that, unlike wages, did not go into consumers' pockets. The banks and financiers were siphoning off purchasing power that would keep the system in equilibrium, hence devices to destroy some of the excess product were needed: wars, or for a later era, "defense spending." Wars produced a strangely beneficent inflation: goods were in short supply, but people had more money, and there was a perceptible rise in the standard of living. Many British workers had a decent diet for the first time ever during the war, in spite of German submarines. Observing such paradoxes, Pound saw even more sinister forces than did Douglas, and concocted a belief in a "usurocracy" that instigated paroxysms of mutual destruction: "The cannibals of Europe are eating one another again" (32/159).[113]

As parasitical bankers and currency manipulators were the villains in this vision of things, it was only a matter of time before the features of the stereotyped Jewish moneylender merged with the shadowy image of the warmonger. Actually Pound seemed to resist this move for some years. There is very little evidence of anti-Semitism in Pound's recorded words before 1918; the genteel sort by which fraternities and suburbs were restricted in America in those days seems to have had little effect on him. The first glimpse is in a Vorticist poem:

> Let us be done with Jews and Jobbery,
> Let us SPIT upon those who fawn on the JEWS for their money.[114]

This probably derives from Pound's uncritical acceptance of Ford's story that *The English Review* had been stolen from him by rich Jews (referred to in Chapter 1). Ford's brief tenure as its editor had been brilliant, except for the financial angle, and the journal had indeed passed into the control of Sir Alfred Mond, though in a more complicated way than Ford's version had it. He disliked Jews to begin with, and was known for fabulism. This story had a fateful effect on Pound, suggesting conspiracies to smother good

113. See Hugh Kenner's lucid chapter "Douglas," in *The Pound Era*; and Surette, *A Light from Eleusis*.
114. "Salutation the Third," which first appeared in *BLAST*, June 20, 1914.

writing. Later these conspiracies became part of the many heads of Geryon. Even so, the *BLAST* lines do not caricature Jews themselves. Except for the labored joke in *Mauberley* about the size of "Brennbaum's" nose, there is nothing in Pound's writing that resembles Eliot's portrait of "Bleistein," who stares uncomprehending at Venetian treasures with a "lustreless protrusive eye" and apelike posture.[115] Nor did Pound ever do any hatchet jobs like the one with which Hemingway turned Harold Loeb into Robert Cohn. Even as late as *Guide to Kulchur* (1938) Pound was still insisting that "race prejudice is red herring. The tool of the man defeated intellectually, and of the cheap politician." Affirming the existence of "racial characteristics," he yet sneered at the polite racialism of his society: "It is nonsense for the anglo-saxon to revile the jew for beating him at his own game."[116] The implication was that Jewish usurers were only exploiting fissures in an already rotted society, and this implication reappears in the *Cantos*, in which Jewish usurers are greatly outnumbered by Presbyterian slumlords, European munitions makers, corrupt Stuarts and Venetians, and the like.

The coming of yet another world war shoved Pound over the line. So monstrous was war to him that he could account for it only by constructing a broad pantheon of villains, including all of the political leaders of England and America and, of course, all rich Jews (though even in the most vituperative of his Rome broadcasts he warned against pogroms directed at "small Jews"). From his Rapallo isolation he had yammered frantically and futilely against the causes of the looming war as he saw them, and the rising tone of hysteria in his writings can be correlated with the approach of the conflict and with his sense of impotence. Roosevelt and Churchill seemed to be conspiring to make sure that America got involved — which was in fact the case — and yet no one seemed to resist effectively.[117] Having failed to persuade anyone with what were, for Pound, moderate tones and reasonable arguments, he threw himself into violent rhetorical excess. The repulsive results have been given wide publicity.

Pound began to believe that Jews had burrowed not only into

---

115. "Burbank with a Baedeker: Bleistein with a Cigar."

116. *Guide to Kulchur*, pp. 242–43.

117. See William Stevenson, *A Man Called Intrepid* (Harcourt Brace Jovanovich, 1976), which boasts of the "secret war" waged by British Intelligence to bring

financial positions of power but also into all the institutions of the West, as vengeance for earlier ill treatment. Eventually he swallowed the "Protocols of the Elders of Zion" and all the other staples of this conspiracy theory. The proof, as with all such theories, was his own ineffectiveness in persuading anyone to his viewpoint. By circular logic, this showed the existence of blackout, concerted silence, which — given the incuriosity of the average person — explained why such plain truth was ignored. Nothing less could explain how the West could allow the encroachment of another war after that stupefyingly bloody first one.

In short, ironic and repellent as it may seem, Pound's anti-Semitism arose as a result of his antiwar crusade, and though it reveals a pathetic egoism in him as well a terrible deficiency in moral sensibility, and some grievous intellectual flaws as well, it was not the product of common prejudice or venomous personal spite. Twisted as Pound's vision and logic were, they have to be seen against his conviction that war must be prevented at any cost, and that anyone who resisted this idea must be corrupt. Like Maud Gonne and others before him, and like many Americans in the 1960s, he became a violent, inflammatory pacifist.

During his time in the mental asylum, Pound maintained a fiercely defensive hostility to Judaism, but of course his anomalous position there continually fed his fantasies of persecution and hence of correctness: if he wasn't right, why was he incarcerated and discredited? His own power of denial kept him from acknowledging that it was the Jews who had been worst victimized in the war, and that he had spoken on behalf of mass murderers. But even this resistance broke down after he was released, when freedom showed that his paranoias were fanciful. Some time afterward, partly as the result of a prostate operation, he fell into geriatric depression, renounced his own works, and repented his collusion with "the stupid, suburban prejudice," calling it the worst of all his mistakes.[118] His depression brought to an end the aggressive rationalizing and vehement pretenses with which he had kept the truth from himself. The mutism of his last years was part of an

---

America into the war and to eliminate isolationists. Among the steps contemplated was the assassination of John L. Lewis, the labor leader (pp. 288 ff.)

118. Quoted in *The Pound Era*, p. 556.

effort at expiation. He realized that he had not known when to shut up, and made himself pay for it.

So his attempt at a great poem was inextricably mixed with his sickening participation in one of the major disgraces of human history. The paradox itself is difficult enough to wrestle with; given the inaccessibility of his writings to any but dedicated readers — those willing to question the conventions that govern so much other literature — only one thing explains his continuing force in literary history, and that is his responsibility for the most important movement of our time. Pound simply cannot be wished away, though there are many, from either moral repugnance or simple laziness, who wish to remove his thorny writings from the record of the age. This point should be self-evident, and although it is equally futile to hector anyone who refuses to pay any attention to him, the history of modern literature cannot be understood without him. We are going to have to come to terms even with his Fascism. To many this in itself will seem a Fascist step, an aestheticization of moral questions. In fact, it is a basic historical one; let us not fall victim to yet another conspiracy theory.

In Solzhenitsyn's *One Day in the Life of Ivan Denisovitch* the question is framed in terms of Eisenstein's film *Ivan the Terrible*, manifestly an apologia for Stalin: can a true work of art be made in the service of a reprehensible political philosophy?[119] One thinks of all the victims of the Gulag, as well as those of the Holocaust, and wants to say no. But in truth things are more complicated. First, the problem is usually not in the philosophy itself but in the inhuman acts that are tolerated in order to defend it. Can any new order be so desirable that defending it justifies the killing of millions of people? Marxism has discredited itself by evading that question. And yet the revolution did have its enemies, and so did Stalin, and Eisenstein made a great film on that premise — not a flawless one, but surely a work of art.

We may believe that Keats has already given the answer, in his insight into "negative capability": the poet has as much delight in the creation of an Iago as an Imogen. Or we may want to deny the implications of that apothegm and to counter it with, say, Kafka's belief that art must chop away at the frozen sea of feeling within

119. Trans. Ralph Parker (Dutton, 1963), pp. 83–84.

all of us.[120] Yet even a work that advocates murder is thinkable — witness the Marquis de Sade. We all want to make artists into moral heroes, and many still cannot accept the fact that Robert Frost, for instance, was not a nice man. As far as politics are concerned, the very idea of art invokes a viewpoint that questions the instrumentalities by which the achievement of human justice is to take place, and scrutinizes all the ambiguities that shadow those very attempts to seek justice. We may be unable to avoid political questions, but we might remind ourselves (and art implicitly does) that those who offer political solutions are essentially salesmen. Not every product offered for sale is faulty, but no salesmen should be trusted absolutely either. Pound would have done well to re-member that, but his antiwar hysteria overcame his instinct, and his belief in the interpenetration of worldly and spiritual realms seemed to justify him.

Nor is it possible to conceive of art so pure that it could pass every moral test suggested by Solzhenitsyn's question. Consider only anti-Semitism: can anyone deny that Wagner was a great mu-sician though an eloquent anti-Semite, or that Heidegger was an important philosopher though a member of the Nazi party, or Ingmar Bergman a notable filmmaker though deeply impressed by Hitler? And if we say that the anti-Semitism that occurs in The Prioress's Tale, the *Merchant of Venice*, and *Oliver Twist* reflects "the times" and not the authors, this might make us wonder whether the attempt to isolate and quarantine Pound is not also a dubious enterprise, even though it is undeniably true that anti-Semitism is far more constitutive of his work than of theirs.[121]

Robert Lowell put the consequences of taking this line of investi-gation in a way that highlights its problems and its possibilities:

> Pound's social credit, his Fascism, all these various things were a tre-mendous gain to him; he'd be a very Parnassian poet without them.

120. Keats, letter to Richard Woodhouse, October 27, 1818; Kafka, letter to Oscar Pollak, January 27, 1904.

121. See Robert Casillo, *The Genealogy of Demons: Anti-Semitism, Fascism, and the Myths of Ezra Pound* (Northwestern University Press, 1988): though prose-cutorial in tone and often dependent on forced readings of Pound's statements, it usefully details the morbid metaphors that infected Pound's view of Judaism. How-ever, it leaves one wondering whether the morbidities were Pound's private demons, or more general.

Even if they're bad beliefs—and some were bad, some weren't, and some were just terrible of course—they made him more human and more to do with life, more to do with the times. They served him. Taking what interested him in these things gave him a kind of realism and life to his poetry that it wouldn't have had otherwise.[122]

The point, clearly, is that we're not simply interested in how good a poet Pound was but rather in how the force of his poetry and of his ideas, for better or worse, are intertwined. That is what really has "more to do with the times." We don't have to abdicate moral judgments to want to know how and why.

To begin with, his views should not be thought of as mere negative, scapegoating manias; there was a positive effort too, as in the heroicization of Mussolini. Why did he idealize Mussolini, and how is this reflected in the *Cantos*? Pound became an admirer not because Mussolini was an anti-Semite. On the contrary, until 1938 when the orbit of Hitler's Germany pulled him in, Mussolini was hailed as one of the Jews' protectors: "In 1933 American Jewish publishers selected him as one of the world's twelve 'greatest Christian champions' of the Jews."[123] (If this fact seems shocking, you have more surprises in store.)

How did Mussolini look then? We have all learned to retch politely at the phrase "he made the trains run on time," but that seems to be the essence of the matter. What is usually forgotten on this point is that his image was formed during the Depression:

The Corporate State in the early thirties seemed a hive of smoking industry. While America floundered, Italy's progress in shipping, aviation, hydroelectric construction, and public works held out an attractive example of direct action and national planning. Compared to the ineptitude with which President Hoover approached the economic crisis, the Italian dictator appeared a paragon of action. Remarked *Fortune* in 1932: "[Mussolini] presents, too, the virtue of force and centralized government acting without conflict for the whole nation at once." Even liberals had become so disgusted with the decrepitude of congressional

122. Quoted by Anthony Woodward, *Ezra Pound and the Pisan Cantos* (Routledge & Kegan Paul, 1980), p. 7.
123. John P. Diggins, *Mussolini and Fascism: The View from America* (Princeton University Press, 1972), p. 40; see also p. 202: "*B'nai B'rith Magazine*, surveying European Fascist movements in 1934, reassured its readers that no anti-Semitism existed within the borders of Italy."

government that the anti-Fascist *Nation* could (perhaps in a fit of absentmindedness) print an article entitled "Wanted: A Mussolini."[124]

But he had an amazing number of admirers even earlier: "From the time of the March on Rome [1922] to the beginning of the Ethiopian War [1935] he was an esteemed figure." Many Englishmen were enthusiasts early on, from Churchill to Shaw (who also liked Stalin), but he was "more popular in America than anywhere else," according to Emil Ludwig. He seemed no more a real dictator than De Gaulle later. Will Rogers declared after interviewing Mussolini in 1926: "Dictator form of government is the greatest form of government; that is, if you have the right Dictator." The Cole Porter tune originally featured the line "You're the tops — / you're Musso — li — ni"; it was changed after the Ethiopian invasion, but good feelings lasted even into the war years: according to polls, "Two months before Italy attacked France 96 percent of Americans expressed a desire to see Italy join the Allies. . . . only 1.2 percent thought Italy the 'worst influence' in Europe, a more favorable ranking than that received even by England (1.8 percent)." Many at this time credited Mussolini with being the engineer of the Munich settlement that had temporarily saved the peace. Meanwhile, the "Pact of Steel" with Hitler and intervention in the Spanish Civil War were explained away, so strong were the favorable hopes for him. "Italy's neutrality at the outbreak of World War II seemed to rekindle hope that Mussolini had retained his saving sense of realism." Whereas Americans always overwhelmingly distrusted Hitler, they saw Mussolini as a counterforce. And his castor-oil purges for his opponents were not nearly as frightening as those that Stalin was mounting. Pound's determination to see only the good in Fascism was shared by a great number. Indeed, it can be argued that "on the whole, the American people approved of Fascism during the years of its ascendancy."[125]

After June 1940 there was a great revulsion, but Pound stayed in Italy, fatefully, and listened to only one side of events. In any case he was convinced, unlike most Americans, that Roosevelt and Churchill were the true villains. He had never liked Mussolini just

124. Diggins, pp. 37–38.
125. Diggins, pp. 59, 22, 27, 287, 324–25, 39–40; the final quotation is from the *New Yorker* review of this prize-winning book, quoted on the back cover.

because other Americans did so, but saw himself as an isolated prophet with unique insights into Fascism because of his possession of the secret of economics. The approach of war enraged and terrified him but also gave him a sense of vindication. No news he got in the war years was likely to change that complex of feelings. So, although he had stated that "no decent man tortures prisoners" in 1938, he heard little of Axis atrocities and no doubt discounted what he did hear.[126] At this point in life, self-doubt was not his métier; he was still convinced that he had to reform the world — hence the Rome broadcasts. Even in St. Elizabeth's he practiced denial. Only release broke his resistance, bringing an end to his defiant certainties and to the *Cantos* as well.

But why the attraction to Fascism in the first place? Given Pound's hatred of the "gold bugs" and of capitalism itself, which he called "black death," why not Marxism?[127] In fact Pound did have conversations with Marxists that led him at times to minimize the differences between his views and theirs. Though both Fascism and Naziism rode to power on the fear of Marxism among the middle and upper classes, Pound was not troubled by this bogey. In the Pisan Cantos, he still fantasized that he could get Stalin to see the light, and quoted Lenin as a seer:

> and but one point needed for Stalin
> you need not, i.e. need not take over the means of production
>
> . . . .
> Never inside the country to raise the standard of living
> but always abroad to increase the profits of usurers,
>   dixit Lenin   (74:426, 429)

You need not take over the factories, because the financial system is the problem: it's the banks that should be nationalized. That was Douglas's improvement on Marx, in Pound's eyes. Mussolini had begun as a socialist, and his new movement was a perverse appropriation of guild socialism; Hitler too began under the banner of socialist labor, and the word *Nazi* stood for *Nationalsozialistische Deutsche Arbeiter Partei.* Sir Oswald Mosley, leader of the British

---

126. *Guide to Kulchur*, p. 255.
127. *Jefferson and/or Mussolini* (Liveright, 1970; originally published, 1935), p. 128. See also Peter Nicholls, *Ezra Pound: Politics, Economics, and Writing* (Macmillan [London], 1984), esp. pp. 47 ff. and 79 ff.

Fascists, had earlier served in a Labour cabinet![128] These points show that our facile groupings of left and right are not helpful in this context: to call Pound a "right-winger" is highly misleading. Eliot wrote of Wordsworth's political conversion: "When a man takes politics and social affairs seriously the difference between revolution and reaction may be by the breadth of a hair."[129]

Fascism was based on the idea of recovery of community, the Gemeinschaft that had been lost by the deracination of workers and other convulsions of industrial capitalism. Its symbol, the Roman *fasces* (an ax handle with a bundle of sticks tied around it, which appears on old American dimes) is as collectivist as one could wish, signifying the synergetic strength of unity. It could absorb not only socialist impulses but also nationalist ones, which is one of the reasons it appealed to Yeats. Eliot too was drawn by the appeal of restored community. Several critics recently have pointed out the patterns of similarity between these poets' thinking and that of Fascists; this corrects the idea that Pound was an isolated anomaly, a loony crank who went off into sick fantasies that his friends would have tastefully avoided. Cairns Craig scoffs at those critics who have seen Yeats and Eliot as "essentially conservative, but never Fascistic. . . . it is a warping of the poets' views to make their politics mere nostalgia for a past age, let alone approval of contemporary conservatisms."[130]

Conor Cruise O'Brien in 1965 laid out the evidence for taking Yeats as a Fascist sympathizer. He showed that both Yeats's nationalist phase and senatorial service manifested predilections toward strong-man rule, hatred of "the mob" and welcome of repressive measures; that his admiration for Kevin O'Higgins and General O'Duffy was based on their potential as Irish Mussolinis; and that his march-writing for the Blueshirts was no aberration. In one march, Yeats defined equality as "muck in the yard," and he quoted with approval Mussolini's boast about trampling on the

128. A. J. P. Taylor, *English History 1914–1945* (Oxford University Press, 1965), pp. 284–85.

129. *The Use of Poetry and the Use of Criticism* (Faber & Faber, 1964; originally published, 1933), p. 73.

130. Craig, *Yeats, Eliot, Pound*, p. 252. The atavistic collectivism of Fascism was emphasized by the ritual of all answering "Presente!" when the name of a dead comrade was called in roll-call (see 78/479).

decomposing body of the Goddess of Liberty.[131] Frankly it is hard to imagine Pound doing any of those things. He lacked Yeats's aristocratic pretensions, and his own orientation was nearer to populism, with its concern for the average person, particularly the farmer, victimized by financiers: here he was closer to Huey Long and Father Coughlin than to Yeats.[132] Yeats grew "disillusioned" with Fascism in 1934, but O'Brien argues this simply meant that he saw that Fascism was unlikely to succeed in Ireland. Whatever the truth of this, Yeats unlike Pound welcomed the looming conflagration of World War II, regarding violence as necessary to usher in the new gyre. "'Send war in our time, O Lord!'"[133] (Williams also contrasts unfavorably with Pound here, as he wrote an unreprinted poem celebrating the blitz on London as a form of renewal through destruction.)[134]

Eliot, always more circumspect, put his trust in the corporate church rather than the corporate state because for him the anarchic forces rotting modern culture had their ultimate source not in Hobbes or Locke, as Yeats thought, but in the great Protestant mistake of making every man his own priest. This leaves each of us at the mercy of our own unregenerate conscience, "the inner voice, which breathes the eternal message of vanity, fear, and lust."[135] Only institutional Christianity can curb the erratic tendencies of the individual soul; all we like sheep have gone astray, every one to his own way. But in this piety there are clear political overtones: Eliot's notions of Christian community entail the same rejection of liberal progressivism and parliamentary democracy that facilitated Fascism. The knights, at the end of *Murder in the Cathedral*, remind the audience that their bloody act enabled the modern state's subordination of the church: "We have been instrumental in bringing about the state of affairs that you approve. We have served your interests; we merit your applause; and if there is any guilt whatever

131. "Passion and Cunning: An Essay on the Politics of W. B. Yeats," in A. Norman Jeffares and K. G. W. Cross, eds., *In Excited Reverie: A Centenary Tribute to William Butler Yeats 1865-1939* (Macmillan [London], 1965), pp. 207-78.

132. *Guide to Kulchur*, p. 302.

133. "Under Ben Bulben," stanza 3.

134. See Reed Whittemore, *William Carlos Williams: Poet from Jersey* (Houghton Mifflin, 1975), pp. 277-78.

135. "The Function of Criticism," in *Selected Essays*, p. 16.

in the matter, you must share it with us."[136] The point is well taken; from some points of view, the revolutionary acts that led to modern democracy look like brutal power plays. This attitude could be made to appear to be mere nostalgia, and Eliot — a great disguiser of himself — wore a white rose on the anniversary of Bosworth, claimed that the Civil War (English) was not over, in short played the role of a crank as he did that of a clubman.[137] But when he did write on modern politics, he championed more repressive ideas than Pound ever held. This point is made by C. K. Stead, who notes that Eliot approved the policy statements of the British Union of Fascists as "wholly admirable," but wanted more of a role for "Kingship and hereditary class." Stead sees Eliot's admiration for Charles Maurras, head of the monarchist, clericalist, anti-Semitic Action Française movement, as far more reprehensible than Pound's admiration for Mussolini: "In every respect *Action Fran-çaise*, which [Eliot] favoured, was more illiberal, more 'reactionary,' than Mussolini's party."[138] If Pound was childishly dazzled by the trappings of power when he looked at Mussolini, Eliot's *Coriolan* is disturbing in a quieter way, dramatizing (a bit like Eisenstein) the burdens of a man on horseback faced with the dangers of anarchic mobs, bureaucratic muddle, and parliamentary dither.

Craig puts the three together, and finds that their poetics shaped their politics, precisely because of those poetics' dependence on atavistic recall:

> Yeats, Eliot, and Pound were driven to politics in order to maintain the institutions and the patterns of society which preserved and promulgated the kinds of memory on which their poetry relied. The open poem demanded for its completion not the free mind of democratic man, but the rich mind of the privileged within a hierarchical society. The open poem demanded as its counterbalance the closed society.[139]

This is oversimplified, but provocative; it falsifies Pound particularly, making him sound conservative rather than populist. His

136. *The Complete Poems and Plays 1909-1950* (Harcourt Brace, 1952), pp. 217-18.

137. See Peter Ackroyd, *T. S. Eliot* (Hamish Hamilton, 1984), p. 166; and Eliot, "Milton II," *On Poetry and Poets* (Noonday Press, 1961), p. 168.

138. *Pound, Yeats, Eliot and the Modernist Movement* (Rutgers University Press, 1986), pp. 204-5.

139. Craig, p. 71.

work depends not on aristocratic memory but on far more esoteric concepts: on the survival of pagan mysteries, the eruption of a subversive literary tradition into the present, and so on. Pound did not defer to the rich and privileged—he called them "ploots"—but scorned them for willful ignorance, failure to patronize artists, and complicity with the iniquitous financial system. Nor did he share all of Yeats's and Eliot's nostalgia for restoration of community: he was less nationalist than they, more individualist and "volition-ist," as he called it, more fascinated with the strong man in history. Nonetheless Craig is right to tie together the poetics and the poli-tics, and he catches the paradox of the *Cantos*: "The poem which in its modernity, in its 'newness,' was also a recovery of all the past found its political model in Fascism. . . . bridging the false society of usury to recover the true spirit of the past while asserting its aggressive modernity in the march towards the future."[140]

As Craig notes, Pound believed that he saw in Mussolini an "artifex," an art- and artist-maker, who would restore the power of true patronage. Mussolini absorbed the figures of Malatesta, warrior and art collector, and Jefferson, statesman and propagator of culture, as well as other heroes of the *Cantos*. A less brutal man would not have served Pound's purpose; his portrait of Malatesta is designed to show how artistic judgment and savage energies can combine. One doesn't have to be a gentlemanly aesthete to be a patron or collector; a crude rapacity helps. Pound's own aggres-siveness was confined to the tennis court, but his violent rhetoric (beginning in Vorticism, which aimed to "save the public's soul by punching its face") could tolerate no dignified nor effete leader: faced with entrenched usury and stupidity, only force would avail.[141] Love of the dynamic and of "transferences of power" led Pound to the belief that form-producing force—the sculptor cut-ting stone, the poet cutting language—was the source of beauty. As in his favorite metaphor of the iron filings: their ugliness could be transformed by the magnet, arranging them into rose-like "lines of force." "An organisation of forms expresses a confluence of forces. . . . The design in the magnetised iron filings expresses a

140. Craig, p. 140. For Pound on the rich, see *Literary Essays*, p. 79; cf. *Letters*, p. 235.

141. *Letters*, p. 13; cf. p. 115: "In dealing with the 'public' one has never said enough. There is nothing but 'rubbing it in' that has the slightest effect."

confluence of energy."[142] From these formulations to the rhetoric of Fascism is a plausible step, although Pound's personal rage for order did not include a wish for a hierarchical, well-behaved society: for that matter, his notions were far more boisterous and bumptious, far more inclusive of the transgressive in both art and politics, than those of Eliot, Yeats, or others such as Stevens. It was the energy, not the order, that he emphasized. Indeed, he jibed that good literature worries "lovers of order," who find it "dangerous, chaotic, subversive."[143]

But if we take the Modernists together, we can explain much of the puzzling and embarrassing mystery of their politics by noting that Fascism was after all an atavistic convulsion, one that held out hopes of actually materializing the past in the present. Despite its futurist decor (and support from Marinetti), Fascism was a revival of Caesarism, with Napoleonic improvements by way of subverting popular protest: that revolution often ends in reaction and dictatorship is a truism not confined to the so-called right; Stalin and Mao present variations. Fascism in Italy proposed to restore the imperial eagles and colossal marmoreality, all the symbols of vanished glory: so also in Germany, where economic distress and revanchism compounded the nostalgia. Ultimately both movements drew much of their power from fear of the "modern" faceless, secularized, cosmopolitan world; like Communism, Fascism and Naziism appealed to those who felt threatened by alienation, anomie, rootlessness. As Norman Cohn has argued, both Hitler and Stalin proffered parodies of medieval millennialist peasants' revolts, mixing apocalyptic religiosity, grandiose visions of the future, and scapegoating as part of the process of restoring community.[144] Their message was: you can go home again, to a glorious Utopia, but first you have to help us stamp out parasites who sap communal strength — Jews, kulaks, or landlords.

These were cynical and opportunistic appeals, as was Fascism's

142. "Affirmations: Vorticism," *New Age*, January 14, 1915, p. 277.

143. *Literary Essays*, p. 21.

144. *The Pursuit of the Millennium: Revolutionary Messianism in Medieval and Reformation Europe and Its Bearing on Modern Totalitarian Movements* (Harper & Row, 1961). On Fascism's revivalist attitude to the past, see Wyndham Lewis, *Time and Western Man*, pp. 35–36. Lewis's insights on this and related matters are, as usual, instructive, but not in the way he intended them to be.

apparent fulfillment of Modernist aesthetics; and the poets fell for it, just as did the masses in Germany and Italy. Fascist ambivalence about past and future deceptively mimicked the hopes for atavistic revival embodied in the most visionary works of the early twentieth century. Fascism was a product of what T. J. Jackson Lears calls "the antimodernism of modernism," with a characteristically divided mind:

> Yet even in its most extreme political manifestations the antimodern quest for authenticity wore a Janus face. Rooted in reaction against modernizing tendencies, it also reinforced them. Mussolini and Hitler were fascinated with machines; more important, despite their visions of an agrarian utopia, they spearheaded the creation of giant mechanized economies and government bureaucracies. . . . fascist activism caricatured the capitalist commitment to ceaseless "growth."[145]

Pound mistook this confusion for his own sense that the past was alive in the present.

Lears has traced the hostility to postindustrial culture through craft movements, Catholic revivals, and other repudiations of sanguine progressivism, showing that strange connections link Marx to Henry Adams, critiques of alienation to veneration of "the premodern unconscious." These phenomena typically eventuate in anti-Semitism, xenophobia, and contempt for liberal democracy: an obvious proto-Fascist pattern. One noteworthy forerunner of Modernism, particularly of Pound's economic obsessions, was the distributism articulated by G. K. Chesterton and Hilaire Belloc. Like the Guild Socialism of Pound's friend A. R. Orage, this had an openly avowed atavistic rationale, proposing to restore medieval localism in order to repeal the effects of modern industrialism. Pound took no interest in it early on, writing off Chesterton as an apologist for Catholicism: "the mumbo-jumbo of superstition dodging behind clumsy fun and paradox."[146] But their movements shared a populist economics, hatred of usury and bankers, anti-Semitism, and disparagement of current politics. Both would have agreed, for instance, that "high taxation is simply the instrument of the usurocracy to ensure the financial enslavement of the citi-

---

145. *No Place of Grace: Antimodernism and the Transformation of American Culture 1880–1920* (Pantheon, 1981), p. 309.
146. *Letters*, p. 116.

zen."[147] The "Chesterbelloc's" fondness for feudalism and Merrie England bore only a slight resemblance to Pound's more primal and unsentimental vision, but Modernism's embrace of atavism is illuminated by such parallels. The revulsion against progressivism left the ground prepared.

Other precedent antimodernisms rejected not only facile notions of progress but also contemporary humanistic and especially vitalistic values: life, warmth, sanguinity, and their congeners were treated as nauseating clichés. This eventuated in Vorticism, but also in the "hardness" of Yeats's poetry after the turn of the century, in which the word "cold" becomes honorific, even appears in strange combinations like "cold and passionate"; Yeats embraced the values of a dehumanized rigidity, fixity, artifice, and permanence. Spurning the transitory "complexities of mire and blood" in favor of "changeless metal," he infused this into his poetry but even more into his plays, inspired by the Japanese Noh theater with its stylized conventions and masks (informed on these points by Pound, who had Fenollosa's notes and translations). Behind the patronizing use of the word *modern* in "Among School Children" ("The children learn to cipher . . . / In the best modern way"), we must hear all the echoes of this animus against humanisms.[148]

Similarly, Eliot used the word *modern* mostly in disparagement, in antihumanistic, antivitalistic diatribes. A prime example is his praise of Baudelaire for courting a "damnation denied to the newspaper editors of Paris," in his morbid sexuality:

> One aphorism which has been especially noticed is the following: *la volupté unique et suprême de l'amour gît dans le certitude de faire le mal.* . . . He was at least able to understand that the sexual act as evil is more dignified, less boring, than as the natural, "life-giving," cheery automatism of the modern world. For Baudelaire, sexual operation is at least something not analogous to Kruschen Salts.

Hence Baudelaire implicitly rebukes "an age of bustle, programmes, platforms, scientific progress, humanitarianism and rev-

---

147. Lorne A. Reznowski, "The 'Chesterbelloc' and Ezra Pound," *Paideuma* 13 (Fall 1984): 293. See also Jay P. Corrin, *G. K. Chesterton and Hilaire Belloc: The Battle Against Modernity* (Ohio University Press, 1981).

148. "Among School Children," stanza 1; on the Noh's transmission, see Carpenter, *A Serious Character*, pp. 218 ff.

olutions which improved nothing, an age of progressive degradation."[149]

In contrast to Yeats's metallic or granitic values and Eliot's rehabilitation of "Sin and Redemption," Pound's attitude toward the "modern" appears far more balanced and focused: his use of the term is almost always favorable. Ironically, his first burst of praise for Eliot contended that he had "modernized himself *on his own*"; for Pound this meant that he had anticipated Ford's *aggiornamento*, jettisoning archaisms of diction and the like.[150] With Pound the paradox of Modernism, embracing the past *in* the present, must be seen in full force. For him, the contemporary world had been rotted by usury and by such forces as Protestant Christianity that operated "semiticly to obliterate values, to efface grades and graduations."[151] But there is less antiquarian nostalgia in this view than in those of Yeats and Eliot, with their idealization of Byzantine "Unity of Being" and of Metaphysical "undissociated sensibility" respectively. Pound does not look back to some island of time in the past; his perception of the effects of usury is not based on a slightly submerged myth of the Fall. On the contrary, usury has been at its evil work in many eras, and not just in the West. Whereas most of the antimodernisms cited by Lears trail off into plaintive Miniver Cheevy dreams of escape, Pound embraces the trends of the modern world except for the deleterious effects of the financial system, against which he sees inventors, scientists, and others struggling. This made him more open, eventually, to scapegoating of the Jews, but less to the overt or covert nostalgias that left Yeats and Eliot unwilling to grasp the full complexity of the atavistic paradox. Moved by their own distaste for contemporary life, they if pressed would be willing to disown the present and return to the past. Not so with Pound, a true atavist, who wanted the present but only with the past alive in it. He made this point specifically in rejecting simplified readings of the *Cantos*: "The poem is not a dualism of past against present. . . . The poem should establish an hierarchy of values, not simply: past is good, present is bad, which I certainly do not believe and never have

---

149. "Baudelaire," in *Selected Essays*, pp. 380, 378.
150. *Letters*, p. 40.
151. *Guide to Kulchur*, p. 185.

believed."[152] As remarked earlier, he was more individualist also than Yeats or Eliot, more entranced by the possibilities of "factive" or "volitionist" personalities and what they could achieve in history; this was part of his sense of the modern world's possibilities, since he was seduced by the dream that Mussolini could break the stranglehold of "usurocracy."

The drive in Modernism to repeal outdated or degenerated conventions, and to replace them with new energies drawn from the primordial and ancient, may be said to be tinged with nostalgia in only a limited sense. The artist who simply accepts the conditions of the time is like Lévi-Strauss's *bricoleur*. This person takes to hand whatever bits and pieces can be picked up, and makes the work out of what are in effect ready-made parts reshuffled. But the most driven of twentieth-century artists are more like the *bricoleur*'s opposite, the engineer (*ingénieur* says it better). The quest of the engineer is to probe and question both the task and the materials, seeking to reinvent the raw materials rather than to accept what is at hand. (Such quests are exemplified most notably by that for the elementary particle in physics, rather than by engineering as such.) As Seurat sought for the elements of an aesthetics of light, and Cubists sought to reinvent form and perspective, so the twelve-tone theorists sought new elementary structures of sound. Pound shares a good deal with Schönberg as well as Picasso: "Schönberg rejected the notion of artist-as-genius and replaced it with the artist as craftsman; he saw music not as the expression of subjectivity, but as a search for knowledge which lay outside the artist, as potential within the object, the material."[153] This describes Pound uncannily well, even to the idea—in his favorite sculptural metaphor—of letting the shape latent in the stone emerge. (See the earlier discussion of his repudiation of subjective predication.) In literature Gertrude Stein is an even more obvious exemplar than Pound, of seeking to reinvent the sentence and the elementary forms of language, while Joyce achieved in *Finnegans Wake* the "abnihilisation of the etym" itself. But Pound, in his quest for a new poetics, was as far-reaching, and better informed about the uses of the past.

152. Quoted in Bush, *The Genesis of Ezra Pound's Cantos*, p. 14.
153. Susan Buck-Morss, quoted by Gregory L. Ulmer, "The Object of Post-Criticism," in Hal Foster, ed., *The Anti-Aesthetic* (Bay Press, 1983), p. 98.

To call this nostalgia seems a bit perverse, as no one afflicted by a sense of loss, or need to escape, would be so perseveringly energetic. This is nostalgic only in the sense that all revolutions are; such drives owe something to the latent Puritanism in the Western heritage that urges us always to go upstream, nearer the source and therefore purer. As it happens, Puritanism was a crucial element in Pound's makeup, and forms the final, most ironic of his atavisms, in that it represented a return of the repressed religious tradition of his American predecessors. The very concept of revolutionary atavism itself, in the forms in which it appeared in Modernism, has a source in Protestant revivalism: this covers even Eliot's religious conversion, much as it would have distressed him to be found in alliance with the Dissenting tradition. For him the whole point was to recover the full force of orthodoxy and continuity; but, of course, that is exactly what the Puritans thought they were doing.

In Pound's case the Puritanism is more open, though no less ironic, given his attacks on Protestant Christianity. Earlier it was remarked that Fenollosa's insistence that "it was not we who made [the sentence form]" joined the two traditions, pagan and Biblical. A latent Puritanism is equally apparent in many other aspects of Pound's work and beliefs: his hatred of ornament and of meretricious appeals; his epistemology, with its suspicion of rhetoric, fear of spurious knowledge and insistence on making the reader work; his referentiality, with its emphatic affirmation of the "out-there"; his literalism, hostile to metaphor and symbol, but delighting in the actually existent, including what he thought of as the realities of economics and politics; and finally the shape of his whole career, which shows the outlines of a displaced evangelical urge. Even his frequent vulgarism, which compounded the repulsiveness of the anti-Semitism, owes something to this urge: he had to show that he was not awed by the niceties of *politesse*. At its worst, this heritage led him into exaggeration of the evil intentions of those who opposed or ignored him, and lent fatal strength to his anti-Semitic conspiracy theory. Since for him the political and religious interacted on the same plane, his covert Puritanism gave force to his self-righteousness.

Of course Pound repudiated his religious heritage whenever he was conscious of it, and especially abominated the dregs of such Calvinist dogmas as the innate depravity of man, seeing in these leavings not only fanatical superstition but also evil-minded cynicism that hindered needed meliorations. Anyone who looks at economics as Pound did must be struck by the gap between our productivity—which has long since been able to turn out all the goods the world could possibly use—and our grievously inequitable distribution systems. For Pound usurers were the villains who perpetuated this situation, but only intellectual and moral torpor could explain why we allowed their activities; he thought that outdated, twisted religious pessimism about human nature kept us sunk in this torpor. Having irritably rejected such traditions, Pound was left with a peculiar blind spot, discernible in his snappish remark about Samuel Johnson's poem of Christian stoicism, that "human wishes are not vain in the least"; to say so, he thought, was to yield cravenly to the obstructionists. Predictably, forfeiting venerable insights into the emptiness and folly of human desire led him into yet another political error. Reed Way Dasenbrock, studying Pound's reading of Dante's *De Monarchia*, has shown that Pound followed Dante in the fallacy of supposing that a powerful ruler would be free from greed because he would already possess so many goods. Because of his blind spot, Pound was unable to distinguish between need and desire, unable to see that *cupiditas* for wealth or power or sensual satisfaction can never be satisfied, and that any honest "ploot" will admit that making money only makes him want more. Thus a dictator like Mussolini will be more, not less, tempted to aggrandize himself. Less idealism about human nature could have kept Pound from his disastrous hero worship.[154]

Yet such conscious repudiation only displaced his underlying Puritanism, forcing it into aesthetic dogmas, and the most dynamic forces in the art of the time reinforced it. Across the spectrum of early twentieth-century artistic "revolts," a hatred of ornament, of nonfunctional decorative elements, prevails, so much so that these qualities have had to be specifically revived in more recent revolts against the revolts. Modernism in art and architecture, even more than in literature, hearkened to the cry of Adolph Loos: "Orna-

154. On Johnson, see *Guide to Kulchur*, p. 180; on human nature, see Donald Pearce and Herbert Schneidau, eds., *Ezra Pound: Letters to John Theobald* (Black Swan, 1984), p. 56. Dasenbrock, essay forthcoming in the *Journal of Modern Literature*, and in a book: *Imitating the Italians: Wyatt, Spenser, Synge, Pound, and Joyce*, forthcoming in 1991 from Johns Hopkins.

ment is excrement!" With religious fervor, form was made to follow function, and the trend eventuated in the visionary, almost Manichean ethereality of the Bauhaus, directing against materiality the famous paradox "less is more." A dead end to this cult was reached by Le Corbusier, whose highminded inhumanism spawned architectural projects of disastrous impracticality, now abandoned or demolished. Pound, likewise important more for his vision than for specific lasting achievements, was the most vocal of literary figures in specifically denouncing ornament, heeding the force of Ford's condemnations of his own derivative and decorative devices. But his crusade had many reverberations, affecting writers from the Imagists to Hemingway and Williams, and finding concordant practices in the works of Eliot and Joyce. No Puritan could have desired a more strenuous insistence than Pound's on unadorned language, eschewal of insidious appeal, and the like. His hatred of prettification was almost a mania.

This ties naturally into his textual epistemology, his certainty that conventional forms of expression were corrupt or moribund, that new means must be found that stir readers to work for what they get. Much has already been said, above, that implies Pound's distaste for homogenizing either his material or its presentation. He sought to invent a new poetics that would embody all his convictions and practices, in order to provide "direct knowledge" for the reader: combining veneration of metamorphic tradition with elimination of subjective predication, and fear of predigested responses with use of fragmentary dissociation, he worked to construct a poem that would register realities, but also rebuke the reader's "degrading thirst after outrageous stimulation" (as Wordsworth would have put it), his appetite for "the caressable," which is the forbidden fruit in this fable. The artist must above all never flatter, cajole, or reassure the reader; instead, facile comprehension must be blunted, the reader forced to slow down, skip around, try out new combinations of elements: as if dealing with an ancient manuscrap. As in the passage quoted in Chapter 1: "I . . . want a poetry where the reader must not only read every word, but must read his English as carefully as if it were a Greek that he could not rapidly be sure of comprehending."[155] Only if the reader were made

155. Quoted in Bush, *The Genesis of Ezra Pound's Cantos*, pp. 10–11.

to labor, imaginatively, could predictable, programmed reactions
be broken up; besides, as Augustine put it, those truths are the
sweetest that are gained with the most labor. As Cubism may be
said to be an attempt to frustrate the viewer's "reading" of the
picture according to the canons of perspective — deliberately disori-
enting the viewer so as to force a creative response — so Pound did
not hesitate to frustrate his readers: he dispersed narrative and
discourse, made tantalizing, puzzling references, put in bits of un-
familiar quotations, and so on. It was his own version of an aesthetic of delay and of postponed gratification, which he knew
about not only from his quasi-scholarly researches but also from
his sense of the visions produced in Troubadour love cults by unconsummated sex. Above all, this poetic insisted that the reader
must be given "new eyes." The ideogrammic method was designed
to get off the "desensitized" parts of the reader's brain, provoke a
fresh reaction: "Make it new," which meant make a fresh presentation of the revived past.[156] Here, the imagery of regeneration — as
in baptism, or conversion — joins that of resurrection already implicit in "the tradition." The reader is given new or regenerate spiritual organs.

Pound's hatred of ornamental or superfluous elements combined
with his epistemological quests to make his poetics one of fanatical
concision and compression. *Dichten = condensare*! His manuscripts show that he was never happier than in cutting words that
could in any way be deemed superfluous, combining two lines into
one, and the like. Ford had taught *progression d'effet*, which became the Imagist point that every word must "contribute to the
presentation." Behind this were the sacred lessons of Flaubert:
show, don't tell, i.e. "make the scene present the emotion"; don't
"comment" to supply to the reader what you have failed to show;
cut adjectives, which are mostly "comment"; confine yourself to
clear "constatation or presentation."[157] But behind these, still further, was the legend of art as a monastic vocation; the force these
lessons had was derived from the figure of Flaubert as the hermit,

---

156. *Guide to Kulchur*, p. 51.

157. See my *Ezra Pound: The Image and the Real*, pp. 24–27; and Pound,
Literary Essays, p. 3.

devoting himself with saintlike intensity to the fanatical "hyper-scientific" precisions by which alone language could be made into immortal art. The lessons' technical prestige was overshadowed by the quasi-religious inspiration that they assumed and required. But what made them doubly forceful for Pound was that compression opened further opportunities to practice dissociation, to write manuscraps of one's own, to force readers to labor for regenerated vision. Both aspects testify to the emergence of subterranean Puritanism, deep within the personality, which Pound called his "plymouth-rock conscience landed on predilection for the arts."[158]

Further consequences of the evangelical urge can be seen in the content of Pound's work, as clearly as in the techniques. Obviously in his didacticism, but also in his referentiality: to some this seems like a remnant of old-fashioned representationalism, but it is simply the Puritan insistence on "truth," mistrust of the figural and fictional, and exhortation to kerygmatic proclamation. The truth must be told; woe to those who do not speak out! His economic and political messages need no belaboring, but the *Cantos* are suffused even in minor points with the idea of testimony, of "bearing witness." It is "not a work of fiction," as there is no room for make-believe. What is there actually exists; as Hugh Kenner says, "Again and again in the *Cantos* single details merely prove that something lies inside the domain of the possible."[159]

Pitying but also condemning the aesthetes and decadents of England for letting themselves be beaten down by the rotted culture — the burden of *Mauberley* — Pound determined to condemn their "taste for the unreal" by grappling, like a lone prophet, with "the relation of the state to the individual." Thus he decided to take "the old man's road," to follow Hardy in giving primacy to "CONTENT, the INSIDES."[160] This choice was the upswelling of unrecognized religious fervor from his own heritage; in youth, he had taken YMCA Christianity "with great seriousness," and it returned to him from all sides.[161] His heroes all bear laconic witness: Acoetes in Canto II kerygmatically proclaims Dionysus: "I have seen what

158. *Letters*, p. 12.
159. *Pound Era*, p. 325.
160. *Letters*, p. 248.
161. *Guide to Kulchur*, p. 300.

I have seen." Though Pound would have squirmed at the connection, the very language recalls the last lines of his early, muscular-Christian pseudoballad, "The Goodly Fere":

> I ha' seen him eat o' the honey-comb
> Sin' they nailed him to the tree.

Pound's debt to Whitman, even, is involved: "I am the man, I suffer'd, I was there" could be used as a note. Whitman's sudden appearance in the Pisan sequence is no coincidence.[162] At many points in the poem we can envision the defiant, ecstatic gestures of Protestantism: "Here I stand, I can do no other."

Pound had a lifelong struggle with himself, divided between his urge to expound (a "Village Explainer," Gertrude Stein called him) and his even stronger admiration for laconism, understatement, and silence — *tempus loquendi, tempus tacendi* — both drives being very American (cf. Anderson and Hemingway) and ultimately Puritan, one deriving from the urgent need to testify and the other from mistrust of words.[163] The *Cantos* are ambivalent: powerfully marked by concision, compression, and particularist concentration, they are also frequently deformed by a garrulous, haranguing tendency. In his poetic as such, admiration was reserved for compression: in Imagist days he admired British understatement, and even before that must have been struck by the dramatic force that Yeats was able to achieve in reticent lines like those of Cuchulain on learning that the warrior he has just fatally struck down is his own son:

> 'I put you from your pain. I can no more.'[164]

The Fenollosa materials multiplied his admiration for leaving things out, as "The Jewel Stairs' Grievance" shows. To the poem itself Pound added a note concluding, "The poem is especially prized because [the lady] utters no direct reproach." The Noh was equally allusive and indirect, like "listening to incense," and the Chinese poems make passion and sorrow seem stronger for being

---

162. "Song of Myself," l. 832; cf. Canto 82/526.

163. "There is a time to speak, and a time to be silent," adapted from Eccles. 3: 7; the motto of Malatesta; 31/153.

164. "Cuchulain's Fight with the Sea" (1892), l. 69.

curbed: a tendency Pound heightened in his *Cathay* translations, as in these lines about harried soldiers:

Surprised. Desert turmoil. Sea sun.
Flying snow bewilders the barbarian heaven.[165]

Such devices foreshadow the truncated lines of *The Waste Land*, and Hemingway's "theory of omission"; Pound spread laconism through the Modernist movement.

His ambivalence about revealing/concealing is also evident in his telegraphic letters. His fear of belaboring the obvious, and his awareness of his own tendency toward garrulity, cause him to rein in suddenly at key moments: "My longsuffering consort sez I so OFTEN leave out the POINT," he laconically admitted to one correspondent.[166] Indeed he did, which is why the letters are good preparation for the *Cantos'* poetry of ellipsis. In striving to get off the dead spots of the reader's mind, he often resorted to suggestive "blanks in the writing." And sometimes he was just not going to tell, from annoyance. Eliot's diagnosis has much relevance:

I once complained to him about an article on the monetary theory of Gesell. . . . "I asked you to write an article which would explain this subject to people who had never heard of it; yet you write as if your readers knew about it already, but had failed to understand it." In the *Cantos* there is an increasing defect of communication. . . . as if the author was so irritated with his readers for not knowing all about anybody so important as [Martin] Van Buren, that he refused to enlighten them.[167]

As so often happens with conspiracy theorists, Pound kept discovering his own ideas in his chosen patrology, then could only conclude that these important lessons had been somehow censored — so should he reveal them? What could more passionately engage Pound's embattled Puritan conscience? The urge to curb himself — and to discipline his readers — often won out over the expansive testifying, sometimes where it would be most helpful for "readability."

Whoever has not experienced Eliot's feelings in reading the *Can-*

165. "South-Folk in Cold Country."
166. Pearce and Schneidau, *Letters to Theobald*, p. 86.
167. "Ezra Pound" (1946), from Sutton, *Ezra Pound*, p. 23.

tos is not being honest. It is idle to pretend that the poem is everywhere successful; how could it not be wildly uneven, with such a
complicated and ambitious poetic and such divisive wars going on
in the poet himself? Pound, complimenting Eliot for *The Waste
Land*, spoke regretfully of his own "deformative secretions," with
reason. He candidly admitted that his great poem had "the defects
inherent in a record of struggle" — struggle within and without.[168]
Pound relished making enemies, not realizing he had enough within
himself.

Some critics, forgetting that the poem is a compendious anthology, a farrago not a unity, want to accept or reject it as a whole.
Perhaps they fear falling into the wistfulness of early commenta-
tors who could admire the lyrical moments but make nothing of
the didacticism. But Pound believed that "no man ever writes very
much poetry that 'matters,'" and the proportion of brilliant pages
in his work is about the same as in a volume of Keats, or Wallace
Stevens.[169] It is clear that Cantos like I and II, and XIII, are clearly
focused in a way that others are not; that the Renaissance Cantos
are divided: the Malatesta ones are boisterous but uneven, while
those dealing with the Borgias and Venice are hopelessly murky.
Others have other problems, and achievements: Cantos XIV and
XV have the force of anecdotal modern painting, like (ironically)
Peter Blume's *Eternal City*, a cartoonish depiction of Mussolini.
The Adams and Chinese Cantos tend to drown in detail, the
Sienese are deformed by irritable reticence, but the Pisan have a
force and grace that derives from yet another fruitful atavism:
memories of pre-1914 London flood Pound's mind as he crawls
from his "broken ant-hill," providing movingly elegiac moments —
indeed these cantos form a pastoral elegy, the green world healing
and redeeming the red one of man's furies and wars. The epic is
naturally elegiac; weeping is as frequent as fighting; from Homer
on there is always a lost world to be remembered, and recovered in
the very laments of its loss.

Pound was wrong about many things, poetical as well as political, and when he was wrong, he was likely to be disastrously and
offensively wrong. Still, as a figure in literary history, he is more

168. *Letters*, p. 169; *Guide to Kulchur*, p. 135.
169. *Literary Essays*, p. 10.

interesting than multitudes of more conventionally meaningful and politically correct poets. What we must finally say of Pound is that his Puritan referentiality was simply wrong, and that he was the victim as well as the legatee of the fundamental truth of literature, that represented experience is more moving and potent than "reality." If he had been able to stomach *Finnegans Wake*, he might have been amused by the mock-patristic exhortation based on that principle that Joyce placed near the end of his work: *Ut vivat volumen, sic pereat pouradosus* ("that the book may live, let paradise [?] be lost").[170]

In any case, he is the figure who best represents the paradox of the importance of the past in Modernism. "In Pound's spatial sense of time the past is here, now; its invisibility is our blindness, not its absence," as Guy Davenport puts it.[171] Modernism belongs to an age when the very meaning of the term *the past* underwent enormous expansion: in the nineteenth century it signified a few millennia at most, but in the twentieth its extent, and significance, has been multiplied exponentially. Pound's work takes on its true import in view of that great shift in the dimensions of our imagined, represented world. If today our new translations help us discover an earthy richness and power in ancient texts, such as those of Homer or the Bible, this is not only a matter of Pound's insistence on the demotic in translation. These texts have new dimensions for us because we see an immense panorama of prehistory behind them, and thus the chthonic matrix from whence they emerged. They are of the earth, earthy in the best sense. Modernism prepared us for the excavation of this treasure.

---

170. (Viking, 1939), p. 610.
171. "Persephone's Ezra," in Eva Hesse, ed., *New Approaches to Ezra Pound* (University of California Press, 1969), p. 157. Davenport says it was Pound's lifework to "treat what had become a world of ghosts as a world eternally present." Cf. Pound, *Selected Prose*, p. 70: "The essence of religion is the *present* tense."

Index

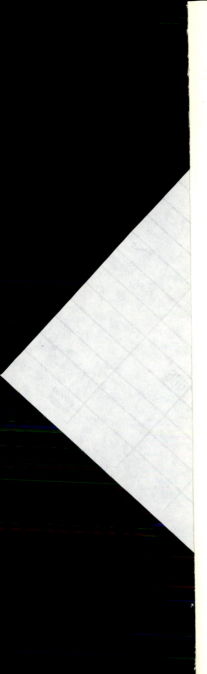